Library of
Davidson College

THE PHILOSOPHY OF LANGUAGE
IN BRITAIN

AMS Studies in the Seventeenth Century, No. 2

ISSN: 0731-2342

Also in this series:
No. 1. T. E. Lawrenson. *The French Stage and Playhouse in the Seventeenth Century.* 1986.
No. 3. William Frost. *John Dryden: Dramatist, Satirist, Translator.* 1986.

The Philosophy of Language in Britain

Major Theories from Hobbes to Thomas Reid

STEPHEN K. LAND

AMS PRESS
NEW YORK

Library of Congress Cataloging-in-Publication Data

Land, Stephen K.
　The Philosophy of Language in Britain.

　(AMS Studies in the Seventeenth Century,
ISSN 0731-2342; No. 2)
　　Bibliography: p.
　　Includes index.
　　1. Linguistics—Great Britain—History.
2. Languages —Philosophy.　I. Title.　II. Series.
P81.G7L28　1986　410′.941　83-45287
ISBN 0-404-61722-0

Copyright © 1986, AMS PRESS, INC.
All rights reserved.

Grateful acknowledgment is made to Penguin Books, Ltd., for permission to reproduce the passage on page 82 from G. J. Warnock's *Berkeley*, p. 83 (Peregrine Books, 1969; © G. J. Warnock, 1953, 1969).

Manufactured in the United States of America

Contents

Preface	vii
Introduction	1
1. Hobbes: Formalism	5
THE THEORY OF MIND	9
THE THEORY OF SIGNS AND NAMES	15
THE THEORY OF LOGIC	22
2. Lockean Theory: Idealism	31
SEMANTIC IDEALISM	35
THE THEORY OF IDEAS	43
THE THEORY OF WORDS	59
THE THEORY OF MIND	65
THE THEORY OF GRAMMAR	74
3. Berkeleian Theory: Structuralism	79
ANALYSIS	80
THE THEORY OF IDEAS	93
THE THEORY OF MIND	100
THE THEORY OF LANGUAGE	118
4. Smith and Monboddo: The Search for Origins	131
ADAM SMITH	133
LORD MONBODDO	159
5. Harris and Reid: Rationalism and Common Sense	193
JAMES HARRIS	193
HERMES	198
THOMAS REID: LANGUAGE AND COMMON SENSE	215
LANGUAGE AND THOUGHT	229
Conclusion	237
Notes	243
Bibliography	249
Index	253

Preface

This book was prepared for publication in 1978, but unavoidable circumstances have delayed its appearance. I must therefore apologize to scholars whose writings in the field covered have appeared since that time. My failure to mention them implies no disregard.

I am grateful to Cora Diamond for reading an early draft of the chapters on Hobbes, Locke, and Berkeley, and for saving me from many untoward assertions. I must, however, take sole responsibility for those which may remain.

Suffolk, England
1985

Introduction

The present study is not a history of the philosophy of language but rather an examination of major theories of language current in Britain in the period from Hobbes to the end of the eighteenth century. No systematic attempt is made to chronicle the passage or development of ideas from one writer to another or to trace conceptual origins. Instead I have tried to analyze in some depth several of the most important theories of the period as they appear in certain seminal British texts.

The theories chosen are those of the philosophers Hobbes, Locke, Berkeley, and Reid, along with the genetic theories of Smith and Monboddo and the philosophical grammar of Harris. In kind and overall historical significance these theories differ considerably one from another, but together they represent the major *types* of theoretical work on language conducted in the period and, within the philosophy of language, the most significant approaches developed.

Within each of these types and approaches the works selected are undoubtedly the most important British examples. It cannot be too much stressed, however, that in the seventeenth and eighteenth centuries original work in philosophy, linguistics, and philology was generally conducted on an international level. French and English-speaking writers (including native Germans, like Leibniz, who wrote mostly in French or Latin) enjoyed a rapid and profitable exchange of ideas, both through published essays and private correspondence. It is not possible to trace the history of ideas concerning language in this period without continually crossing national frontiers. The present work does not offer such a history and limits its attention to British writers—a limitation which, from the wider point of view of the history of ideas, must be recognized as largely arbitrary.

The purpose of a study within the methodological and geographical boundaries just described is twofold. First, and most important, is the provision of a close analysis of the major theories of the period, with comparison and cross-reference among them on basic issues, so that the outlines and fundamental assumptions of each can be displayed. Some of these writers, like Monboddo, have been neglected, or like Berkeley seriously misconstrued. In other cases, notably that of Locke, a fair amount of useful scholarship is already available; but even where recent scholarly discussion has been abundant there remains a good deal of confusion in the history of the philosophy of language of this period, a confusion due in large part to Noam Chomsky's brilliant and controversial observations. The present study does not seek to provide the final word but offers an interim exposition and description of each theory such as would be the precondition for consideration of the theory's place in history and its philosophical validity.

Second, the selection of theories taken here displays something of the range and variety of issues in language theory current in the seventeenth and eighteenth centuries. The disciplinary categories of our own time—"philosophy of language," "linguistics," "linguistic philosophy," "anthropological linguistics," "philology"—are all represented to some extent in the period, but not within the compartments to which the structure of contemporary academia now tends to confine them. Many modern studies of the period are *either* philosophical *or* linguistic in orientation—although there are valuable exceptions, Chomsky's historical writings among them. The present work is impartial with respect to twentieth-century disciplinary categories in both selection and exposition. Again, it is too easy to classify theories of language in the period simply as either rationalist or empiricist (following Funke) or as Cartesian or Lockean (following Chomsky). The display of several theories here shows that the picture is more complex and that the range of theoretical positions covered in the period was not conspicuously less broad than that of which our contemporary theorists of language must take account.

The period chosen for consideration has certain natural boundaries, which can be useful so long as they are not allowed to obscure vital continuities. The new philosophy of the seventeenth century prompted extensive thinking about language, represented in England chiefly by Hobbes, the many linguists who worked in association with the Royal Society, and Locke. The conceptual aspects of this movement, particularly the notion of philosophical grammar, have roots in the medieval period, but it remains true that a new phase in the philosophy of language was introduced largely as a result of the writings of Bacon and Descartes in the early seventeenth century. At the other extremity of our period the late eighteenth century sees the beginnings of comparative philology and the movement which leads directly into linguistic science as we now know it. Again the boundaries are not clear-cut; the beginnings of comparative philology are evident in Monboddo, who himself works in a conceptual climate created by Condillac and Locke. But by the second quarter of the nineteenth century the change is unmistakable, and one of its results was the disciplinary divergence of linguistic and philological studies from the philosophy of language, with which they had remained closely bound throughout the eighteenth century.

Because of both their currency and intrinsic relevance, Noam Chomsky's remarks on this period will be encountered at several points in what follows. The present study stands in a dual relation to the Chomskyan account of the history of linguistic theory: on the one hand it is in large part an extension of Chomsky's perception that many philosophies of language in the seventeenth and eighteenth centuries are in a very real sense expounding what he has called a "generative" concept of grammar, but on the other hand (accepting the criticisms of Chomsky advanced by Hans Aarsleff and others) it aims to show that his discussion of the subject in terms of an antithesis between Cartesian and empiricist positions is seriously inadequate.

What I take to be the distortions in Chomsky's view of the period may well stem from his approach, which is avowedly to seek precursors of particular twentieth-century notions. Thus nowhere does he give full expositions of the theories he cites, and, as he often points out, the traditional interpretations are frequently unreliable. The procedure adopted here is primarily expository, and one of the chief points of substance to emerge from it is the aforementioned modification of Chomsky's conclusion.

Finally, a word on the method of exposition. Because of the nature of the texts under consideration no sharp line can be drawn here between exposition, criticism, and reconstruction. Several of the writers discussed have only a secondary interest in language. Locke, for example, is chiefly concerned to outline a theory of human knowledge which will serve philosophy as a basis for certainty in argument, and he discusses language only in so far as he finds it necessary to do so for this purpose. Consequently his remarks on language, as is also true in the writings of Hobbes and Berkeley, are usually scattered and incidental to various other ends. Bringing these remarks together to build a coherent picture of the theory of language adopted in any particular case therefore requires a degree of selection and even speculation. In what follows I have tried to ground discussion in the texts as far as possible and to mark the more crucial points at which reconstruction becomes hypothetical.

For the same reason, the fact that philosophers in the period did not always study language for its own sake, several of the following chapters give a summary indication of how the theory of language in question arises from the wider issues addressed. This is particularly important in the cases of Locke and Berkeley, whose theories of language rest upon, and are not without distortion separable from, their philosophies of mind.

The expositions offered are critical in that an attempt is made to indicate the foundations, and therefore the limitations and presuppositions, of each writer discussed. There is, however, no endeavor to offer new solutions to the philosophical or linguistic problems raised. In this sense the book is basically historical.

1. Hobbes: Formalism

INTRODUCTION

The first serious challenge to the Aristotelian tradition in western logic came in the sixteenth century. Scholars of the Renaissance, imbued with the humanism of the new learning, came to prefer the poetry and breadth of conception found in the newly recovered writings of Plato and Lucretius to the formalities of the Schoolmen. The first influential reaction against Aristotle was that of Petrus Ramus (1515–1572), but it is now generally agreed that the new scheme of logic he offered involved only "a specious rearrangement of the old material, which was no gain."[1] The real challenge to traditional logic came not from Ramus but from Bacon. Ramus attempted to replace the system of Aristotle with an alternative system of his own, but Bacon attacked formal logic itself. In the *Novum Organum* (1620) he proposed not a modification of traditional logic nor even a total reconstruction, but a new kind of logic altogether. Part of his purpose, Bacon announced, concerned "the better and more perfect use of human reason in the inquisition of things, and the true helps of the understanding."

> The art which I introduce with this view (which I call "Interpretation of Nature") is a kind of logic, though the difference between it and the ordinary logic is great, indeed, immense. For the ordinary logic professes to contrive and prepare helps and guards for the understanding, as mine does; and in this one point they agree. But mine differs from it in three points especially—viz., in the end aimed at, in the order of demonstration, and in the starting point of the inquiry.
> For the end which this science of mine proposes is the

> invention not of arguments but of arts; not of things in accordance with principles, but of principles themselves; not of probable reasons, but of designations and directions for works. And as the intention is different, so, accordingly, is the effect; the effect of the one being to overcome an opponent in argument, of the other to command nature in action.
>
> In accordance with this end is also the nature and order of the demonstrations. For in the ordinary logic almost all the work is spent about the syllogism. Of induction, the logicians seem hardly to have taken any serious thought, but they pass it by with a slight notice and hasten on to the formulae of disputation. I, on the contrary, reject demonstration by syllogism as acting too confusedly and letting nature slip out of its hands. For although no one can doubt that things which agree in a middle term agree with one another (which is a proposition of mathematical certainty), yet it leaves an opening for deception, which is this: the syllogism consists of propositions—propositions of words; and words are the tokens and signs of notions. Now if the very notions of the mind (which are as the soul of words and the basis of the whole structure) be improperly and overhastily abstracted from the facts, vague, not sufficiently definite, faulty—in short, in many ways, the whole ediface tumbles.[2]

Bacon therefore rejects the syllogism "in dealing with the nature of things" and turns to induction as "that form of demonstration which upholds the sense, and closes with nature, and comes to the very brink of operation, if it does not actually deal with it."[3]

The criticisms Bacon levelled against formal logic became standard in the seventeenth and eighteenth centuries among those who felt that the old logic was not adequate to the new purposes of science and philosophy. Traditional logic, they claimed, was too much concerned with the formal deduction of the syllogism, too little with facts. In particular they followed Bacon in holding traditional logic to be too much concerned with words—and therefore too much inclined to the mere "formulae of disputation"—when logic should rest upon what Bacon called "notions of the mind," which are in effect what Descartes and Locke later called "ideas."

The attack on the Aristotelian tradition of logic was succeeded by many formulations of "heuristic methodology"[4]—attempts to replace formal logic as a ground of certainty in argument with a theory of ideas and operations upon ideas. The foremost examples are the *Regulae ad directionem ingenii* (written circa 1628) and *Meditationes* (1641) of Descartes, and Locke's *Essay concerning Human Understanding* (1690). The old logic continued to be taught into the nineteenth century, but in England at least few philosophers of importance gave it much attention.[5] The issue between the new logic and the old is complex and receives different statements from different philosophers. At its heart, however, lay a matter which was to affect the philosophy of language in England for over two centuries following Bacon's attack: the old logic was formal, relying on certain formulae (such as the syllogism) to guarantee the validity of arguments, but the new logic cast doubt upon these "forms of disputation" as mere words, and in seeking certainty in induction or in regulated comparisons of ideas claimed to be turning from weak words to hard facts. The suspicion cast on words by the new logic, which can be clearly seen in the passage quoted from Bacon, was the reason for the reappraisal of language undertaken by the Royal Society[6] and was a major conditioning factor in the approach to language adopted in Locke's *Essay*.

Having rejected formalism in logic Descartes and Locke, the foremost among the new logicians, turned to a theory of ideas as a basis for certainty. In their writings certainty became a psychological matter involving ideas and the ways in which they relate to one another in the mind, a matter of "intuition" or the "light" of reason. Yet although the foundations of logic now lay in ideas and not in language, language of some kind remained necessarily the medium in which any logical argument must manifest itself. Theoretically the Cartesian philosopher is responsible to no one but himself and needs no authority but his own for arguments which he formulates in his mind without the offices of language and without an intention to communicate his findings. In practice, however, it was recognized that language remained integral to logic not only for purposes of communication (if desired) but also because—as the philosophers of ideas were well aware—a man who reasons with himself alone is liable to deficiency of memory. How can he be sure at the end of his chain of reasoning that the memory he has of coming correctly to his conclusion is not deceptive? To ensure that memory does not deceive him he must record his reasoning in the public domain—he must use language, whether it be ordinary languge or some special logical language or notation. Hence the urgency with which philosophers of the period sought a sound method of linguistic analysis, a set of procedures to mediate between the psychological foundation which was the proper source of certainty and the language upon which logic depended for both communication and a guarantee against the fallibility of memory. The method of analysis required would consist in rules for translating between the "deep-structure" level of ideas and mental operations and the "surface-structure" level of verbal propositions.

The burst of linguistic study in England and France in the latter half of the seventeenth century was governed largely by pursuit of such a method. The philosophy of language, in its phase between the Renaissance and the rise of comparative philology at the end of the eighteenth century, was chiefly concerned with exploration of the relation between linguistic structures and underlying thought processes. Locke's philosophy of language must be seen in this perspective. His *Essay* is an attempt to fill the vacuum left by the failure of the old logic after the criticisms of Bacon and Descartes to supply grounds for certainty. Suspicious of words, Locke turns instead to ideas and mental operations. Language is reintroduced in relation to these new psychological substructures, and the purpose of the philosophy of language is to show how it *should* serve to record and communicate the products of the cognitive faculties.[7]

Not all the major philosophers of the period accepted uncritically the strictures against formal logic advanced by Bacon and Descartes. The most notable exception is Hobbes, at once one of the most radical thinkers of the age and yet among the major figures perhaps the one in closest touch with his Scholastic forebears. Hobbes is content to accept a modified version of the logic which Locke and Berkeley (following Bacon and Descartes) reject, with the result that his theory of language rests upon a different set of presuppositions and is wholly unlike theirs in character. Locke and Berkeley, seeking to ground reasoning upon ideas and mental operations, considered language exclusively in the light of its underlying mental machinery. Hobbes, however, adopts an approach to language which by contrast might be labelled "formal."

Hobbes' writings on language are mostly distributed through three of his essays, sometimes overlapping, sometimes supplementing, sometimes contradicting each other. They are: *Human Nature* (chapters 1–6), first published in 1640 as part of the *Elements of Law*; *Leviathan* (chapters 1–7), published in 1651; and *De Corpore* (chapters 1–5), published in 1655 and translated in 1656 as *Elements of Philosophy, The First Section, Concerning Body*.[8] We begin with a brief account of his theory of mind in order to show the place of language in Hobbes' philosophy, and then proceed in section 3 to his theory of signs and names. An outline of Hobbes' account of reasoning below will show the formalism of his theory in operation.

THE THEORY OF MIND

The origin of all knowledge for Hobbes is *sense*.

> CONCERNING the thoughts of man.... *Singly*, they are every one a representation or appearance, of some quality, or other accident of a body without us, which is commonly called an object. Which object worketh on the eyes, ears, and other parts of a man's body; and by diversity of working, produceth diversity of appearances.
> The original of them all, is that which we call SENSE, for there is no conception in a man's mind, which hath not at first, totally, or by parts, been begotten upon the organs of sense. The rest are derived from that original. (III.1)

The world, according to Hobbes' materialism, consists entirely of body and motion. Sense, therefore, like all other phenomena, is to be explained in terms of the motion of bodies.

> The cause of sense, is the external body, or object, which presseth the organ proper to each sense, either immediately, as in the taste and touch; or mediately, as in seeing, hearing, and smelling; which pressure, by the mediation of nerves, and other strings and membranes of the body, continued inwards

> to the brain, and heart, causeth there a resistance, or counter-pressure, or endeavour of the heart to deliver itself, which endeavour, because *outward*, seemeth to be some matter without. And this *seeming*, or *fancy*, is that which men call *sense*.
> (III.1–2)

Sense is defined as "a phantasm, made by the reaction and endeavour outwards in the organ of sense, caused by an endeavour inwards from the object, remaining for some time more or less" (I.391). Motions of bodies in the external world affect our senses and give rise to appearances or "phantasms" in the mind. (Mind and its phantasms are of course simply matter in motion.) Because the "inward" motion from the object to the brain and heart provokes a counter motion "outward" the appearances may seem to be outside us although in fact they are all necessarily in the mind. (Hobbes agrees in general with the distinction drawn by Galileo and Descartes between primary and secondary qualities and with the conclusion that whereas ideas of primary qualities represent real qualities of the body perceived the ideas of secondary qualities have nothing corresponding to them outside the mind. Hobbes does not pause to explore the details and difficulties of this position.)

The definition of sense includes the requirement that the phantasm should remain "for some time more or less" after the object which originally caused it has ceased to act upon the senses. Conception in the absence of the object causing it is properly called not *sense* but *imagination*. Retention of the appearance after removal of the object is important because it provides Hobbes with a foundation for the distinction of mind from a merely passive receiver of sensations. He explains the phenomenon in terms of the law of inertia derived from Galileo.

> When a body is once in motion, it moveth, unless something else hinder it, eternally; and whatsoever hindreth it, cannot in an instant, but in time, and by degrees, quite extinguish it; and as we see in the water, though the wind cease, the waves give not over rolling for a long time after: so also it happeneth in that motion, which is made in the internal parts of a man, then, when he sees, dreams, &c. For after the object is re-

> moved, or the eyes shut, we still retain an image of the thing seen, though more obscure than when we see it. And this is it, the Latins call *imagination*, from the image made in seeing; and apply the same, though improperly, to all the other senses. But the Greeks call it fancy; which signifies appearance, and is as proper to one sense, as to another. IMAGINATION therefore is nothing but *decaying sense*; and is found in men, and many other living creatures, as well sleeping, as waking. (III.4–5; *cf.* IV.9)

The motions of sense "decay" eventually not because they run down or fade away of themselves (which would be contrary to the law of inertia) but because they meet resistance in the form of other motions of sense which take their place. Such an explanation presupposes that the mind cannot hold an indefinite number of phantasms at one time. Hobbes in fact believes that we experience phantasms singly and that each one decays as a stronger motion of sense replaces it.

> And yet such is the nature of sense, that it does not permit a man to discern many things at once. For seeing the nature of sense consists in motion; as long as the organs are employed about one object, they cannot be so moved by another at the same time, as to make by both their motions one sincere phantasm of each of them at once. And therefore two several phantasms will not be made by two objects working together, but only one phantasm compounded from the action of both.
> (I.394)

The strongest motion of sense, that which at any given moment replaces all others and presents its phantasm to the imagination, is that caused by an object currently affecting the organs of sense.

"Thoughts" or "conceptions" succeed one another in the mind and this succession Hobbes calls "mental discourse" (III.11) or "discursion." The succession is not random even when not dictated by sense, for "as we have no imagination, whereof we have not formerly had sense, in whole, or in parts; so we have no transition from one imagination to another, whereof we never had the like before in our senses" (III.11). There follows Hobbes' account of what was later to become known as the "association" of ideas.

> All fancies are motions within us, relics of those made in the sense: and those motions that immediately succeeded one another in the sense, continue also together after sense: insomuch as the former coming again to take place, and be predominant, the latter followeth, by coherence of matter moved, in such manner, as water upon a plain table is drawn which way any one part of it is guided by the finger.
> (III.11–12; *cf.* I.397–398)

The explanation depends upon the crucial ability to retain the idea after the object has ceased to work upon the senses. The overlap of the decaying idea and the new sense impression provides the "cohesion" among ideas which gives rise to their subsequent association.

Hobbes distinguishes two types of succession: the "casual" or "unguided" and the "orderly" or "regulated" (IV.14 and III.12–13). Although no association is possible which has not been first encountered in sensation Hobbes points out that after a little experience every sensation is potentially associated with a great many others. As a result "it comes to pass in time, that in the imagining of any thing, there is no certainty what we shall imagine next" (III.12). So many associations are made available by experience that the "unguided" mind can ramble virtually without restriction. Unlike Hume, Hobbes has no interest in finding the principles of this apparently free association. He is concerned only with "regulated" thought sequences, which in *Leviathan* he divides into two kinds: "one, when of an effect imagined we seek the causes, or means that produce it: and this is common to man and beast. The other is, when imagining any thing whatsoever, we seek all the possible effects, that can be produced; that is to say, we imagine what we can do with it" (III.13).

Although experience is its necessary precondition, regulated association is not a mechanical process but is governed by what Hobbes calls "appetite" (IV.15; *cf.* III.13), by our desire to follow a particular direction or to achieve a specific end in our train of thought. In its power to direct or regulate its thinking to predetermined ends the mind becomes independent of sensation in that it does not require the presence of sensations to direct its thought but can, as it were, create ideas to or from which it may proceed. This is done by means of *marks*, which are in Hobbes' terminology signs created by the individual for his own mnemonic use.

> SEEING the *succession* of conceptions in the *mind* are caused, as hath been said before, by the succession they *had* one to another when they were produced by the *senses*, and that there is no conception that hath not been produced immediately before or after innumerable others, by the innumerable acts of sense; it must needs follow, that one *conception* followeth *not* another, according to our election, and the need we have of them, *but* as it *chanceth* us to hear or see such things as shall bring them to our mind. The experience we have hereof, is in such brute beasts, which, having the providence to hide the remains and superfluity of their meat, do nevertheless want the remembrance of the place where they hid it, and thereby make no benefit thereof in their hunger: but man, who in this point beginneth to rank himself somewhat above the nature of beasts, hath observed and remembered the cause of this defect, and to amend the same, hath imagined or devised to set up a visible or other sensible mark, the which, when he seeth it again, may bring to his mind the thought he had when he set it up. (IV.19–20)

How far ideas may be regulated by our appetites, fears, and desires alone is not sharply determined. Some animals share with man the ability to learn from experience and to regulate thought to the extent of recalling past successions of ideas and anticipating those to come. But the higher faculties in Hobbes' view depend upon the use not only of marks (private signs) but also of *speech*, which is a uniquely human function. Without language man would be endowed with only sense, imagination, memory, and prudence (the ability to anticipate on the basis of past experience). Other higher faculties depend upon the use of language.

> Those other faculties, of which I shall speak by and by, and which seem proper to men only, are acquired and increased by study and industry; and of most men learned by instruction, and discipline; and proceed all from the invention of

> words, and speech. For besides sense, and thoughts, the mind of man has no other motion; though by the help of speech, and method, the same faculties may be improved to such a hight, as to distinguish men from all other living creatures.
> (III.16)

The use of private marks for the guidance of regulated thought is necessarily limited by the fallibility of memory. The use of *signs*, which are in Hobbes' terminology essentially public (I.14–15), is therefore a precondition for any thinking advanced much beyond the animal level. *Names* are the kind of sign most commonly used by men for these purposes (I.15).

Hobbes is aware of the difficulty raised for the notion of private thought or "discursion" by its inevitable reliance on memory.[9] How can we be sure, having arrived at the end of our chain of thought, that we did in fact arrive there by due process and that there were no breaks in the chain? How can we be certain of the conclusions of our reasoning? Of course we remember our thought processes—but memory, as we know, is fallible. What might guarantee our memory in such a case? For Descartes in the *Regulae* the answer lies in the flash of intuition which, giving us an instantaneous grasp of the whole argument, avoids reliance upon memory. For Hobbes, who does not share the Cartesian suspicion of language and formal logic, the answer lies in words, in the use of a system of public signs.

> How unconstant and fading men's thoughts are, and how much the recovery of them depends upon chance, there is none but knows by infallible experience in himself. For no man is able to remember quantities without sensible and present measures, nor colours without sensible and present patterns, nor number without the names of numbers disposed in order and learned by heart. So that whatsoever a man has put together in his mind by ratiocination without such help, will presently slip from him, and not be revocable but by beginning his ratiocination anew. From which it follows, that, for the acquiring of philosophy, some sensible moniments are necessary, by which our past thoughts may be not only reduced, but also registered every one in its own order.
> (I.13–14)

Here, however, Hobbes' argument breaks down as he goes on to say that such "moniments" are what he calls "marks" which are "sensible things taken at pleasure, that, by the sense of them, such thoughts may be recalled to our mind as are like those thoughts for which we took them" and are "for our own [not public] use" (I.14–15). The mark so defined is itself subject to memory, for its meaning might be forgotten. What Hobbes needs here is the "sign," the public mark whose sense is guaranteed against memory by its use in the public domain. The fallibility of memory then justifies the Hobbesian conclusion that *understanding* is dependent upon speech (III.28; *cf.* III.11).

In Hobbes' conclusion that the mind relies upon language to redress memory obviously lies a source for several of Locke's observations on the relation between words and ideas. When Locke points out that our ability to conceive ideas of mixed and simple modes is often dependent upon our having learnt names for them he is borrowing one aspect of Hobbes' more general argument.[10] Locke wishes to retain thought as the basis for language and therefore admits language as a necessary prop for thought only in a number of exceptional cases (although we are left free to observe that the exceptions cover a significantly large portion of the lexicon). Hobbes on the other hand sees the fallibility of memory as fundamental and as indicating that the mind's ability to pursue even the simplest thought processes is severely limited in the absence of the use of signs. Locke insists that all statements should be resolvable into the ideas and mental operations in which their meaning and structure are grounded, whereas Hobbes insists, in a manner to be explained below, that the truth grounds of statements lie in the meaning and structure of language.

THE THEORY OF SIGNS AND NAMES

> Now, those things we call SIGNS are the *antecedents of their consequents, and the consequents of their antecedents, as often as we observe them to go before or follow after in the same manner.*
> (I.14; *cf.* III.15)

This, the Hobbesian definition of a sign, is much the same as that which Locke approached in his theory of judgment (but finally rejected) and which Berkeley later accepted. It is an associationist definition; a sign is anything regularly associated (in temporal occurrence) with anything else. The Lockean definition holds a sign to be that which stands for an idea *in the mind of the speaker*; the associationist definition set out by Hobbes and evidently followed by Berkeley (whose concept of "suggestion" is a version of associationism) is neutral between speaker and audience. A sign is that which indicates an idea in *any* mind.

As it stands in Hobbes however the definition is too broad, for not only does it avoid specifying the mind in which the association is to occur but it also fails to state that the association should have any special purpose—with the result that *any* observed connection is by definition a sign. The mind is consequently flooded with signs—not only those used in communication but all the regular connections among ideas established in experience. This is the situation Locke wishes to avoid when he tries to distinguish association from judgment; judgments are common property, uses of signs derived from general experience, but what he calls associations are idiosyncratic, and although otherwise indistinguishable from judgments are to be rejected as akin to madness.[11]

Hobbes' distinction between natural and arbitrary signs is designed to alleviate this situation by allowing us to distinguish among the class of signs the smaller class of man-made signs to which most if not all of the signs of language belong. After the definition quoted above Hobbes continues:

> For example, a thick cloud is a sign of rain to follow, and rain a sign that a cloud has gone before, for this reason only, that we seldom see clouds without the consequence of rain, nor rain at anytime but when a cloud has gone before. And of signs, some are *natural*, whereof I have already given an example, others are *arbitrary*, namely, those we make choice of at our own pleasure, as a bush hung up, signifies that wine is to be sold there; a stone set in the ground signifies the bound of a field; and words so and so connected, signify the cogitations and motions of our mind. (I.14–15)

The distinction between these two kinds of signs serves to show that the original definition of signs is far too broad. Natural and arbitrary signs are so very different from one another that we are left wondering whether there is any useful sense in which the name "sign" should be applied to both. It is essential to natural signs that the two elements, the signifier and the signified (*e.g.*, the dark cloud and the rain) should regularly occur together—or at least in quick succession. The sign will survive an occasional occurrence of either element in the absence of the other, but if in something approaching half the cases of the sighting of dark clouds no rain follows then the future sighting of a cloud will no more lead me to anticipate rain than its absence. As Hobbes says, the sign functions *"for this reason only,* that we seldom see clouds without the consequence of rain, nor rain at any time but when a cloud has gone before" (my italics). The arbitrary sign, however, does not depend on regular coincidence of signified and signifier; indeed, the very point of the institution of such signs would seem to be to enable us to signify that which is not present. My use of the word "horse," for example, does not in any way depend upon the regular—or even occasional—coincidence of horses with the word in my experience. (It might be argued that my learning the word in the first place depended upon its being used in my experience in the presence of horses; it may be answered first that we are talking not of the learning of signs but of their normal use, and second that this objection is very hard to maintain in cases of words which do not name or refer to physical objects.) Put in this way the difference between natural and arbitrary signs seems more striking than any similarity, and the original definition now seems to fit the natural sign much more comfortably than the artificial. The artificial sign, we are inclined to say, has very little to do with the co-occurrence of consequents and antecedents.

In order to maintain his original definition of signs against this objection Hobbes might have argued that artificial signs are normally accompanied by ideas or conceptions; although the word "horse" often occurs in the absence of real horses, he might have said, it rarely occurs meaningfully in my experience without my having more or less concurrently an idea of a horse. In this way the artificial sign might be held to conform to the definition in terms of consequents and antecedents. We have already suggested, however, that in the final analysis Hobbes will not favor this view that words need be regularly accompanied by ideas. In so far as this is so there is a conflict between his account of *signs*, which seem to require the accompanying ideas, and his theory of *language* in which the necessity for such ideas is denied.

In Hobbes' discussion of names (which are a species of signs) there is an interesting passage which at first appears to assert a virtually Lockean semantic theory in requiring the concomitance of words and ideas in the meaningful use of language.

> But seeing names ordered in speech (as is defined) are signs of our conceptions, it is manifest they are not signs of the things themselves; for that the sound of this word *stone* should be the sign of a stone, cannot be understood in any sense but this, that he that hears it collects that he that pronounces it thinks of a stone. (I.17)

Words cannot signify *things* because there are meaningful words such as "future" and "nothing," as well as negative terms, to which no things correspond (I.17–19). Hobbes appears to say that words must therefore stand for *ideas*. What he actually says, however, is that a word is a sign of something only because "he that hears it *collects that* he that pronounces it thinks of a stone" (my italics), which is very different from the Lockean position because it presents the word in terms of its interpretation rather than its utterance. A word is seen as that by means of which a hearer understands a speaker. The problems of semantic idealism do not arise; if by chance I use the word "horse" without an accompanying idea of a horse the word is nonetheless understood in the usual way. In this passage at least Hobbes has been careful to avoid commitment to the view that requires a meaningful word to be accompanied by an idea. The problem we found in the previous paragraph concerning the definition of a sign still remains, however.

We can avoid the problem of signs defined in terms of antecedents and consequents by concentrating instead upon *names*. A name is defined as "a word taken at pleasure to serve for a mark, which may raise in our mind a thought like some thought we had before, and which being pronounced to others, may be to them a sign of what thought the speaker had, or had not before his mind" (I.16).[12] Names are always *arbitrary* signs, which means that in dealing with language we may ignore the general definition of signs which is fitted rather to the *natural* sign. Names are arbitrary signs and are defined consistently with the passage from I.17 just quoted; they are the means whereby a hearer forms a belief as to what the speaker has in mind.

Hobbes classifies names as positive or negative (I.18) and as common or proper (I.19). The latter distinction leads him into an assertion of nominalism. Hobbes was the chief reviver of nominalism in seventeenth-century English philosophy. In developing the consequences of nominalist doctrines for the philosophy of language he was to have several important followers, including Berkeley and Dugald Stewart. Here is Hobbes' best statement of his position:

> Secondly, of names, some are *common* to many things, as a *man*, a *tree*; others *proper* to one thing, as *he that writ the Iliad, Homer, this man, that man*. And a common name, being the name of many things severally taken, but not collectively of all together (as man is not the name of all mankind, but of every one, as of Peter, John, and the rest severally) is therefore called an *universal name*; and therefore this word *universal* is never the name of any thing existent in nature, nor of any idea or phantasm formed in the mind, but always the name of some word or name; so that when *a living creature, a stone, a spirit*, or any other thing, is said to be *universal*, it is not to be understood, that any man, stone, &c. ever was or can be universal, but only that these words, *living creature, stone, &c*, are *universal names*, that is names common to many things; and the conceptions answering them in our mind, are the images and phantasms of several living creatures, or other things. And therefore, for the understanding of the extent of an universal name, we need no other faculty but that of our imagination, by which we remember that such names bring sometimes one thing, sometimes another into our mind.
> (I.19–20)

Some names name only one thing (*e.g.*, *Homer*), but others (*tree, man*) are names of a number of things. The latter we call "universal," but universality consists only in the applicability of the name to a plurality of things; nothing in reality (and nothing in the mind) other than the name is universal. The crux of the matter lies in the last sentence of the passage quoted; the working of the name depends upon our ability, which Hobbes assigns to "imagination," to identify the particulars to which a given universal name applies. The word "man" names a number of particulars and signifies to me a certain conception in the mind of a speaker, but it does so successfully only if I know the class of particulars it denotes. Where do I derive my knowledge of these classifications? When a new particular comes into my experience how do I know whether or not the name "man" applies to it? If indeed I do know this it can only be because the new particular corresponds (or fails to correspond) in specific ways to all of those particulars to which the name "man" is already given—*i.e.*, because the name is in fact bestowed by virtue of features common to all the particulars named by it. Such at least is Hobbes' opinion: "One universal name is imposed on many things, for their similitude in some quality, or other accident" (III.21). But this is a thinly disguised return to the philosophy of realism: the features by virtue of which particulars receive their common names are the universals whose real existence was initially denied.[13]

Hobbes usually ignores the problems and takes the nominalist position as sufficiently established, an assumption which greatly reinforces his belief that thought depends heavily upon language. If there are no universals and no conception of universals outside language then all general knowledge, all knowledge which goes beyond the level of particulars, can be reached and formulated only through names. Without language I might, *ceteris paribus*, be able to obtain knowledge of particular things, but I could know nothing about any class or collection of things, nothing which would be true of *any* member of such a class or collection.

> For example: a man that hath no use of speech at all, such as is born and remains perfectly deaf and dumb, if he set before his eyes a triangle, and by it two right angles, such as are the corners of a square figure, he may, by meditation, compare and find, that the three angles of that triangle, are equal to

those two right angles that stand by it. But if another triangle be shown him, different in shape from the former, he cannot know, without a new labour, whether the three angles of that also be equal to the same. But he that hath the use of words, when he observes, that such equality was consequent, not to the length of the sides, nor to any other particular thing in his triangle; but only to this, that the sides were straight, and the angles three; and that that was all, for which he named it a triangle; will boldly conclude universally, that such equality of angles is in all triangles whatsoever; and register his invention in these general terms, *every triangle hath its three angles equal to two right angles.* (III.22)

The dependence of all general knowledge upon universal names leads directly into Hobbes' account of formal reasoning, which will be considered in the next section.

Signs and marks, in conclusion, name *things* but achieve their effect in use by signifying or suggesting to a hearer *what the speaker has in mind*. (In the special and problematic case of marks, speaker and hearer are one person who seeks to call to mind what he himself was thinking on a previous occasion.) Signs and marks may be either natural or arbitrary. All names are arbitrary, and may be classified in several ways, of which the most important is according to whether they name one thing or many. Overall the chief distinctions of Hobbes' theory of signs may be tabulated as shown in Figure 1.

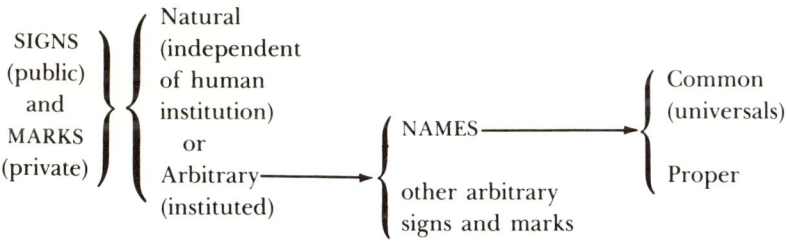

Fig. 1

Figure 1 shows how Hobbes' theory of names fits into a wider account of signs and marks, although these wider concepts, for reasons we have suggested, are not very profitable. The theory of names is also part of the theory of language, or of what Hobbes calls "speech"—not the whole of it, for Hobbes is as well aware as Locke that language comprises more than names alone. *Speech* consists "of *names* or *appellations*, and their connexion; whereby men register their thoughts; recall them when they are past; and also declare them to one another for mutual utility and conversation" (III.18). Like Locke, therefore, Hobbes classifies all words as either names or connectives, but he pursues the matter of the connectives no further than to isolate the copula, which is essential to his account of reasoning.

THE THEORY OF LOGIC

Besides "speech" in general there are also "speeches," particular utterances or kinds of utterance in language. Of these the most important for Hobbes is the *proposition*.

> A PROPOSITION is a speech consisting of two names copulated, by which he that speaketh signifies he conceives the latter name to be the name of the same thing whereof the former is the name; or (which is all one) that the former name is comprehended by the latter. For example, this speech, *man is a living creature*, in which two names are copulated by the verb *is*, is a *proposition*, for this reason, that he that speaks it conceives both *living creature* and *man* to be names of the same thing, or that the former name, *man*, is comprehended by the latter name, *living creature*. Now the former name is commonly called the *subject*, or *antecedent*, or the *contained name*, and the latter the *predicate, consequent*, or *containing name*. The sign of connection amongst most nations is either some word, as the word *is* in the proposition *man is a living creature*, or some case or termination of a word, as in this proposition, *man walketh* (which is equivalent to this, *man is walking*); the termination by which it is said he *walketh*, rather than *is walking*, signifieth that those two are understood to be copulated, or to be names of the same thing. (I.30–31)

Hobbes' traditional view of the structure of the proposition anticipates that of Locke and the Port-Royal grammarians. Unlike Locke, however, Hobbes avoids the Cartesian language of the "perception" or "intuition" of "agreement or disagreement" between the things or ideas named. For Hobbes the proposition works not by virtue of any underlying psychological machinery but because by means of the copula the extensions of the names are said to overlap.

The reasons why this must be so lie in Hobbes' nominalism. When I say "man is a living creature" I can be talking about nothing but particular things. What I say of them is simply that all those which can be designated by the first term can also be designated by the second. Universals are common names which differ among themselves by being "more or less common" (I.20)—*i.e.*, in being the names of a greater or lesser number of things. "Living creature" is more common than "man," and since all the things designated by the latter are also designated by the former the name "living creature" *comprehends* the name "man" (III.21). It is a matter of what we would now call class inclusion.

The different kinds of proposition (Hobbes accepts the traditional classifications: universal and particular, affirmative and negative) simply say that the collection of particulars named by one term is or is not wholly or partially coincident with the collection of particulars named by the other. A proposition is true if as a matter of fact the names are so used: "man is a living creature" is true if all the things called "man" are also called "living creature." Since Hobbes believes that names are assigned arbitrarily he is led directly to the "conventional" theory of truth, which he states as follows:

> Now these words *true, truth,* and *true proposition,* are equivalent to one another; for truth consists in speech, and not in the things spoken of; and though *true* be sometimes opposed to *apparent* or *feigned,* yet it is always to be referred to the truth of a proposition; for the image of a man in a glass, or a ghost, is therefore denied to be a very man, because this proposition, *a ghost is a man,* is not true; for it cannot be denied but that a ghost is a very ghost. And therefore truth or verity is not any affection of the thing, but of the proposition concerning it. . . .
>
> And from hence it is evident, that truth and falsity have no place but amongst such living creatures as use speech. . . .

> From hence also this may be deduced, that the first truths were arbitrarily made by those that first of all imposed names upon things, or received them from the imposition of others. For it is true (for example) that *man is a living creature*, but it is for this reason, that it pleased men to impose both those names on the same thing. (I.35–36)

The man in the street would say that "man is a living creature" is true because, as a matter of fact, man *is* a living creature. Developing the Cartesian position, Locke holds that a proposition is true if it correctly states the agreement or disagreement of the ideas signified by its terms; "man is a living creature" is true because the idea of man "agrees with" the idea of a living creature. Hobbes says that truth is a function of language: a proposition is true if convention assigns to its terms denotations related (by inclusion, exclusion, or partial inclusion) in the way stated by the proposition.

In Hobbes' nominalism and conventionalism lie the grounds for his assertion that the faculty of "reason" is "nothing but *reckoning*, that is adding and subtracting, of the consequences of general names agreed upon for the *marking* and *signifying* of our thoughts" (III.30). Reasoning is a formal process in much the same way as is a mathematical calculation, a process consisting in the manipulation of symbols according to determined rules. If in solving a mathematical problem we follow the rules appropriate to the symbols we shall arrive at the correct answer even though we may know nothing of the circumstances which gave rise to the problem. Similarly, Hobbes suggests, we can work with propositions in terms of class inclusion without worrying about what the terms refer to. For example, just as we can solve the equation $2x + 3 = 11$ without enquiring what it is that is being numbered, so we can determine the truth of "man is a living creature" by comparing the extensions of the terms without further concern for the natures of men and living creatures. It is true that to understand a proposition we must understand the meanings of the terms to the extent of knowing to which particulars they are applicable, but since this is a matter fixed solely by human institution (by convention) it amounts to no more than simply knowing the language. Reasoning for Hobbes may therefore be said to be a *formal* procedure conducted in the linguistic medium.

Computation of the truth of propositions is only a beginning. A series of propositions connected by common terms can form arguments the validity of which may be "reckoned" in the same way, the conclusion being guaranteed as in a mathematical calculation by the correct application of the rules to the symbols. The classical example of such a formalized argument is the syllogism, and thus Hobbes in the generation after Bacon and Descartes readmits by way of nominalism and conventionalism the formal logic which they had denounced. Bacon and Descartes in different ways had both rejected traditional logic because of its formalism, because—to put it simply—in operating with signs and formulae (words and syllogisms) one is liable to lose sight of what one is talking about. They feared that the words would take over and the meaning be lost.

An interesting confrontation occurs when Hobbes states his view in his Objections to Descartes' *Meditationes* in 1641. Hobbes writes:

> But what shall we now say, if reasoning chance to be nothing more than the uniting and stringing together of names or designations by the word is? It will be a consequence of this that reason gives us no conclusion about the nature of things, but only about the terms that designate them, whether, indeed, or not there is a convention (arbitrarily made about their meanings) according to which we join these names together. If this be so, as is possible, reasoning will depend on names, names on the imagination, and imagination, perchance, as I think, on the motion of the corporeal organs.

Reasoning depends upon names because it is about the denotations of terms. Names depend upon imagination presumably in the sense of the passage on I.20 which defines imagination as that "by which we remember that such names bring sometimes one thing, sometimes another, into our mind," as the faculty whereby we apprehend the extension of a general term. Imagination is a faculty of the mind which is in turn nothing but matter in motion.

This is a stark exhibition of Hobbes' account of reason along with some of its implications. Not only is the rational process formal but it is also mechanical. Here we can briefly glimpse the debate in a wider context: formalism in logic could be seen as debasing human nature by reducing its highest mental faculty to a mechanical operation and thus opening the way to atheism and materialism. Against formalism, in this broader perspective, Descartes and Locke asserted the indispensability of the divine spark of human reason, the flash of "intuition" or "perception" which made the mental connections on the basis of which propositions were built. Reasoning is not about names nor even dependent upon them, they held, but is a pre-verbal mental process which deals, through the necessary mediation of ideas, with the nature of reality. To Hobbes' Objection Descartes replies:

> Moreover, in reasoning we unite not names but the things signified by the names; and I marvel that the opposite can occur to anyone. For who doubts whether a Frenchman and a German are able to reason in exactly the same way about the same things, though they yet conceive the words in an entirely diverse way? And has not my opponent condemned himself in talking of conventions arbitrarily made about the meanings of words? For, if he admits that words signify anything, why will he not allow our reasonings to refer to this something that is signified, rather than to the words alone?[14]

(The two last sentences from Descartes miss the mark, for Hobbes' claim that reasoning depends upon names does not deny that the names used in reasoning might refer to things. The first two sentences of the passage point out that Hobbes' conventionalism appears to commit him to a degree of linguistic relativism and therefore to leave him with problems of interlinguistic communication to explain.)

This completes an outline of a Hobbesian theory of language. Alternative versions could no doubt be formulated by emphasizing different passages, for Hobbes is at once cursory, repetitious, and inconsistent in his treatment of the subject. He is not always clear, for instance, about the distinction between extensional and intensional readings of terms in propositions. The reading given here, however, in this and other cases, is that to which Hobbes seems most strongly committed. From the theory outlined two related conclusions follow concerning the place of language in rational thought. First, from the doctrine of nominalism it follows that all reasoning beyond the level of particulars must depend upon names, because all things (including ideas) are particular. Second, following from the foregoing in conjunction with the conventional theory of truth is the belief that reasoning is primarily a formal, linguistic process; the mind functions in reasoning only by recognizing symbols (understanding denotations) and applying to them the appropriate rules (of what Hobbes calls "reckoning"). The first of these conclusions is in effect an extreme form of the idea also found in Locke and Berkeley that certain areas of thought are not possible without language. The second involves a more radical departure and is what sets Hobbesian theory most distinctively apart from other philosophies of language in the period.

In different ways Bacon and Descartes had both challenged traditional logic precisely because of its strong tendency towards formalism, and in its place they had suggested modes of reasoning which were deliberately non-formal in their constant attention to the referents of terms. This same fear of formalism no doubt influenced Locke and Berkeley to maintain the ideational view of analysis as the foundation of linguistic theory in spite of the many cases they discovered in which words appeared to be more fundamental than ideas. Hobbes himself is evidently not comfortable with the extreme position at which he arrives, very probably because he too felt apprehensive at the prospect of purely formal reasoning. His hesitations, which we ignored in our exposition of his theory, manifest themselves in several ways. He defines "speech," for instance, as "words so connected that they become signs *of our thoughts*" (I.15; my italics), even though his nominalism dictates that there can be no "thoughts" corresponding in any precise way to general terms. Even more equivocal is Hobbes' insistence that knowledge necessarily implies both truth and *evidence*. Truth, as we have seen, he believes to be conventional— a verbal phenomenon—but evidence is conceptual.

> [Evidence] is concomitance of a man's *conception* with the *words* that signify such conception in the act of ratiocination: for

> when a man reasoneth with his lips only, to which the mind suggesteth only the beginning, and followeth not the words of his mouth with the conceptions of his mind, out of custom of so speaking; though he begin his ratiocination with true propositions, and proceed with certain syllogisms, and thereby make always true conclusions; yet are not his conclusions *evident* to him, for want of the *concomitance of conception* with his words: for if the words alone were sufficient, a *parrot* might be taught as well to know truth as to speak it. (IV.28)

He appears to be raising the common-sense objection to formal reasoning that to conduct an argument formally is of no profit because at the end of it the conclusion, although technically valid, will not be understood or appreciated. Yet Hobbes admits that formal reasoning can guarantee "true conclusions," and he makes no attempt to reconcile this demand for accompanying conceptions with what he says elsewhere about the dependence of general reasoning upon signs.

Similar uncertainties occur in Hobbes' account of the syllogism. He first presents the syllogism as a formula, the structure of which, in certain figures, guarantees the validity of its conclusions. But here again, as in his doctrine of evidence, Hobbes makes an apparent concession to the logic of ideas and the correspondence theory of truth, devoting a paragraph to "the thoughts in the mind answering to a direct syllogism" (I.49–50) and giving an account of the way in which "phantasms" corresponding to the terms of the syllogism succeed one another in the mind. As in the case of "evidence" this psychological account of reasoning appears to conflict with the general claim that reasoning is verbal.

The example Hobbes gives, however, shows that his psychological claims may be more limited than they at first appear.

> For example, when this syllogism is made, *man is a living creature, a living creature is a body*, therefore, *man is a body*, the mind conceives first an image of a man speaking or discoursing, and remembers that that, which so appears, is called *man;* then it has the image of the same man moving, and remembers that that, which appears so, is called *living creature*; thirdly, it conceives an image of the same man, as filling some place or space, and remembers that what appears so is called

body; and lastly, when it remembers that that thing, which was extended, and moved and spake, was one and the same thing, and that therefore *man is a living creature* is a true proposition.
(I.50)

A syllogism necessarily contains at least one universal term (I.47), but to a strict nominalism nothing outside language corresponds to this universality. Therefore, as is evident from the description Hobbes gives, the mind in considering general terms necessarily proceeds by taking particular instances as tokens of the classes which the terms denote. It remains finally true for Hobbes "that living creatures that have not the use of speech, have no conception or thought in the mind, answering to a syllogism made of universal propositions" (I.50).

Hobbes' reservations are significant of the strength in his day of the distrust of language introduced into modern philosophy by Bacon and Descartes and fundamental to most philosophizing on the subject for well over a century thereafter. In spite of these reservations Hobbes succeeds in presenting some important alternatives to generally current linguistic theories. He shows that from bases in nominalism and conventionalism can be derived an inversion of the generally accepted relations between language and thought, placing words prior to ideas and language prior to reason. Such a notion would hardly have gained ground in the age of Locke even had it not been associated with the disreputable author of *Leviathan*. And in fact the Hobbesian theory of language was, in England, largely eclipsed by that of Locke.[15]

2. Lockean Theory: Idealism

INTRODUCTION

Locke's great *Essay concerning Human Understanding*[1] (1690) is divided into four books. The first and shortest argues that there is no innate knowledge. The second and longest presents and explores the fundamental Lockean tenet that all knowledge derives from experience, which in turn consists in "ideas" derived from sensation and reflection (II.i.2). Here Locke in justifying this thesis conducts a critical classification of the contents of the mind, which he calls "ideas," with the object of showing how the different kinds of ideas, which together provide all the material of human knowledge, are obtained from experience. Ideas provide the material of human knowledge but not knowledge itself; to have an idea is not necessarily to *know* anything. The fourth book outlines a theory of knowledge in terms of mental operations performed upon ideas. It offers in effect a theory of logic which crowns the ediface of Lockean empiricism.

Locke's original design for the work had no place for an account of language, but having discovered in the composition of Book II how closely the analysis of thought was bound up with linguistic issues he decided to insert between the theory of ideas and the theory of knowledge an outline of linguistic theory. At the end of the second book he wrote:

> Having thus given an account of the original, sorts, and extent of our *Ideas*, with several other Considerations about these (I know not whether I may say) Instruments, or Materials, of our Knowledge, the method I at first proposed to my self, would now require, that I should immediately proceed to shew, what use the Understanding makes of them, and what

> Knowledge we have by them. This was that, which, in the first general view I had of this Subject, was all that I thought I should have to do: but upon a nearer approach, I find, that there is so close a connexion between *Ideas* and Words; and our abstract *Ideas*, and general Words, have so constant a relation one to another, that it is impossible to speak clearly and distinctly of our Knowledge, which all consists in Propositions, without considering, first, the Nature, Use, and Signification of Language; which therefore must be the business of the next Book. (II.xxxiii.19)

Book III accordingly presents a theory of *words*—not strictly of *language*, for to find an account of language it is necessary both to look back to the classification of ideas to which words are said to correspond and to look forward to the account of knowledge, the process whereby ideas are meaningfully combined, which provides the mental substructure for language.

Later writers on language blamed Locke for not revising his plan more radically after he had stumbled across the inevitability of linguistic theory. Condillac in 1746 wrote that Locke should have treated words along with ideas in his second book instead of relegating them to an afterthought in the third,[2] and in 1786 Horne Tooke claimed that

> perhaps it was for mankind a lucky mistake (for it was a mistake) which Mr. Locke made when he called his book, An Essay on Human *Understanding*. For some part of the inestimable benefit of that book has, merely on account of its title, reached to many thousands more than, I fear, it would have done, had he called it (what it is merely) A *Grammatical* Essay, or a Treatise on *Words*, or on *Language*.[3]

Such strictures are not directed merely at the structural organization of the *Essay* but call for a theory of language very different from that which Locke held. In spite of the admittedly belated conception of Book III the account of words in the *Essay* is rightly placed after the account of ideas, for language in Locke's view is essentially a reflection of its ideational base. He does indeed admit that in a number of specific ways words may condition ideas, but these instances are qualifications of the general principle that language is secondary to thought. Both Condillac and Tooke believed that language has a much greater influence on thought than Locke would be willing to admit.

Locke's principle is stated at the beginning of Book III:

> God having designed Man for a sociable Creature, made him not only with an inclination, and under a necessity to have fellowship with those of his own kind; but furnished him also with Language, which was to be the great Instrument and common Tye of Society. *Man* therefore had by Nature his Organs so fashioned, as to be *fit to frame articulate Sounds*, which we call Words. But this was not enough to produce Language; for Parrots, and several other Birds, will be taught to make articulate Sounds distinct enough, which yet, by no means, are capable of Language.
>
> Besides articulate Sounds therefore, it was farther necessary, that he should be *able to use these Sounds, as Signs of internal Conceptions*; and to make them stand as marks for the *Ideas* within his own Mind, whereby they might be made known to others, and the Thoughts of Men's Minds be conveyed from one to another. (III.i.1–2)

The underlying conceptions distinguish language proper from mere articulate sound. It is a condition of the sound's being counted as language that it should on the occasion in question be used to signify conceptions. Locke thus defines language in terms of its purpose, the communication of ideas.

A further component of his initial definition is that the relation between language and conception is arbitrary. Words serve as signs for ideas "not by any natural connexion, that there is between particular articulate Sounds and certain *Ideas*, for then there would be but one Language amongst all Men; but by a voluntary Imposition, whereby such a Word is made arbitrarily the Mark of such an *Idea*" (III.ii.1). None of the writers with whom we shall deal seriously doubts this position, but it is helpful to remember that contrary views, entailing some form of natural and non-arbitrary connection between the sign and the thing signified, were widely current in the latter half of the seventeenth century. Locke's emphatic rejection of any such connection is fundamental to his philosophy, for "not to have dismissed the last remnant of the doctrine of natural language would have allowed innateness to creep in by the back door."[4] If words are naturally connected to the reality they denote, then for one who has acquired a language words may become a third source of knowledge independent of sense and reflection.

Locke's evidence for this position in the fact that different peoples speak different languages misses the point of the argument advanced by many of his opponents. Leibniz for instance believed that the different languages in use among men might in principle be derived from a single primal language. That different words are now used by different peoples ceases to be a bar to the natural language theory as soon as we adopt an etymological perspective which presents the possibility of deriving these different words from common roots.

Locke's reference to the diversity of languages at this early stage of his discussion of words may be misleading, especially if taken in conjunction with his advocation elsewhere (*e.g.*, II.xxii.6) of what appears to be linguistic relativism—the view that there are expressions in some languages which *cannot* be adequately rendered in others. It may seem that Locke's emphasis on the diversity and relativity of languages must set him against the universal grammarians of the period who believed in rules and underlying structures common to all languages.[5] We shall see, however, not only that Locke's approach to language is consistent with the notion of universal grammar but also that his theory of language demands interpretation in the light of the principles of the celebrated *Grammaire* of Port-Royal.

The opening chapters of Book III define words as arbitrary signs for ideas. As we have presented it so far the definition is both problematic and incomplete. It is incomplete because words are part of language, and language, as Locke was not unaware, is more than a collection of words. The definition of words must be considered in the wider context of the discussions of language elsewhere in the *Essay*. The chief source of problems in the definition is the notion of reference to *ideas*, which Locke makes the primary purpose of language. Before considering Locke's wider view of language we will outline the difficulties arising from the place of ideas in his account of meaning.

SEMANTIC IDEALISM

That words should signify ideas is necessary to the purpose of language as Locke sees it: the communication of our thoughts. Man needs to *communicate* his ideas because ideas "are all within his own Breast, invisible, and hidden from others, nor can of themselves be made to appear" (III.ii.1). The privacy of ideas makes necessary their reflection in some public medium by means of *signs*. Because ideas, of themselves, are not common, the signs must reflect first and foremost the ideas in some particular mind, which with the same inevitability is that of the "speaker" (if we assume a verbal medium; other media, such as written words or representative pictures, are tacitly comprehended in the theory). Therefore Locke is bound to take the step, however awkward its consequences, of limiting the primary significance of the sign to the idea in the speaker's mind. The purposes of communication and of language itself are served to the extent that the signs given by the speaker give rise to *the same* ideas in the mind of another. At this point the initial assumption of the privacy of ideas confronts us with an insurmountable obstacle: if ideas are necessarily peculiar to the mind in which they occur and can never properly be said to be common to two or more minds, the "sameness" of ideas in different minds required by the theory of communication is an empty notion. What criteria of comparison could we possibly apply here?[6]

The contradiction inherent in the Lockean view of communication was addressed neither by Locke himself nor by any of his eighteenth-century successors in the theory of language. The difficulty of holding that ideas are both private and yet comparable is simply not noticed in the period. The more obvious problem arising from Locke's claim that words signify ideas in the mind of the speaker is that it appears to commit him to what is sometimes called "semantic idealism." If it is the case simply that my words signify *my* ideas then anything I say is first and foremost about my state of mind. When I say for example "Today is Tuesday," I must mean "I am thinking that today is Tuesday" or more fully "I have an idea of today which agrees with another idea

I have of Tuesday." It might seem as though these consequences could be avoided by way of the notion of intention; when I say "Today is Tuesday" I *intend* to state what day it is and not to convey information about my state of mind. It would not therefore be wholly true to say that I *mean* "I am thinking that today is Tuesday." But Locke may have left no room for this distinction between meaning and intention (or between two senses of "mean" in common parlance) because he establishes the virtual identity of the meaning of the word with the idea to which it refers. In the light of this identity any intention I may have beyond that of referring to the idea must be seen as irrelevant to meaning. The identity of meaning and reference is apparently asserted in the following passages:

> *Words in their primary or immediate Signification, stand for nothing, but the* Ideas *in the Mind of him that uses them*. . . . That then which Words are the Marks of, are the *Ideas* of the Speaker. (III.ii.2)

> But so far as Words are of Use and Signification, so far there is a constant connexion between the Sound and the *Idea*; and a Designation, that the one stand for the other: without which Application of them, they are nothing but so much insignificant Noise. (III.ii.7)

> He that hath Names without *Ideas*, wants meaning in his Words, and speaks only empty Sounds. (III.x.31)[7]

When the identification of meaning with reference is combined with the theory that reference is to ideas in the mind of the speaker we are led inevitably to two obviously undesirable consequences, both of which are aspects of semantic idealism: (i) that I can refer only to my own state of mind; and (ii) that a hearer cannot distinguish meaningful words from nonsense. The first consequence was illustrated above. The second follows clearly: if the meaning of the word *is* the idea in the speaker's mind then because the idea is private and inaccessible to all but the speaker himself the hearer is unable to distinguish between words which have meaning (corresponding ideas) and those which do not. If I say "Today is Tuesday" while thinking of something totally different or of nothing at all my words will be mere articulate sounds, which because unsupported by ideas are not meaningful words at all—they will not fall within language as Locke defined it. But how is my audience supposed to know this?

A reading of the *Essay* which avoids at least the first of these two consequences is suggested by Norman Kretzmann.[8] He argues that Locke's semantic theory rests upon two interdependent but separate arguments. First is the argument from the *use* of language in communication (III.ii.1–2). The fact that words are used to communicate shows that they *can* be used to signify ideas in the mind of the speaker (but not that they must be so used or that they can be used in no other way). Second is the argument from the doctrine of representative ideas. This holds that we have no direct perception of anything except by way of ideas: "since the Things, the Mind contemplates, are none of them, besides it self, present to the Understanding, 'tis necessary that something else, as a Sign or Representation of the thing it considers, should be present to it: And these are *Ideas*" (IV.xxi.4). Therefore no word can be applied *immediately* to anything other than an idea. Words cannot be applied "as Marks, immediately to any thing else, but the *Ideas*, that [the speaker] him self hath: For this would be to make them Signs of his own Conceptions, and yet apply them to other *Ideas*; which would be to make them Signs, and not Signs of his *Ideas* at the same time; and so in effect, to have no Signification at all" (III.ii.2). In Kretzmann's words: "if X is something other than an idea of mine, to suppose that I can apply a word to signify X *immediately* is to suppose that I can apply a word to signify X while I have no idea of X, which is impossible."[9]

Together these two arguments yield the thesis that "*Words in their primary or immediate Signification, stand for nothing, but the Ideas in the Mind of* him that uses them" (III.ii.2). Kretzmann's reading of Locke requires that we give weight to the implied distinction between "primary" or "immediate" and "secondary" or "mediate" uses of words: the primary use is to signify the speaker's ideas, the secondary to signify things in the public domain. The distinction is plausible because Locke undeniably holds that just as words are signs for ideas so ideas are signs for things (IV.xxi.4). The primary signification of the word is the idea in the mind of the speaker, without which the word would be a mere sound, and the secondary or mediate signification, by way of this idea, is the thing of which the idea itself is a sign.

If we adopt Kretzmann's reading Locke is at least partly exonerated from the absurdities of semantic idealism. The suggested distinction between primary and secondary significations appears to negate the identity of meaning and reference. As a result of this distinction in Lockean theory words may be said to *refer* to ideas in the mind of the speaker but to have *sense* in the public domain beyond their reference. When I say "Today is Tuesday" I am necessarily *referring* to my ideas, but the *sense* of my statement is not that *I am thinking* that today is Tuesday but simply *that* today is Tuesday.

Kretzmann's reading is impressive and evidently offers a possible alternative construction of Locke's position on meaning and reference. Three main observations arise from it.

The first concerns Locke's claim that not only are words *signs* for ideas but also ideas are *signs* for the things of which they are ideas. We are presented with this picture:

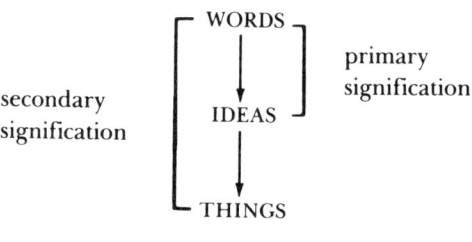

Fig. 2

The secondary signification (which, Kretzmann would suggest, constitutes the sense as distinct from the reference of the word) depends upon the relation between ideas and things, without which the word would be applicable to nothing beyond the idea. To this relation Locke himself gives the same name as to that between words and ideas, and the two relations are accordingly represented in the same way in the figure. Words are "signs" for ideas and ideas are "signs" for things (II.xxxii.19; IV.xxi.4). But the two relations must in fact, as Kretzmann observes, be radically different. The difference is most obvious if we consider that whereas the relation between word and idea is for Locke necessarily arbitrary, the relation between idea and thing is necessarily natural. Words signify ideas only by virtue of the conventions of language, but no conventional element appears in the relation between the idea and the thing of which it is an idea. Consequently, although word-signs can correctly be said to be parts of a "language" in the Lockean sense, there is no corresponding way for Locke to see idea-signs as parts of an ideational "language" having non-ideational reality for its object. For the same reason it would not be correct to infer from the figure that words are part of some kind of metalanguage with respect to reality. The two kinds of sign differ, moreover, in that only in the case of word-signs is it possible to have in mind both the signifier (the idea of the word) and the signified (the idea of the thing). In the case of idea-signs it is not possible for the mind to apprehend the signified (the thing) except through the signifier (the idea), and it is consequently not at all clear in what sense the term "sign" is being employed here. We must conclude that Locke's use of the term to cover both relationships is careless and confusing, especially when at the end of the *Essay* he tries to pull both cases together under the "branch of learning" called *semiotics* or the *doctrine of signs* (IV.xxi.4).

The second observation concerns Kretzmann's suggestion that Locke intends a distinction between primary and secondary signification. This is hard to reconcile with passages (such as III.ii.7 and III.x.31, both quoted above) where Locke appears to identify meaning with reference by claiming that without its referent (the corresponding idea) the word is "empty sound" or "insignificant noise." Such passages can, however, be read in the light of Kretzmann's suggestion. Locke may be saying no more than is implied in his argument from the doctrine of representative ideas: that a *word* cannot occur without an idea and that what purports to be a word without an idea is really not part of *language* at all. In terms of the figure, Locke may be pointing out that when the idea is absent the word has no connection with the thing. In short, he may be saying not that sense is *identical* with reference but that sense is *dependent upon* the referential use of the word.

Third, though Kretzmann's reading of Locke has encountered no insuperable obstacle, its purpose, to rescue Locke from the pitfalls of semantic idealism, is only partially achieved. By means of the distinction between primary and secondary signification we can excuse Locke from commitment to the view that we can talk only about our own states of mind, but this does not help him avoid the second facet of semantic idealism, the definition of meaning in such a way that the speaker is the only judge of the meaning of his words. The problem is seen most clearly from the position outlined in the second observation, above: if a word with its corresponding idea is a part of language but the same articulate sound without the idea is an "insignificant sound," who but the speaker of the word can distinguish among articulate sounds between words and noises?

We may accept the distinction between primary and secondary signification as part of Locke's theory, but we must then face the problem that the primary signification has no appreciable function. The burden of communication rests wholly upon the secondary signification simply because, given the nature of ideas, it can make no difference to the hearer whether the words spoken have primary signification or not. The trouble here, apart from the difficulties inherent in the theory of ideas, arises largely from Locke's tendency to see the process of communication solely from the speaker's point of view. Whenever Locke talks about the *uses* of words he considers only their uses to the speaker: their service in recording thoughts or in making thoughts manifest to others (III.ii.2).[10] The result of this one-sided approach, as we have seen, is that the allegedly *primary* function of words in communication is in fact no *function* at all.

Why does Locke insist that the primary function of words is to signify the speaker's ideas? Presumably pressure from traditional theory of language and from the linguistic work of his colleagues in the Royal Society left him no alternative but to base his semantic theory on reference (or "signification"); but his theory of ideas, of which the foundation is that an idea is "*whatsoever* is the Object of the Understanding when a Man thinks" (I.i.8, my italics), did not permit Locke the usual course of seeking the referents in the public domain. Words must refer to *ideas* because it is only of ideas that we have direct knowledge. And because ideas are "private" the ideas referred to must be those of the speaker. The root of Locke's problem is not so much the notion of reference, which is a reasonably flexible concept in the history of semantic theory, as the theory of ideas. It is no accident that when the common sense school of Reid and Stewart attacked the theory of ideas towards the end of the eighteenth century they also came up with semantic theories radically different from that of Locke.[11]

As a result of Locke's view that a word signifies primarily the idea in the mind of the one who utters it the word remains a mysterious and indefinable entity in the context of his philosophy.[12] The difficulty is best presented in more general terms as a problem of the nature of *signs* (of which words in Locke's view are a particular species). A sign is that which stands for an idea in the mind of one who uses it. There is therefore no objective criterion to enable anyone other than the user to distinguish signs from non-signs—to distinguish between, for example, words and mere articulate noises, or between representative symbols and mere marks. If for the sake of illustration we adopt the theory of meaning shown in Figure 2, we seem to have two possible ways of explaining how we might recognize signs (other than those which we ourselves utter) when they occur: we may either look to the intention behind the utterance or consider the language or set of conventions of which the alleged sign may be a part. For example, if I utter any articulate sound "x" my audience may have two ways of determining whether this occurrence of "x" is a word or a mere noise. They may ask whether I *intend to say something* by uttering "x" or they may ask whether "x" is a term *in the language* I am using (or in any language that I am likely to use). Of these two ways of deciding the question the first agrees more obviously with Lockean doctrine, for to ask whether I intend "x" as a sign is in effect to ask if I have in mind as I utter "x" an idea to which it corresponds. But the problem is insoluble by this method for the obvious reason that the only evidence my audience has of my ideas is the signs I give them; they cannot, without circularity, be supposed to use my ideas as a means to recognition of the signs I utter. We are thrown back upon the second procedure, the recognition of signs as parts of known languages, codes, or sign systems. If, for example, it is known that I speak only English and French the question of whether or not my "x" is a word may be decided by asking whether "x" is a part of either language. But this is to admit that a sign can be recognized as such only by one who already knows the whole corpus of signs—we have not achieved an objective definition of a sign by this method but have simply stated that a sign is any member of the class of signs. Whereas members of other classes can be recognized as such by their possession of specifiable qualities, the members of the class of signs have no distinguishing features. Among our ideas, those which are signs cannot be collected under any definition but must simply be recognized as they occur.

Thus the assumption that a sign involves a relation between a sensible phenomenon, such as an articulate sound, and an idea in the mind of the person who utters the sign fails to yield any objective criterion whereby signs may be distinguished. Locke's one-sided view of communication includes an account of how and why signs are employed by a "speaker" but offers no explanation of their recognition and interpretation by his audience. If Locke were to adopt a different approach to the sign this difficulty might be circumvented. If he were to say that a sign is any idea which regularly leads anyone (not only the "speaker") to conceive another idea he would have given an adequate criterion for the recognition of signs. In fact such an approach is implicit in Locke's theory of what he calls "judgment," but he does not himself connect this part of the *Essay* with the theory of what he calls "signs." (The connection was to be made by Berkeley, and in this important respect Berkeley's semantic theory is a development of a line of thought suggested but not pursued by Locke.)

Locke's theory of judgment will be examined later; the next step in the construction of a Lockean theory of language must be a discussion of the theory of ideas. Words stand for ideas, and the classification of words must therefore depend at least in part upon the classification of ideas. Locke does, however, allow certain classifications of words independent of the theory of ideas because, significantly, he does not hold that *all* words stand for ideas. After discussing the classifications based upon ideas, which come largely from Book II, we shall therefore proceed to the further, purely grammatical classifications which Locke introduces in Book III. When the classification of words is complete we can turn to the theory of language proper, which depends heavily upon material from Book IV.

THE THEORY OF IDEAS

Locke's theory of ideas is detailed and controversial. All that need be attempted here, however, is an outline of its categories, upon which the theory of words may then be based.

Locke takes over from Descartes the comprehensive use of the term "idea" to cover "whatsoever is the Object of the Understanding when a Man thinks." "I have," he continues, "used it to express whatever is meant by *Phantasm, Notion, Species,* or whatever it is, which the Mind can be employ'd about in thinking; and I could not avoid frequently using it" (I.i.8). Clearly there can be no thought without ideas. And thought is necessarily conscious: "Our being sensible of it is not necessary to any thing, but to our thoughts; and to them it is; and to them it will always be necessary, until we can think without being conscious of it," and "'tis altogether as intelligible to say, that a body is extended without parts, as that any thing *thinks without being conscious of it,* or perceiving, that it does so" (I.i.10 and 19). Ideas are essential to thought and are essentially conscious.

Ideas occur successively and distinctly in the mind. "Every one that has any Knowledge at all, has, as the Foundation of it, various and distinct *Ideas*: And it is the first act of the Mind, (without which, it can never be capable of any Knowledge,) to know every one of its *Ideas* by it self, and distinguish it from others" (IV.vii.4). The apprehension of ideas as discrete is immediate and inescapable; confusion is not properly predicable of ideas but of words. "Now every *Idea* a Man has, being visibly what it is, and distinct from all other *Ideas* but it self, that which makes it *confused* is, when it is such, that it may as well be called by another Name, as that which it is expressed by" (II.xxix.6). To have an idea is necessarily to comprehend it (II.ii.5) and to be able to distinguish it from any different idea. Locke admits that ideas may be "obscure" in the sense of inexact or unclear with reference to some assumed standard of precision (II.xxix.2–3), but no idea can properly be said to be "confused" in the sense of "not sufficiently distinguishable from another, from which it should be different" (II.xxix.5).

Ideas are therefore events in the conscious mind, distinct both in being clear and definite and in being separate from one another. Locke classifies them first of all as either simple or complex; all ideas are either simple or compounded of simples (II.ii.1). This doctrine we may call *ideational atomism*, because it is avowedly modeled on the atomist theories current in both philosophy and the sciences in the latter half of the seventeenth century.

> When the Understanding is once stored with these simple *Ideas*, it has the power to repeat, compare, and unite them even to an almost infinite Variety, and so can make at Pleasure new complex *Ideas*. But it is not in the Power of the most exalted Wit, or enlarged Understanding, by any quickness or variety of Thought, to *invent or frame one new simple* Idea in the mind, not taken in by the ways before mentioned [*i.e.*, sensation and reflection]: nor can any force of the Understanding, *destroy* those that are there. The Dominion of Man, in this little World of his own Understanding, being much what the same, as it is in the great World of visible things; wherein his Power, however managed by Art and Skill, reaches no farther, than to compound and divide the Materials, that are made to his Hand; but can do nothing towards the making the least Particle of new Matter, or destroying one Atome of what is already in Being. (II.ii.2)

Complex ideas are then subclassified according to their objects (*i.e.*, to what they are ideas of), as either modes, substances, or relations (II.xii.3). These categories, which Locke accepts rather uncritically from the Aristotelian tradition, are best defined briefly in his own words. *Modes* are

> such complex *Ideas*, which however compounded, contain not in them the supposition of subsisting by themselves, but are

considered as Dependences on, or Affections of Substances; such are the *Ideas* signified by the Words *Triangle, Gratitude, Murder, etc.* (II.xii.4)

Substances are

> such combinations of simple *Ideas*, as are taken to represent distinct particular things subsisting by themselves; in which the supposed, or confused *Idea* of Substance, such as it is, is always the first and chief. (II.xii.7)

Relations are ideas which consist "in the consideration and comparing one *Idea* with another" (II.xii.7).

Modes, moreover, subdivide into simple and mixed (II.xii.5). The evident intention in the first edition of the *Essay* is that the subcategorization of complex ideas into modes, substances, and relations should be regarded as complete and exhaustive and should therefore yield the simple scheme of Figure 3.

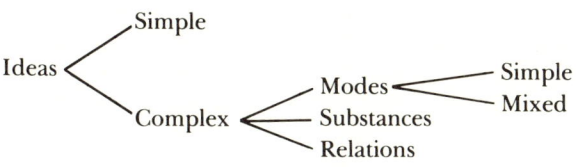

Fig. 3

There are, however, a number of obvious difficulties in this scheme, some of which are reflected in the *Essay* or in Locke's later revisions of the text. In the first place it is not clear how the classification of Figure 3 sits with the no less basic classification of ideas as derived from either sensation or reflection. The scheme, as Locke elaborates it, is evidently designed to fit ideas of sensation, but he nowhere says that it does not apply to ideas of reflection, nor does he explain how it could be so applied. Second, there is an obvious difficulty in the two occurrences of the term "simple" in that *simple* modes are said to be a subcategory of *complex* ideas. To this we shall return when we consider what Locke means by a simple idea. Third, the scheme makes no reference to general ideas. It is not clear whether these constitute a third category along with simple and complex, or form a subcategory of complex ideas, or are somehow distributed among the categories given. Finally, it is not clear that relations are complex ideas as the scheme suggests, for a relation-idea (*e.g.*, "husband") is not *compounded* of several ideas but is rather one idea considered *in relation to* another. On the other hand, because more than one idea is necessarily involved, relations can hardly be simple.

The first of these problems Locke appears to have overlooked, and his intentions regarding ideas of reflection remain similarly uncertain. The third and fourth problems, concerning general ideas and relations, evidently troubled him, and some alterations of the scheme of Figure 3 are accordingly suggested by revisions in later editions of the *Essay*. Aaron cites an important addition to the fourth edition (1700):[13]

> The Acts of the Mind wherein it exerts its Power over its simple *Ideas* are chiefly these three, 1. Combining several simple *Ideas* into one compound one, and thus all Complex *Ideas* are made. 2. The 2*d.* is bringing two *Ideas*, whether simple or complex, together; and setting them by one another, so as to take a view of them at once, without uniting them into one; by which way it gets all its *Ideas* of Relations. 3. The 3*d.* is separating them from all other *Ideas* that accompany them in their real existence; this is called *Abstraction*: And thus all its General *Ideas* are made. (II.xii.1)

This second scheme, which is based upon different principles from the first, is presented in Figure 4, in which the "acts" or operations of the mind upon its ideas are capitalized.

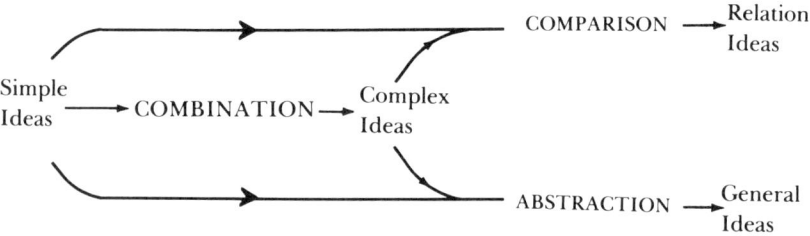

Fig. 4

Substances and the problematic modes are absent from the scheme of Figure 4, tacitly subsumed under complex ideas. Moreover, the scheme of Figure 4 is inconsistent with that of Figure 3 because the later scheme makes it impossible to treat either general ideas or relations simply as subcategories of complex ideas. The later scheme is supported by several passages elsewhere in the *Essay* (*e.g.*, II.xxv.1, where it is expressly held that relations are neither simple nor complex ideas but an independent third category) but Locke did not trouble to revise systematically the original classification of ideas in the text. Both versions remain in the *Essay* as he left it, the earlier being the more prominent and the one usually cited.

Common to both schemes is the distinction between simple and complex ideas. Locke apparently came to admit by 1700 that not all non-simple ideas are complex, but he never explicitly abandoned the atomist position that all ideas are either simple or reducible to simples. Given the general position that words refer to ideas, ideational atomism is of the first importance to semantic theory. If Locke holds, as he does in some passages at least, that the meaning of a word is the idea it refers to, his atomist theory of ideas leads inevitably to the position that there are semantic simples, or units of meaning, from which all other meanings are somehow constructed.

Seen in this light the semantic theory of the *Essay* has something in common with the *Tractatus Logico-Philosophicus* in that both Locke and Wittgenstein believe that the world which language describes is composed of atoms (Locke's "simple ideas" and Wittgenstein's "objects") and that meaningful utterances are correspondingly analyzable into combinations of names for these atoms. Both Locke and Wittgenstein are noticeably reticent to produce such an atom or to give an instance of a simple name, and it is therefore interesting to ask in each case why they believe that the atoms exist.

Wittgenstein argues that language depicts the world and that the meaning of an utterance is the state of affairs it depicts. If, in analyzing the state of affairs, we were never to arrive at a level beyond which we could not proceed, a level of atoms or "objects," then we could discover no final and specific meaning for an utterance depicting that state of affairs. But Wittgenstein believes it must be true that what can be said can be said precisely—*i.e.*, that specific meaning is possible. Therefore there must be an end to the process of analysis; there must be "objects."

Locke's route to simple ideas appears to have been very different. His chief premise in this connection is that all ideas must come from experience. But to this it may be objected that I have ideas of unicorns and golden mountains even although I have no experience of either. The answer to this objection lies in the claim that such ideas are compounds of several ideas each one of which is either derived from experience or itself compounded of others which are. The empiricist premise is satisfied so long as it can be held that every idea is either derived from experience or somehow reducible ultimately to ideas which are so derived. The *simplicity* of the "simple idea" to which *this* line of argument leads consists only in the idea's being derived directly from experience; the argument itself does not entail that the idea should be "atomic" in any further sense. But Locke was considerably influenced by the leading seventeenth-century atomists—particularly by Gassendi and his follower François Bernier and in England by Robert Boyle[14]—and it was probably under this influence that he deliberately grafted his account of the compounding of ideas onto the theoretical structure of atomism (II.ii.2 and II.xii.1).

The grafting was not altogether successful, for the strict atomism which results in Locke's theory of ideas goes somewhat beyond his purposes and becomes awkward to handle in certain areas of the *Essay*. Because of the importance of ideational atomism to Locke's semantic theory it is unfortunately necessary to pause over the tangled question of what precisely he means by a simple idea. (At the same time we can address the problem of "simple" modes which arises from the scheme of Figure 2.) We shall see that Locke offers two different and mutually inconsistent accounts of ideational simplicity.

The initial and "official" definition occurs in the second chapter of Book II:

> Though the Qualities that affect our Senses, are, in the things themselves, so united and blended, that there is no separation,

no distance between them; yet 'tis plain, the *Ideas* they produce in the Mind, enter by the Senses simple and unmixed. For, though the Sight and Touch often take in from the same Object, at the same time, different *Ideas*: as a Man sees at once Motion and Colour; the Hand feels Softness and Warmth in the same piece of Wax: Yet the simple *Ideas* thus united in the same Subject, are as perfectly distinct, as those that come in by different Senses. The coldness and hardness, which a Man feels in a piece of *Ice*, being as distinct *Ideas* in the Mind, as the Smell and Whiteness of a Lily; or as the taste of Sugar, and smell of a Rose: And there is nothing can be plainer to a Man, than the clear and distinct Perception he has of those simple *Ideas*; which, being each in it self uncompounded, contains in it nothing but *one uniform Appearance*, or Conception in the mind, and is not distinguishable into different *Ideas*. (II.ii.1)

Here Locke rests ideational simplicity upon what he assumes to be inherent conceptual limitations. We can break down a complex idea of perception into the components provided by the different senses: if I perceive a block of ice I can distinguish its visual appearance (color and apparent shape) from the way it feels (cold and hard). We can, moreover, distinguish *distinct* ideas provided contemporaneously by a single sense: if I touch the block of ice I can differentiate between the hardness and the coldness. (*Why* we are able to make this distinction, and why such ideas are distinct, is not explained.) Further than this we cannot go; we have reached the conceptual limits and isolated simple ideas. What these limits are would have to be discovered in each case. We might begin, from the above examples, by listing *temperature* and *solidity* as simple ideas of perception derived from the sense of touch. In much the same way *color* and *shape* would presumably be simple ideas of perception derived from sight.

The world may be analyzed in an indefinite number of different ways, however, and a method of analysis which reveals the "simples" required for certain purposes may fail to reveal "simples" required for other purposes. The conceptual analysis outlined in II.ii.1, for instance, serves to tell us that a tactile idea of, say, a block of ice comprises the conceptual elements *temperature* and *solidity*, which are, as it were, the qualitative categories into which the idea falls. But this kind of analysis will not tell us how the idea I get by touching a block of ice differs from that obtained by touching a smooth block of wood or a warm metal ingot. In each case (leaving apart considerations of weight, size, and texture) the ideas will include the same conceptual elements of temperature and solidity. To differentiate among them I must adopt a new principle of analysis. Locke is no doubt correct in a sense when he says that temperature and solidity are unanalyzable conceptual simples, but it is nonetheless possible to ask *what* temperature, and *what degree of* solidity, I find in my ideas. Here, then, is a problem: do we want to say that an idea of temperature *per se* is a simple idea, or do we want to hold that an idea of 54° Fahrenheit is one simple idea, an idea of 55° another, and so on?

Locke faces the issues in the field of what he calls simple "modes," under which he tries to deal with matters of quantity, number, degree, extension, and duration. Simple modes are defined as complex ideas of modes which are "only variations, or different combinations of the same simple *Idea*, without the mixture of any other, as a dozen, or a score; which are nothing but the *Ideas* of so many distinct Unites added together, and these I call *simple Modes*, as being contained within the bounds of one simple *Idea*" (II.xii.5). Thus, if *length* is a conceptual simple, the ideas of particular lengths are simple modes. But is an idea of *some particular length* simple or complex? The term "simple mode" suggests it is simple, and this view is reinforced by II.xiii.1, which clearly implies that simple modes *are* simple ideas. Yet modes are expressly said to be a species of complex ideas (II.xii.3–4).

The difficulty may be put this way. Locke suggests that *length* is a conceptual simple. If a particular length is a complex idea it is difficult to explain how it can be an instance of the (simple) idea *length*; conversely, if the particular length is simple it is no easier to explain how a compound of two such simple lengths, also a particular length, can also be simple.

In this dilemma Locke occasionally tries an alternative notion of simplicity. Instead of seeking conceptual simples such as temperature, solidity, and length, he looks rather for perceptual simples, the least quantities or degrees that can be *perceived*. In the case of extension he suggests a *minimum sensible*, a "sensible point," as a simple idea; in the case of time a "moment," the least interval we can apprehend (II.xv.9); and in the case of number an idea of "unity" (II.xvi.1). The perceptual simple, however, creates serious conflicts with the notions of continuity and infinite divisibility of space, time, and number, to which Locke in the shadow of Newton was much inclined, and for this reason the chapters on simple modes are confused and indecisive.[15] The perceptual simple does not appear elsewhere in the *Essay* because it would not serve Locke's wider purposes: it has no application in the sphere of reflection, and its application to ideas other than those of measurable quantity is not at all clear. Evidently Locke preferred the conceptual view of simpicity stated in II.ii.1 but was driven to the perceptual alternative by the special problems of the ideas he called simple modes.

Having indicated the kinds of difficulty that occur in Locke's theory of ideas we can now go on to examine the theory of words which, in the *Essay*, is largely based upon the foregoing account of ideas. We will take the scheme of Figure 4 as representing Locke's classification of ideas, but with the addition, imported from the scheme of Figure 3, that complex ideas subdivide into modes—simple and mixed—and substances. Consequently we have five categories of ideas to deal with: simple ideas, relations, simple modes, mixed modes, and substances. General ideas need not be considered as a separate category because any general idea will fall into one of these five divisions.

Locke's fundamental position is that words signify ideas (he allows certain exceptions which are examined in the next section), but the relation between words and ideas varies as we move through the five ideational categories. What seems at first a simple referential theory is complicated by detailed considerations of how different kinds of words work in different ways.

The simplest case, as would be expected, is that of the simple idea. Because the idea is uncompounded it can be obtained only by direct experience. Complex ideas, being compounded, need not be derived directly from experience, for provided I have experienced all the requisite simple ideas I can myself construct the complex by the mental operation Locke calls combination. Consequently, whereas names for complex ideas can be defined in terms of the simples of which the ideas are compounded, names of simple ideas are incapable of definition (III.iv.7). This in turn means that the simple name cannot be understood unless the mind has already acquired the idea; simple ideas can never be learnt from their names.

The simple name straightforwardly signifies an idea, which must precede it in the mind and without which it cannot be understood. But names for other kinds of ideas depart in various ways from these requirements. The picture begins to alter as soon as we move on to ideas of relations. An idea of relation is an idea of any thing considered in relation to anything else:

> When the Mind so considers one thing, that it does, as it were, bring it to, and set it by another, carry its view from one to t'other: This is, as the Words import, *Relation* and *Respect*; and the Denominations given to positive Things, intimating that Respect; and serving as Marks to lead the Thoughts beyond the Subject it self dominated, to something distinct from it, are what we call *Relatives*; and the Things so brought together, Related." (II.xxv.1)

As examples of pairs of relatives Locke gives "husband" and "wife," and "father" and son," and observes that many other terms, like "concubine," are in fact relatives but are not commonly seen to be so because in their cases "Languages have failed to give correlative Names" (II.xxv.2). The formation of relatives is attuned to "the use of common Life, and not to the truth and extent of Things" (II.xxviii.2). This, Locke observes,

> may give us some light into the different state and growth of Languages, which being suited only to the convenience of Communication, are proportioned to the Notions Men have, and the commerce of Thoughts familiar amongst them; and not to the reality or extent of Things, nor to the various Respects might be found among them; nor the different abstract Considerations might be framed about them. Where they had no philosophical Notions, there they had no Terms to express them: And 'tis no wonder Men should have framed no Names for those Things, they found no occasion to discourse of. (*Ibid.*)

Implicit in Locke's remarks is a weak form of linguistic relativism: each society evolves a vocabulary suited to its own culture and philosophy in such a way that its members cannot without deliberate effort conceive reality in ways other than those embodied in their language. Words still depend upon the priority of ideas, but it now seems that the words of one's language may to some extent condition the ideas of relation that one acquires.

The element of linguistic relativism which Locke introduces in discussion of relations is enlarged in connection with mixed modes. Modes are complex ideas which are not substances—*i.e.*, do not subsist by themselves—but are "considered as Dependences on, or Affectations of Substances" (II.xii.4). *Mixed* modes are those which comprise "several Combinations of simple *Ideas* of different kinds" (II.xxii.1). Among the examples Locke gives are *triangle, gratitude, murder, obligation, drunkenness,* and *a lie.* Such things do not exist in the real world in the same way as do substances. Complex ideas of modes are "made by the Mind" and "have no particular foundation in Nature" (III.v.10). Consequently such ideas, not being simply data of experience but depending largely upon the social structures from which they arise, are liable to be lost quickly with the passing generations. Mixed modes are bundles of ideas not given as such but collected by the mind; as soon as the mind moves on the bundle is released, falls apart, and is unlikely to be exactly recreated a second time. But in fact, Locke claims, a high degree of permanence is lent the mixed mode by its name, "which is, as it were the Knot, that ties [the component simple ideas] fast together" (III.v.10).

It follows that, although the idea must be formulated before the name can come into use, once the name has become part of language, the idea may be learnt from the name and its definition, provided only that the learner has already acquired ideas of all the requisite simples (II.xxii.2). This is true of all complex ideas, but by their very nature mixed modes are particularly suited to be acquired from language rather than directly from experience of non-verbal reality.

> I could not avoid to take thus much notice here of the names of *mixed Modes,* which being fleeting, and transient Combina-

> tions of simple *Ideas*, which have but a short existence any where, but in the Minds of Men, and there too have no longer any existence, than whilst they are thought on, *have not so much any where the appearance of a constant and lasting existence, as in their Names*: which are therefore, in these sort of *Ideas*, very apt to be taken for the *Ideas* themselves. . . .
>
> Indeed, now that Languages are made, and abound with words standing for such Combinations, *an usual way of getting these complex* Ideas *is by the explication of those terms that stand for them*. For consisting of a company of simple *Ideas* combined, they may by words, standing for those simple *Ideas*, be represented to the Mind of one who understands those words, though that complex Combination of simple *Ideas* were never offered to his Mind by the real existence of things.
> (II.xxii.8 and 3; *cf.* III.v.15)

Moreover, because ideas of mixed modes are not fixed by the physical environment but are combinations made by the mind prompted by social and ideological factors, they are likely to vary considerably between different cultures, and such variations will tend to increase through time as they are entrenched and proliferated by linguistic differences. Here the note of linguistic relativism sounds more strongly:

> This shews us *how it comes to pass that there are in every Language many particular words, which cannot be rendered by any one single word of another*. For the several Fashions, Customs, and Manners of one Nation, making several Combinations of *Ideas* familiar and necessary in one, which another people have had never any occasion to make, or, perhaps, so much as take notice of, Names come of course to be annexed to them, to avoid long Periphrases in things of daily Conversation; and so they become so many distinct complex *Ideas* in their Minds. Thus ὀστρακισμός amongst the *Greeks* and *Proscriptio* amongst the *Romans*, were words which other Languages had no names that exactly answered; because they stood for complex *Ideas*, which were not in the Minds of the Men of other Nations.   (II.xxii.6)

Languages, as they stand, are not intertranslatable with respect to mixed modes, and since ideas of mixed modes are usually acquired from language such ideas are likely in fact to be a function of the language we speak.

Since we have raised the specter of linguistic relativism it may be as well to add that Locke could never approach the extreme version of the theory, which holds that different languages are inherently unintertranslatable and that our language places inescapable conditions on the way we think. Locke holds that before a word can come into being it must be associated with an idea (II.xxii.2; III.v.15), and that all complex ideas are reducible to simples (II.xxii.9; IV.vii.4). Simple ideas derive directly from experience and (leaving apart cases of sensory or mental deficiency) the same experiences are potentially available to all men. Add to this that the mind suffers no restriction in its capacity to combine simple ideas, "for it being once furnished with simple *Ideas*, it can put them together in several Compositions, and so make variety of complex *Ideas*, without examining whether they exist so together in Nature" (II.xxii.2). It follows, first, that all ideas are potentially available to all minds, regardless of language, and second that all conceptual systems (and therefore all languages) have a common denominator in the simples to which they may all be reduced. Names for simple ideas would in effect be semantic universals, and on their account Locke can never go too far along the road to relativism.

Mixed modes and relations have in common that they are to a large extent "made by the understanding," whereas simple ideas and substances must conform to patterns having "real existence" outside the mind. It is for this reason that, after its initial invention, the mixed mode or relation depends for its continued currency upon its name. Ideas of simple modes are in similar case but are somewhat more complicated. Under the heading of simple modes Locke treats extension, duration, number, and a host of "other simple modes" such as motion, sound, color, taste, and smell, all of which appear to have in common that they occur in quantities or degrees which may in some way be measured. Locke's treatment of these ideas is brief and inadquate, but his position appears to be that the existence of any particular idea of this kind depends upon there being first a system of names covering the mode to which it belongs and second a name within the system isolating the idea in question. Number presents the most straightforward example.

> By the repeating, as has been said, of the *Idea* of an unite, and joining it to another unite, we make thereof one collective *Idea*, marked by the Name *Two*. And whosoever can do this, and proceed on, still adding one more to the last collective *Idea*, which he had of any Number, and gave a Name to it, may count, or have *Ideas* for several Collections of unites, distinguished one from another, as far as he hath a Series of Names for following Numbers, and a Memory to retain that Series, with their several Names: All *Numeration* being but still the adding of one Unite more, and giving to the whole together, as comprehended in one *Idea*, a new or distinct Name or Sign, whereby to know it from those before and after, and distinguish it from every smaller or greater multitude of Unites. . . . For without such Names or Marks, we can hardly well make use of Numbers in reckoning, especially where the Combination is made up of any great multitude of Unites, which put together without a Name or Mark, to distinguish that precise Collection, will hardly be kept from being a heap in Confusion. (II.xvi.5)

The languages of highly developed cultures include sophisticated systems for the handling of numbers, although even these begin to break down when we try to *talk* of very high numbers, very small fractions, or elaborate mathematical operations. It is clear that without such languages (and their associated notations) we would be unable, because of conceptual limitations and uncertainty of memory, to work with any but the smallest and simplest numbers. Locke reinforces the point by comparison with other modes. In English we have a reasonably well developed set of expressions to designate colors, for instance, but it is a matter of common experience that there are perceptibly different shades of color between which the common man (not being a painter, physicist, or anything such) has no verbal means of distinguishing. A more extreme case is that of the sense of smell, an area in which our English vocabulary is scanty. Because in our way of life the classification of smells is generally unimportant we have names for very few smells, and our language reinforces the tendency to ignore, in normal circumstances, all but the plainest variations of odor (II.xviii.4–5).

Locke leaves a multitude of issues unexplored. He does not

deny, for example, that in the case of color the *ideas* of the different shades may be experienced as distinct ideas even though there are no known names to distinguish them. He also cites the case of arts or sciences which do in fact evolve specialized vocabularies to make fine distinctions within particular modes (II.xviii.7). In such cases we cannot say that the idea depends on the word, for the ideas are evidently experienced even though not named. (The option of saying that the finer distinctions among such ideas are experienced *but not noticed* in the absence of names is not open to Locke because of his emphatic requirement that all ideas be conscious—I.ii.5.) In the case of number, on the other hand, Locke's intention is that there should be *no* ideas beyond the simplest without the support of a system of names or numerals—and the same would therefore be true in modes such as duration which depend for our conception of them upon some kind of quantitative measurement. Evidently there are differences of which Locke takes no explicit notice among what he calls simple modes.

Names of substances are in a different case altogether from names of modes and relations because substances have real existence and are not simply mental constructs (III.iv.1–2). As a direct consequence

> The *Names of simple* Ideas *and Modes, signify always the real, as well as nominal Essence of their Species*. But the *Names of natural Substances, signify* rarely, if ever, any thing but *barely the nominal Essences* of those Species. (III.iv.3)

The distinction between real and nominal essences is introduced in III.iii.15: the real essence "may be taken for the very being of any thing, whereby it is, what it is" whereas the nominal essence is "that abstract *Idea*, which the General . . . Name stands for." The distinction operates only in the case of substances, for in simple ideas and in all modes and relations the idea necessarily represents the reality (III.iii.18). We have no way of assessing the representational accuracy of simple ideas, which must therefore be taken at face value; and ideas of modes and relations are themselves constitutive of the reality they represent. Ideas of substances, however, need not coincide with the real essences of substances— which is a way of saying that our classifications of physical nature are imposed upon a reality the complexity and composition of which is only partly known to us.

The distinction between the real and nominal essences of substances is of importance to the theory of language because, in the case of substances, our words purport to convey the real nature of their referents but usually refer only to nominal essences. Nominal essences, especially of more complex substances, vary greatly from one man to another (III.ix.13); each man is likely to take his own idea as the real essence and fruitless misunderstandings ensue (III.ix.16). The duality of reference of names of substances is one of the "imperfections of words" (III.ix.5) for which the solution is for each man to realize that real essences are generally inaccessible, that words refer to nominal essences (*i.e.*, to our own ideas) and that clear definitions should therefore be a prelude to any philosophical discussion of substances. In Locke's philosophy of language the distinction between real and nominal essences of substances becomes in effect a case of the distinction between primary and secondary signification presented in Figure 2. The primary signification of the name is the idea (the nominal essence) but its secondary signification—commonly taken as its meaning— is the thing itself (the real essence). It is not altogether clear why Locke asserts this dichotomy in the case of substances but explicitly denies it in the cases of all other ideas, for it could be argued that in the other cases, no less than in the case of substances, the words which do in fact (according to Locke) signify ideas alone are generally taken to signify things or events in non-ideational reality. The common man supposes that *gratitude* (a mixed mode) and *husband* (a relation) exist in the real world in much the same way as do *dogs* and *gold* (substances). Locke is evidently concerned not so much with the common man as with the philosopher, who may be taken to appreciate the unsubstantial nature of modes and relations but not to observe in every case the distinction between the real and nominal essences of substance.

We have seen that the relation between word and idea is different in each of the five main types of ideas which Locke isolates. The paradigmatic case is that of simple ideas, in which the word signifies an idea upon whose prior presence in the mind the word depends for its meaning. Other cases depart from this: in modes and relations the word may to some extent be a precondition for the acquisition and retention of the idea which is its meaning, and in substances there is a complicating duality of reference as the word signifies variously both the idea and the unapprehended reality. In no case, however, does Locke abandon the first premise of his semantic theory, that the meaning of the word depends upon the corresponding idea in the mind of the speaker: the word may be the means to realizing the idea, as in the case of mixed modes, but the idea must still be *present* if the word is to be uttered in a meaningful way. He comes closest to controverting this principle in the elusive case of simple modes, where his account of number appears to say that we have *no* ideas of numbers beyond the lowest except in so far as our language includes a system of numeration. But the passage, which is not clear and occurs in the weakest section of the whole *Essay*, will not bear much weight in an overall assessment of Locke's position. Subsequent writers in the Lockean tradition, such as Condillac, were to place greater emphasis on the extent to which language conditions thought, but Locke, although he admits that in certain cases the subsequent learner may take the shortcut of acquiring the idea from his language, insists that in general the idea must be obtained from experience before it can be named in the language, and that the presence of the idea in the speaker's mind remains thereafter a condition of the word's having meaning in use.

THE THEORY OF WORDS

The theory of ideas examined in the last section is part of Locke's theory of words in so far as words which are names for ideas are classified according to the kinds of ideas they name. But not all words are names for ideas. Two types of exception are mentioned in Book III: negatives and particles.

Negative words are apparently names, but it is hard to say, in some cases, what *ideas* they could be names of. "Gratitude," for example, may signify an idea of a certain mode of behavior and a certain attitude of mind, but if "ingratitude" means simply "absence of gratitude" what idea corresponds to it? "Ingratitude" cannot signify the *same* ideas as "gratitude," for the word means *absence* of the qualities signified by "gratitude." But in what would an *idea* of the absence of qualities consist? The answer that "ingratitude," although a negative word, signifies a positive line of conduct no less than does its opposite is not explored by Locke. The answer, in any event, would not have helped him to deal with absolute negatives such as "nothing." Locke does no more than glance at the problems and provide an inadequate blanket answer:

> Besides these names which stand for *Ideas*, there be other words which Men make use of, not to signify any *Idea*, but the want or absence of some *Ideas* simple or complex, or all *Ideas* together; such as are *Nihil* in Latin, and in English, *Ignorance* and *Barrenness*. All which negative or privative Words, cannot be said properly to belong to, or signify no *Ideas*: for then they would be perfectly insignificant Sounds; but they relate to positive *Ideas*, and signify their absence. (III.i.4)

This "answer," that negative words signify the absence of the ideas concerned, is if not paradoxical at least circular—for "absence" is itself one of the negative words in question.

To the case of "particles" Locke gives more serious attention. Negatives are still *names*—although whether they name *ideas* is doubtful—but particles are a different kind of word altogether. In Locke's view they stand not for ideas but for the various mental operations which the mind performs upon its ideas in the construction of mental propositions and arguments:

> Besides Words, which are names of *Ideas* in the Mind, there are a great many others that are made use of, to signify the *connexion* that the Mind gives to *Ideas, or Propositions, one with another*. The Mind, in communicating its thought to others, does not only need signs of the *Ideas* it has then before it, but others also, to shew or intimate some particular action of its own, at that time, relating to those *Ideas*. (III.vii.1)

The distinction between names (sometimes called "integral" words) and particles was a commonplace of seventeenth-century grammatical theory. Locke was no doubt aware of its embodiment in the *Essay towards a Real Character and a Philosophical Language* (1668) by John Wilkins, a fellow member of the Royal Society. A more potent influence, however, was surely the *Grammaire générale et raisonnée*, the celebrated Port-Royal Grammar of 1660, by Arnauld and Lancelot, in which the same distinction—between nouns, articles, prepositions, pronouns, participles, and adverbs on the one hand and verbs, conjunctions, and interjections on the other—is drawn on the basis of a distinction between the contents of the mind ("conceptions") and its actions upon them ("judgment" and "reasoning").[16]

There are two kinds of particles, with each of which we must deal separately: those which signify the combination of ideas in propositions and those which signify the connection of propositions in compound propositions or arguments. The passage last quoted continues:

> This it [the mind] does in several ways; as, *Is*, and *Is not*, are the general marks of the Mind, affirming or denying. But besides affirmation, or negation, without which, there is in Words no Truth or Falsehood,[17] the Mind does, in declaring its Sentiments to others, connect, not only the parts of Propositions, but whole Sentences one to another, with their several Relations and Dependencies, to make a coherent Discourse. (III.vii.1)

The distinction is again reflected in the classification of mental operations given in the Port-Royal Grammar, which may be worth quoting in full at this point.

> Tous les Philosophes enseignent qu'il y a trois operations de nostre esprit: CONCEVOIR, JUGER, RAISONNER.
>
> CONCEVOIR, n'est autre chose qu'un simple regard de nostre esprit sur les choses, soit d'une maniere purement intellectuelle; comme quand je connois l'estre, la durée, la pensée, Dieu: soit avec des images corporelles, comme quand je m'imagine un quarré, un rond, un chien, un cheval.
>
> JUGER, c'est affirmer qu'une chose que nous concevons, est telle, ou n'est pas telle. Comme lors qu'ayant conceu ce que c'est que la *terre*, & ce que c'est que *rondeur*, j'affirme de *la terre* qu'elle *est ronde*.

RAISONNER, est se servir de deux jugemens pour en faire un troisiéme. Comme lors qu'ayant jugé que toute vertu est loüable, & que la patience est une vertu, j'en conclus que la patience est loüable.[18]

Conception is simply having ideas (or "conceptions"). Judgment is the affirmation or denial of one idea with respect to another. Reasoning is the interconnection of propositions in an argument (*e.g.*, a syllogism) so as to derive a further proposition in conclusion. The distinction between conception and judgment is the basis for the distinction between integral words and their combination in propositions by means of the first kind of particles. The further distinction between copulative particles and propositional connectives is an extension of that between judgment and reasoning.

Locke's theory of words is represented in Figure 5.

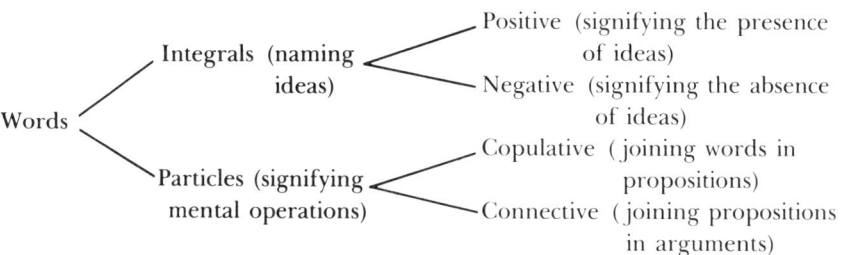

FIG. 5

In its discussion of particles the theory of words is already involved with a theory of grammar. Locke himself points out, moreover, that grammar, the way integral words and propositions are respectively joined by particles, must be considered in the light of a theory of mind. Particles, he says, "are all *marks of some Action, or Intimation of the Mind*; and therefore to understand them rightly, the several views, postures, stands, turns, limitations, and exceptions, and several other Thoughts of the Mind, for which we have either none, or very deficient Names, are diligently to be studied" (III.vii.4). Our next step prior to the construction of a Lockean grammar must therefore be a survey of Locke's theory of mind; this is necessary to an understanding of particles in much the same way as an outline of his theory of ideas is necessary to an appreciation of his account of names ("integrals").

Before we proceed to the theory of mind (in the next section) we must first take care of the matter of verbs. The Port-Royal Grammar includes verbs under the heading of words signifying judgments, but Locke nowhere assigns verbs in general to any category. The chapter on particles gives "is" and "is not" as "general marks" of affirmation and denial, but with these special exceptions all particles mentioned are prepositions or conjunctions. Kretzmann points out that since verbs are not treated as names of ideas in Book III they might have been intentionally omitted from the class of integrals, but he also notes passages elsewhere in which Locke clearly supposes verbs to have corresponding ideas.[19] In connection with simple modes, for instance, Locke says: "To *slide, roll, tumble, walk, creep, run, dance, leap, skip*, and abundance of others, that might be named, are Words, which are no sooner heard, but every one, who understands *English*, has presently in his Mind distinct *Ideas*, which are all but the different modifications of Motion" (II.xvii.2).

Just as Locke's discussion of particles in III.vii.1 can be clarified by comparison with the views given in greater detail in the Port-Royal Grammar, so the account of the verb given in that work may well elucidate Locke's intentions here.[20] Arnauld and Lancelot define a verb as "un mot dont le principal usage est de signifier l'affirmation."[21] (They acknowledge that this may apply to the verb only in its indicative mood and that there are secondary uses of verbs to signify other moods, other "mouvemens de nostre ame.") We must distinguish, however, between the pure or logical verb, which signifies only affirmation (or denial), and the grammatical verb, which because of a natural tendency in language towards abbreviation frequently includes more in its signification.[22] Besides the affirmation, the grammatical verb may include, for example, the attribute affirmed—as the verb in "Petrus vivit" comprehends both the affirmation and the attribute, which may be distinctly rendered in the French "Pierre est vivant." Again, the grammatical verb may include its subject—as the verb in "homo sum" includes the subject which in the French "je suis homme" is represented by a distinct pronoun. Finally, the grammatical verb usually includes a specific tense, whereas the logical verb is theoretically tenseless. The logical verb, as defined by the *Grammaire*, is without tense and is independent of any particular subject or attribute; it expresses only affirmation or denial.

The logical analysis of the verb supposes that any simple proposition in which a finite indicative verb occurs has the underlying form SUBJECT + (AFFIRMATION or DENIAL) + ATTRIBUTE. In this structure the subject and attribute terms both name ideas but the logical verb signifies only the affirmation or denial. The verb in ordinary language which comes closest to representing the logical verb is the third person present of "to be": "il n'y a que le verbe *estre* qu'on appelle substantif qui soit demeuré dans cette simplicité, & encore l'on peut dire qu'il n'y est proprement demeuré que dans la troisiéme personne du present *est*, & en de certaines recontres."[23] The logical verb is the copula, the "is" of predication, to which all verbs in propositions may be reduced.

When the Port-Royal Grammar assigns verbs along with prepositions and conjunctions to the class of words which signify the *manner* of our conceptions it evidently means the logical verb, the copula, and not the grammatical verb. Locke's remarks on verbs become intelligible and consistent if read in the light of this same distinction. He assigns the copula ("is" and "is not") to the class of words signifying the *actions* of the mind (III.vii.1), and when he speaks elsewhere of verbs signifying ideas he is evidently considering the unanalyzed grammatical verb, which always denotes an action as well as signifying an affirmation. We will assume in the following sections that it was Locke's intention to adopt this distinction and the corresponding logical analysis of the proposition.

The basic division of words into those which signify ideas and those which signify actions of the mind upon ideas is attended with certain difficulties in the context of Locke's theory of ideas, and once again it must be admitted that Locke has not given sufficient attention to the reconciliation of his account of language with other parts of his system. The difficulties, however, are not in this case insuperable. They stem largely from Locke's broad use of "signify" to cover both the relation between integral words and ideas and that between particles and mental actions. We must appreciate that the "is" in, for example, "John is running" does not signify the act of affirmation in anything like the way in which "John" signifies my idea of John or in which "running" signifies my idea of running. The point is made by comparing the "is" of predication with the noun "affirmation"; in Locke's loose terminology both words "signify" affirmation but they do not *mean* the same thing. The same terminological confusion arises in the *Grammaire*, but Arnauld and Lancelot make an effort to clarify it:

> Et c'est proprement ce que c'est le verbe, *un mot dont le principal usage est de signifier l'affirmation*: c'est à dire, de marquer que le discours où ce mot est employé, est le discours d'un homme qui ne conçoit pas seulment les choses, mais qui en juge & qui les affirme. En quoy le verbe est distingué de quelques noms qui signifient aussi l'affirmation; comme *affirmans, affirmatio*; parce qu'ils ne la signifient qu'entant que par une reflexion d'esprit elle est devenuë l'objet de nostre pensée; & ainsi ne marquent pas que celuy qui se sert de ces mots affirme, mais seulement qu'il conçoit une affirmation.[24]

The distinction concealed by the ambiguous use of "signify" is between words which *refer to* ideas (including ideas *of* mental actions) and words which *indicate that an action is being performed*. The copula in "roses are red" does not *refer* to my affirmation of the proposition but *shows* that I do affirm it.

THE THEORY OF MIND

In Locke's *Essay* the theory of ideas given in Book II is completed by a theory of mental operations given in Book IV whereby ideas may be brought into meaningful combinations. In the same way the theory of integral words, or names, is completed by a theory of grammar accounting for the meaningful combination of names in propositions. Just as the theory of integrals is based upon the theory of ideas, so the theory of grammar, which Locke comprehends under what he calls "particles," rests upon the theory of mental operations. In this section the account of these operations is outlined; this done, there is sufficient material with which to construct a Lockean grammar in the next section.

In II.xii.1 (quoted above) Locke lists three "acts of the mind, wherein it exerts its power over its simple *ideas*." Of these three operations the first two, combination and comparison, are ways of bringing ideas together. The third, abstraction, is of a different kind, being a means of drawing a single "general" idea out of a number of complex ideas. Combination, however, brings ideas together into *single* compound ideas. Locke emphasizes at several points that a complex idea is still a single idea (II.xii.1; III.vi.28). Combination, therefore, like abstraction, is an operation performed upon two or more ideas to produce a further idea, but unlike comparison is not a way of forming connections between two or more ideas which remain distinct. The operation of comparison therefore lies uniquely at the root of Locke's accounts of grammar and logic.

A passage added in the fourth edition finds two ways of forming connections among distinct ideas:

> Some of our *Ideas* have a natural Correspondence and Connexion one with another: It is the Office and Excellency of our Reason to trace these, and hold them together in that Union and Correspondence which is founded in their peculiar Beings. Besides this there is another Connexion of *Ideas* wholly owing to Chance or Custom; *Ideas* that in themselves are not at all of kin, come to be so united in some Men's Minds, that 'tis very hard to separate them, they always keep in company, and the one no sooner at any time comes into the Understanding but its Associate appears with it; and if they are more than two which are thus united, the whole gang always inseparable shew themselves together. (II.xxxiii.5)

The former connections are made by the faculty of reason, and we shall see that what Locke calls reason is a function of the operation of comparison. The latter connections are made involuntarily, by no operation as such but by virtue of the phenomenon which Locke called "the association of ideas." Locke's account of language, as we shall see, is concerned only with statements and, moreover, with the kind of statement which might occur in philosophical discussion. It is a study not of ordinary speech but of something like the "philosophical language" projected by Wilkins and other members of the Royal Society—the difference being that whereas Wilkins set out to devise a new language on a philosophical base Locke is content to indicate how the old language might be used in a strictly philosophical way. For this reason the connections established by association are of no interest to Locke. Association is automatic and idiosyncratic whereas the language which Locke desires the philosopher to use must be both rational and, in its underlying principles, universal. There will be more to say later of association, but for the present we are left with comparison as the only operation productive of ideational connections relevant to the theory of grammar.

There are two kinds of comparison operation, those which give rise to knowledge, and those, discussed in chapter xxv of Book II, which give rise to ideas of relations (defined as ideas which the mind "gets from their comparison one with another"). This second kind of comparison is that which has its place in the scheme of Figure 4, as the source of relations. We are now concerned only with the former kind, which connects ideas but does not merge them into a further idea.

When two ideas are compared in this way they may *either* agree or disagree *or* they may do neither. Cases of agreement and disagreement form the foundation of knowledge. Locke leaves us uncertain as to how agreement and disagreement are detected; he does give examples and a brief classification (IV.i.1–7), but neither is very helpful. His examples are "white is not black" (disagreement) and "the three angles of a triangle are equal to two right ones" (agreement), which suggests that cases of agreement and disagreement are all and only those which can be represented in analytic statements. Agreement and disagreement are classified into "four sorts:" *Identity*, or *Diversity*; *Relation; Co-existence*, or *necessary connexion*; and *Real Existence*. These categories turn out to be unhelpful. The fourth is utterly mysterious; how our knowledge of real existence—knowledge that the idea we have is of something other than an idea—may be accounted a perception of agreement *between ideas* is never explained. The first and third are, by Locke's own admission, special cases of the second (IV.i.7). We are left with the second category, and with the trouble of distinguishing "relation" in this sense from the sense of "relation" in II.xxv.1. It is better to pass over these terms altogether and hold to the notion that where the comparison of ideas yields the basis for an analytic statement we have a case of agreement or disagreement.

Where agreement or disagreement between ideas is *perceived* we have knowledge: "*Knowledge* then seems to me to be nothing but *the perception of the connexion and agreement, or disagreement and repugnancy of any of our Ideas*" (IV.i.2). This perception need not be immediate:

> For if we will reflect on our own ways of Thinking, we shall find, that sometimes the Mind perceives the Agreement or Disagreement of two *Ideas* immediately by themselves, without the intervention of any other: And this, I think, we may call *intuitive Knowledge*. . . . The next degree of Knowledge is, where the Mind perceives the Agreement or Disagreement of any *Ideas*, but not immediately. Though where-ever the Mind perceives the Agreement or Disagreement of any of its *Ideas*, there be certain Knowledge; Yet it does not always happen, that the Mind sees that Agreement or Disagreement, which there is between them, even where it is discoverable; and in that case, remains in Ignorance, and at most, gets no farther than a probable conjecture. (IV.ii.1–2)

Where there is perception of agreement or disagreement but it is not immediate the "probable conjecture" may be converted to certainty by the supply of intermediate ideas. "Those intervening *Ideas*, which serve to show the Agreement of any two others, are called *Proofs*; and where the Agreement or Disagreement is by this means plainly and clearly perceived, it is called *Demonstration*" (IV.ii.3). In this way Locke distinguishes two "degrees of knowledge," the first called *intuitive* and the second *demonstrative*. All certain knowledge belongs to one of these two modes of perception of agreement or disagreement: "whatever comes short of one of these, with what assurance soever embraced, is but Faith, or Opinion, but not Knowledge, at least in all general Truths" (IV.ii.14). A third degree, *sensitive* knowledge, is subsequently admitted, which consists in knowledge "of the existence of particular external Objects" (IV.ii.14). But this is obviously problematic in the light of the theory of representative ideas, and Locke seems to avoid allowing it to be a third source of *certain* knowledge (*cf*. IV.iii.29).

The outline of the theory of mind is not yet complete, for we have so far dealt only with *knowledge* which consists in the *perception* of agreement or disagreement among ideas. Knowledge is but one of two "faculties" whereby mental propositions are constructed.

> Thus the Mind has two Faculties, conversant about Truth and Falsehood.
> *First, Knowledge,* whereby it certainly perceives, and is undoubtedly satisfied of the Agreement or Disagreement of any *Ideas.*
> *Secondly, Judgment,* which is the putting *Ideas* together, or separating them from one another in the *Mind,* when their certain Agreement or Disagreement is not perceived, but *presumed* to be so; which is, as the Word imports, taken to be so before it certainly appears. And if it so unites, or separates them, as in Reality Things are, it is *right Judgment*. (IV.xiv.4)

With these additions, the theory of mind, so far as it is concerned with the construction of mental propositions, is represented in Figure 6.

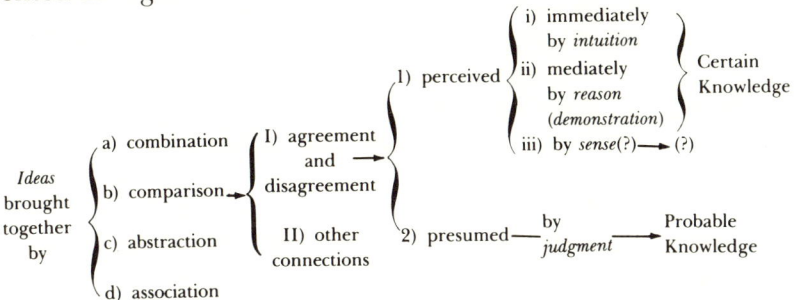

Fig. 6

Knowledge and judgment are the two faculties concerned with truth and falsehood—*i.e.,* with propositions. The difference between them lies in their respective modes of apprehending the agreement and disagreement of ideas; when agreement or disagreement is *perceived* the outcome (leaving aside the ambiguous case of "sensitive" knowledge) is *certainty,* but when it is *presumed* we attain only to *probability* (IV.xiv.2).

To complete the account represented in Figure 6 we must introduce and define two further concepts, *truth* and *proposition.*

> *Truth* then seems to me, in the proper import of the Word, to signify nothing but *the joining or separating of Signs, as the Things signified by them, do agree or disagree one with another*. The *joining* or *separating* of signs here meant is what by another name, we call Proposition. So that Truth properly belongs only to Propositions: whereof there are two sorts, *viz*. Mental and Verbal; as there are two sorts of Signs commonly made use of, *viz*. *Ideas* and Words. (IV.v.2)

Ideas are connected by the operation of comparison, and since ideas are signs the result of the operation is a proposition. Propositions are connections between signs which may be said to be true or false. Since words are also signs there are two kinds of propositions, mental and verbal (*cf*. IV.v.5). The junction is thus established between Locke's theory of mind, of which the account of the formation of propositions is a crucial part, and his theory of language. The manner of the juncture at once suggests two general points, both of which will be discussed in the next section: first, that Locke's theory of language is concerned primarily, if not exclusively, with the construction of *propositions*; and second, that Lockean grammar will evidently conform to what we would now call the "deep-structure" or "generative" model in that its task must be to show how verbal propositions are constructed on the basis of underlying mental propositions. The second of these points sheds light on the purpose of the present section: the theory of mind (of which the theory of ideas is a part) provides the substructural foundations upon which the theory of grammar must rest.

The comparison of ideas does not by itself yield a mental proposition; a proposition occurs only if agreement or disagreement is either perceived or presumed. The perception or presumption of agreement or disagreement, however, not only formulates a proposition but also decides whether the proposition is to be affirmed or denied. The perception or presumption will necessarily be of *either* agreement *or* disagreement—if of agreement, the proposition is affirmed; if of disagreement, it is denied. Affirmation and denial are therefore not, in Locke's account, operations distinct from the perception or presumption which formulates the mental proposition.

As it stands in the scheme of Figure 6 judgment is merely a subordinate branch of Locke's theory of mind, but its real importance in the theory of language is greater than the scheme suggests. In his discussion of judgment Locke provides an alternative theory of signs which circumvents the difficulties of the theory outlined in the first two sections above, and this alternative theory was later adopted by Berkeley as the basis for a radically new account of language.

In approaching Locke's account of judgment we must, once again, dispose of his tendency to use key words in more than one sense. At one point *judgment* is defined in opposition to *wit* (a pair of terms frequently juxtaposed in literary discussions of the period):

> For *Wit* lying most in the assemblage of *Ideas*, and putting those together with quickness and variety, wherein can be found any resemblance or congruity, thereby to make up pleasant Pictures, and agreeable Visions in the Fancy: *Judgment*, on the contrary, lies quite on the other side, in separating carefully, one from another, *Ideas*, wherein can be found the least difference, thereby to avoid being misled by Similitude, and by affinity to take one thing for another. (II.xi.2)

Judgment in this sense occurs in the context of a discussion of "discerning and other operations of the mind" and is totally different from judgment in the sense with which we are now concerned. This, the more important sense of judgment, is first introduced in II.ix.8, but the definitions occur in Book IV—in the passage quoted above from IV.xiv.4 (in the chapter "Of Judgment") and in IV.xvii.17, where judgment is said to be "the thinking or taking two *Ideas* to agree, or disagree, by the intervention of one or more *Ideas*, whose certain Agreement, or Disagreement with them it does not perceive, but hath observed to be frequent and usual."

Judgment as the faculty for discovering probabilities is best illustrated from the passage in which Locke first introduces it in the *Essay*:

> We are farther to consider concerning Perception, that the *Ideas we receive by sensation, are often* in grown People *alter'd by*

> *the Judgment*, without our taking notice of it. When we set before our Eyes a round Globe, of any uniform colour, *v.g.*. Gold, Alabaster, or Jet, 'tis certain, that the *Idea* thereby imprinted in our mind, is of a flat Circle variously shadow'd, with several degrees of Light and Brightness coming to our Eyes. But we having by use been accustomed to perceive, what kind of appearance convex Bodies are wont to make in us; what alterations are made in the reflections of Light, by the difference of the sensible Figures of Bodies, the Judgment presently, by an habitual custom, alters the Appearances into their Causes: So that from that, which truly is variety of shadow or colour, collecting the Figure, it makes it pass for a mark of Figure, and frames to it self the perception of a convex Figure, and an uniform Colour; when the *Idea* we receive from thence, is only a Plane variously colour'd, as is evident in Painting. (II.ix.8)

The situation might be described as follows. When an idea X (*e.g.*, of a variously shaded flat disc) is constantly associated in our experience with another idea Y (*e.g.*, of "a round globe of any uniform colour") it comes to happen that whenever X is presented to our senses by an act of judgment we think of Y. The connection between these two ideas, once established through past experience, becomes habitual and is normally both instantaneous and imperceptible.

> This in many cases, by a settled habit, in things whereof we have frequent experience, is performed so constantly, and so quick, that we take that for the Perception of our Sensation, which is an *Idea* formed by our Judgment; so that one, *viz.* that of Sensation, serves only to excite the other, and is scarce taken notice of itself; as a Man who reads or hears with attention and understanding, takes little notice of the Characters, or Sounds, but of the *Ideas*, that are excited in him by them. (II.ix.9)

To maintain this account of judgment in the *Essay* Locke would have to clarify two areas of difficulty, neither of which he appears to notice. First, it may be objected that if we are said to take *no* notice of the idea of sensation, as Locke implies (II.ix.10), we are apparently left with an unconscious idea, for our *experiencing* the idea of sensation is a precondition of the act of judgment. Yet Locke denies the possibility of unconscious ideas—of experience of which we take no notice (I.i.10 and 19). The potential contradiction was observed by Condillac in 1746.[25] Locke might avoid it by rewriting passages such as II.ix.9–10 so as to make clear that the idea of sensation is not totally unnoticed.

The second problem is more pressing. The mechanism of *judgment* as Locke outlines it is indistinguishable from that of *association*, yet judgment is a respectable "faculty" conversant about truth and falsehood, whereas association stands in "opposition to reason" and deserves to be called "madness" (II.xxxiii.4). In both cases a concurrence of ideas in past experience causes the mind in future to move automatically, whenever one idea occurs, to the other. The only discoverable difference, apparent from the examples given in the chapter on association, is that connections formed by association tend to be eccentric and idiosyncratic while those formed by judgment, barring unusual cases such as those of sensory deprivation, are common to all people. As a means of differentiating between association and judgment, however, this offers no sharp distinction; judgment shades off into association as the subject's past experience varies from the norm and as his susceptibilities increase. The *Essay* affords no further clarification, and we can only note in conclusion that the discussion of association which raises difficulties for the concept of judgment was a late addition to the text, making its first appearance in the fourth edition of 1700.

Locke himself does not connect judgment with the theory of signs, but the hint was given for his successors to find: "a Man who reads or hears with attention and understanding, takes little notice of the Characters or Sounds, but of the *Ideas*, that are excited in him by them" (II.ix.9). The man reading or hearing words is interpreting signs, and the theory of judgment explains how he does this while the official theory of signs leaves us in doubt. We saw in the second section that the definition of a word as a sign for an idea in the mind of the speaker leaves the interpreter with no way of distinguishing signs from mere sounds or shapes. But if we now define signs in terms of judgment we can avoid the pitfalls of semantic idealism. If we let a *sign* be any idea which, by an operation of judgment, leads us to some other idea, we have a definition which is neutral as regards speaker and hearer. The sentence last quoted shows how judgment functions in the reception and interpretation of signs; a later sentence applies the same concept to the utterance of signs: "Men, that by custom have got the use of a By-word, do almost in every sentence, pronounce sounds, though taken notice of by others, they themselves neither hear, nor observe" (II.ix.10).

Why did Locke himself not develop these hints which Berkeley was to put to striking use only twenty years later? A possible reason is that the definition of signs just proposed would not square well with Locke's insistence that not only are words signs for ideas but also ideas for things. If a sign is a connection by way of judgment between two *ideas* there is no way in which anything other than an idea can be signified. Locke may in fact be committed to this latter position already, and his claim that ideas are signs for things is probably one which he has not left himself room to advance. But he may nonetheless have reacted against a definition which would expressly confine meaning to the realm of ideas. He may also have felt that to explain the meaning of any sign in terms of other signs was a dangerous hermeneutic circularity. Berkeley, as we shall see, had no such qualms, largely because his denial of material substance left him with a very different world to account for.

THE THEORY OF GRAMMAR

Putting together the materials surveyed in the last three sections we may now attempt an outline of Lockean grammar. This will consist essentially of two parts: an account of the generation and structure of mental propositions, and the rules whereby verbal propositions corresponding to mental propositions may be produced. The result is what would now be called a "generative" grammar. It is not "transformational," however, as that of Port-Royal may be said to be,[26] because Locke does not involve himself with the grammatical intricacies of ordinary language; he is content to provide for the generation of propositions—i.e., of statements and compound statements.

Ideas are either obtained directly from experience (sense and reflection) or are derived from other ideas already so obtained in the manner outlined in Figure 4. They fall into five classes: simple, simple modes, mixed modes, substances, and relations, and they may be either particular or general. When ideas are compared one with another they may be perceived or presumed to agree or disagree (Figure 6), in which case a mental proposition is formed. The proposition is affirmed if the ideas agree, denied if they disagree. A mental proposition therefore consists of two ideas connected by affirmation or denial.

The mental proposition (the "base-structure" in Lockean grammar) may be represented:

$$\text{IDEA}_1 + \text{AFFIRMATION/DENIAL} + \text{IDEA}_2.$$

The structure of the mental proposition corresponds closely to that which we have found reason to believe Locke accepted as the logical structure of a simple verbal proposition, namely:

$$\text{SUBJECT} + \text{COPULA} + \text{ATTRIBUTE}.$$

Because the structures correspond we need only simple substitution rules to take us from the mental base to the verbal proposition. In each of the three places in the mental structure a word must be inserted. Words are classified (Figure 5) as either names for ideas or particles. Obviously only names, or integral words, can be substituted for ideas, and we are told that the copula, a special kind of particle, stands for the affirmation or denial. The copula has two forms, positive and negative (*e.g.*, "is" and "is not"), which represent affirmation and denial respectively (III.vii.1). The form of a verbal proposition is therefore more fully represented as:

$$\text{NAME for IDEA}_1 + \textit{is/is not} + \text{NAME for IDEA}_2.$$

The substitution of names is governed by the kind of idea for which the name is to stand; the integral words (positive and negative) in any language would fall into five classes corresponding to the five kinds of idea in such a way that a name could be substituted for an idea only if the name belonged to the class corresponding to the class to which the idea belonged. We have seen that Locke spends much time in Books II and III explaining how the relations between words and ideas vary among these five classes.

Finally, Locke mentions one further step: the use of particles (other than the copula) to join propositions into compound propositions (III.vii.1). He gives an example in his analysis of "but": *All Animals have sense;* BUT *a Dog is an Animal* (III.vii.5). The structure of such a sentence may be represented as:

VERBAL PROPOSITION$_1$ + PARTICLE + VERBAL PROPOSITION$_2$

of which the underlying structure would be:

MENTAL PROPOSITION$_1$ + ACTION + MENTAL PROPOSITION$_2$.

Locke does not go into detail, but clearly there are a number of different ways (mental actions) whereby the mind may combine propositions, ways represented by such expressions as "and," "or," and "if . . . then." A complete logical grammar would give a classification of these actions and their corresponding expressions.

This completes the grammar which can be discovered in the *Essay concerning Human Understanding*. Two obvious comments are invited: Lockean grammar adopts a deep-structure model, and it is concerned to generate not the sentences of ordinary language but only a certain kind of statement. The first point would need no emphasis were it not for the suggestion, implicit in the historical writings of Chomsky, that Locke belongs to an empiricist tradition in the philosophy of language somehow opposed to the procedures of a "rationalist" or "Cartesian" tradition represented by the *Grammaire* of Port-Royal.[27] It is here claimed that Lockean grammar is consistent in its fundamental principles with that of Arnauld and Lancelot.

The aims of the *Essay*, however, differ from those of the Port-Royal Grammar. While the latter undertakes to set out the rational principles behind natural language, Locke is concerned only with language used to communicate, in the form of propositions, information about the agreement and disagreement of ideas. Any other use, or any use of language which detracts from the efficacy of such communication, is held by Locke to constitute an "abuse of words" for the purposes of philosophy:

> The *ends of Language in our Discourse with others*, being chiefly these three: *First, To make known* one Man's Thoughts or *Ideas* to another. *Secondly*, To do it *with* as much ease and *quickness*, as is possible; and *Thirdly*, Thereby *to convey* the *Knowledge* of Things. Language is either abused, or deficient, when it fails of any of these Three. (III.x.23)

In other passages Locke allows that words may also be used to record thoughts for the assistance of memory (III.ii.2), and his discussion of modes and relations shows that in certain cases words may assist in the formation and acquisition of ideas as well as in their retention. These are the only uses of words envisaged in the *Essay*, and for this reason we may legitimately ask whether Locke is dealing with *language* at all. He approaches the subject as if his pronouncements were to cover all human speech (*e.g.*, in III.i.1–3), but as we read on it becomes increasingly clear that his concern is with a highly restricted class of utterances. He is interested not in language so much as in logic. The same is true of many, perhaps of most, of the works written before the Second World War and considered as contributions to the philosophy of language.

Locke was himself no doubt uncertain as to how far his linguistic principles could be applied to common speech. Our realization that, whatever he may imply to the contrary, Locke's interest in language was confined to a relatively rare linguistic function, the communication by means of propositions of agreement and disagreement between ideas, may make many of the inadequacies of the general theory seem less serious. For instance, it is almost certainly not true that every word used in common speech should— or could—signify an idea or action in the mind of the speaker, but there might well be some advantage in imposing such requirements on certain kinds of utterances such as propositions in philosophical argument.

3. Berkeleian Theory: Structuralism

INTRODUCTION

Berkeley's theory of language shares several fundamentals with that of Locke. First, it is primarily concerned with the function of language in communicating information by way of statements which are either true or false. Berkeley does show a little more interest than Locke in other uses—*e.g.*, in certain kinds of rhetorical statements and in words used in the course of games—but there can be no doubt that, like Locke, he approached the philosophy of language because in order to account for human knowledge he found it necessary to deal with the communication of what can be known. Consequently his interest in language is largely confined to its function in recording or communicating propositions.

This brings us to the second point of similarity. Like Locke, Berkeley believes that language (in the limited sense just indicated) gets its meaning from the mental events and operations which it serves to make manifest. Just as Locke holds that words (with special exceptions) signify mental phenomena called "ideas," so Berkeley (again with certain reservations) argues broadly that "ideas" provide the semantic base down to which all meaningful utterances can in principle be analyzed. A third common principle lies implicit in the first two: because the purpose of language is to externalize the thoughts which constitute knowledge, it follows that the structure of language must be explicable in terms of the structure of thought, and that for Berkeley as for Locke the theory of grammar must adopt a generative deep-structure model in which thought supplies the base.

In spite of these common features, however, the Berkeleian theory of language differs radically from the Lockean. We shall see that the differences spring largely from three basic points on which Berkeley takes an independent stand. First, he denies the existence of material reality, which denial has important repercussions in semantic theory. Second, although he agrees that words are signs which (for the most part) signify ideas, Berkeley does not add that the idea signified must be in the mind of the speaker. As was suggested in Chapter 2, Berkeley does not adopt the "official" Lockean theory of signs but instead draws a new theory from Locke's account of "judgment." Third, the mental base structures of Berkeleian grammar differ from those of Locke because Berkeley departs from Locke on several particulars within his theories of ideas and of the mind.

Our first task in constructing Berkeley's theory of language must be to show that it does indeed have in common with the Lockean theory the three features mentioned in the first paragraph above. It is particularly important to do so because the few significant published commentaries on Berkeley's view of language are in fundamental disagreement as to the extent to which his theory departs from that of Locke. The three features which Berkeley's theory has in common with Locke's—primary concern with use of language to communicate propositions, belief that words signify mental contents and operations, and adoption of the mental level as the deep structure in a generative theory of grammar—are interrelated positions which may be discussed together under the heading of "analysis." It is shown in the next section that Berkeley's view of analysis, which entails these positions, is virtually identical with Locke's. Subsequent sections explore the ways in which Berkeley's premises differ from Locke's and lead him, in spite of their common views on analysis, to a radically new account of language.

ANALYSIS

Locke believes that the utterances of language can and should, for purposes of philosophical discussion, be analyzed down to corresponding mental events which are integral to (if not identical with) the meanings of the utterances. This general belief, which constitutes a broad theory of linguistic analysis, entails three positions in particular. (i) "Language," for purposes of the theory, means the language of philosophers, which apparently consists largely if not exclusively of true or false propositions. (ii) Words signify mental events (in Locke's account "ideas" and "mental acts"). (As we saw in Chapter 2, this statement by itself is highly ambiguous. It may mean that the idea *is* the meaning of the word, or that the presence of the idea is a condition of the word's having meaning. Neither does the statement as it stands say *whose* mental events are signified.) (iii) Language is related to the underlying mental events in a specifiable way (perhaps by *rules* of substitution or transformation).

The evidence for Locke's acceptance of these tenets and some exploration of the forms they take in his theory of language were offered in Chapter 2. That Berkeley adopted much the same view of analysis is best shown from passages towards the end of the Introduction to the *Principles of Human Knowledge*.[1]

> Since therefore words are so apt to impose on the understanding, whatever ideas I consider, I shall endeavour to take them bare and naked into my view, keeping out of my thoughts, so far as I am able, those names which long and constant use hath so strictly united with them. . . . Of late many have been very sensible of the absurd opinions and insignificant disputes, which grow out of the abuse of words. And in order to remedy these evils they advise well, that we attend to the ideas signified, and draw off our attention from the words which signify them. . . . It were therefore to be wished that every one would use his utmost endeavours, to obtain a clear view of the ideas he would consider, separating from them all that dress and encumbrance of words which so much contribute to blind the judgment and divide the attention. In vain do we extend our view into the heavens, and pry into the entrails of the earth, in vain do we consult the writings of learned men, and trace the dark footsteps of antiquity; we need only draw the curtain of words, to behold the fairest tree of knowledge, whose fruit is excellent, and within the reach of our hand. (*Intro.* 21–24)

No stronger statement could be required of Berkeley's concurrence in both the Baconian-Cartesian rejection of verbal formulae as the ground of certainty and the Lockean purpose of reconstructing logic on a foundation of ideas. Knowledge, Berkeley is saying, finds its materials not in words but in ideas. It follows that when knowledge is necessarily embodied in words, for purposes of record or communication, the words must be systematically chosen so as to convey precisely the ideas involved. There must, in other words, be a specific method of "translating" between verbal and ideational structures, a method of analyzing any meaningful utterance down to its underlying mental events.

Some scholars have held that Berkeley does not accept this position and, in particular, that he rejects the second of the three components of the Lockean view of analysis outlined above. Their contention rests largely upon a number of passages in which Berkeley appears to expressly reject the view that all meaningful words signify ideas. G. J. Warnock, for example, claims in his chapter "Berkeley's Account of Language" that the originality of Berkeley's view of language lies chiefly in his departure from Locke on the matter of the relation between words and ideas:

> The essential thing is [Berkeley's] contention that the assumptions about meaning, which led Locke to propound his doctrine, are wrong. Locke asks what it is of which general words are names; and the crux of Berkeley's contention is, not that he answers this question wrongly, but that the *question itself* is wholly wrong. For it is already implied in the form of Locke's question that any word must stand for, be the name of, something; and this assumption, which Locke never questioned, is precisely what Berkeley rejects.[2]

Kretzmann speaks in a similar way of Berkeley as having "early rejected Locke's semantics" and as "abandoning, or at least supplementing, the attempt to account for all linguistic meaning in terms of the relation between names and their bearers."[3]

One preliminary matter pertaining to the term "idea" must be clarified. Berkeley, no more than Locke, holds that *all* words signify *ideas*. Just as Locke admits a class of words which do not signify ideas but stand for mental actions upon ideas so Berkeley allows that some words stand not for ideas but for mental operations (or for what he calls "notions"). Both philosophers, however, would be satisfied with the proposition that all words signify mental events or mental operations, and it is for Berkeley's adherence to this general form of analysis that we here contend. Some of the passages in which Berkeley denies that all words signify *ideas* are in fact dealing with words which do signify mental operations or "notions."

The several stated exceptions to the Lockean semantic rule in Berkeley's writings have prompted the view that Berkeley does not accept the rule, the theory of analysis, at all. This conclusion can be avoided by a scrutiny of the particular cases with reference to which the rule is apparently denied. The following are most often cited: cases in which the word derives its meaning from its use and can, as a matter of fact, function in use even although the user has no ideas corresponding to it; rhetorical uses, where the purpose is not to raise in the audience ideas corresponding to the words used but rather to produce an effect— arouse an emotion, produce a conviction, provoke an action, *etc.*; general names; and names for "spirits."

A clear passage in which instances of most of these cases are raised occurs in the seventh Dialogue of *Alciphron*, a passage particularly relevant to the present purpose because it appears to be an outright rejection of Lockean linguistic theory. Alciphron, the freethinker, who puts the views which Berkeley, in the character of Euphranor, is concerned to oppose, here gives a virtual paraphrase of the Lockean position (A.VII.2–3). His immediate purpose is to show that certain key terms in Euphranor's philosophy, words such as "grace" (in a theological sense), are without ideas and therefore without meaning (A.VII.4). Euphranor's answer, as far as we shall quote it, makes two points: first it presents Alciphron with a number of cases, from the list just given, of words which seem to have meaning without ideas; and second it takes the example of the word "force," which has a place in mechanics comparable to that of "grace" in theology, and attempts to show that Alciphron's application of Lockean semantics must find "force" a no less empty word than "grace."

> EUPHRANOR: ... Words, it is agreed, are signs: it may not therefore be amiss to examine the use of other signs, in order

to know that of words. Counters, for instance, at a card-table are used, not for their own sake, but only as signs substituted for money, as words are for ideas. Say now, Alciphron, is it necessary every time these counters are used throughout the progress of a game, to frame an idea of the distinct sum or value that each represents? . . . From hence it seems to follow, that words may not be insignificant, although they should not, every time they are used, excite the ideas they signify in our minds; it being sufficient that we have it in our power to substitute things or ideas for their signs when there is occasion. It seems also to follow that there may be another use of words besides that of marking and suggesting distinct ideas, to wit, the influencing our conduct and actions, which may be done either by forming rules for us to act by, or by raising certain passions, dispositions, and emotions in our minds. A discourse, therefore, that directs how to act or excites to the doing or forbearance of an action may, it seems, be useful and significant, although the words whereof it is composed should not bring each a distinct idea into our minds.

ALCIPHRON: It seems so.

EUPHRANOR: Pray tell me, Alciphron, is not an idea altogether inactive?

ALCIPHRON: It is.

EUPHRANOR: An agent therefore, an active mind or spirit, cannot be an idea, or like an idea. Whence it should seem to follow that those words which denote an active principle, soul, or spirit do not, in a strict and proper sense, stand for ideas. And yet they are not insignificant neither; since I understand what is signified by the term *I*, or *myself*, or know what it means, although it be no idea, or like an idea, but that which thinks, and wills, and apprehends ideas, and operates about them. . . .

ALCIPHRON: What would you infer from this?

EUPHRANOR: What hath been inferred already—that words may be significant, although they do not stand for ideas. The contrary whereof having been presumed seems to have produced the doctrine of abstract ideas. . . .

ALCIPHRON: And yet it is a current opinion that every substantive name marks out and exhibits to the mind one distinct idea separate from all others.

EUPHRANOR: Pray, Alciphron, is not the word *number* such a substantive name?

ALCIPHRON: It is.

EUPHRANOR: Do but try now whether you can frame an idea of number in abstract, exclusive of all signs, words, and things numbered. I profess for my own part I cannot. . . . But, to come to your own instance, let us examine what idea we can frame of force abstracted from body, motion, and outward sensible effects. For myself I do not find that I have or can have any such idea.
ALCIPHRON: Surely every one knows what is meant by force.
EUPHRANOR: And yet I question whether every one can form a distinct idea of force. (A.VII.5–6)

The obvious conclusion from such a passage is that Berkeley rejects the principle that words depend for meaning upon underlying ideas. Two considerations, however, suggest that this conclusion should be avoided if possible: first, that it is inconsistent with what Berkeley says elsewhere (*e.g.*, in *Intro.* 21–24, quoted above), and second, that if we take away from Berkeley the ideational theory of meaning we leave his philosophy with no coherent alternative account of how words work. (It will not do to answer the first point by saying that *Alciphron* appeared twenty-two years after the *Principles* and that Berkeley had in the meantime rejected Lockean semantics. All the points made in the passage from *Alciphron* are also stated in the *Principles*: Berkeley evidently thought the two arguments consistent.)

One way to avoid the conclusion in the case of the *Alciphron* passage is to look to its wider context. It occurs as part of an extended dialogue in which Euphranor, frequently on the defensive, is concerned less to expound a system than, from moment to moment, to meet his opponents' arguments. The passage quoted succeeds in dislodging Alciphron from the position he adopts in A.VII.1–4 but does not necessarily give Berkeley's own final position on the semantic question. Berkeley is notorious for giving such partial statements of his complex system in order to meet immediate problems, the most striking instance being the publication in 1709 of the *New Theory of Vision* which makes assumptions incompatible with the fuller exposition published in the next year in the *Principles of Human Knowledge*. The *Principles* may indeed be the only major philosophical work in which the reader can be sure at any point that Berkeley is concerned to tell the whole truth as he sees it and not merely to win conviction. A number of Berkeley's apparent rejections of the Lockean principle elsewhere can also be dealt with in this way, by looking at the context of the argument and its immediate purposes.

More persuasive than such a tedious process of piecemeal textual criticism, however, is an avoidance of the anti-Lockean conclusion by showing that each of the kinds of apparent exceptions to the ideational principle can in fact be made consistent with that principle as stated in *Intro.* 21–24. If this can be done it is then a simple matter to show that Berkeley's apparent denials of the principle are in fact objections to its wrongful application. In the *Alciphron* passage, for instance, Berkeley is not saying that there are *no* ideas corresponding to rhetorical utterances or to "force" and "grace," but that Alciphron's failure to find such ideas should not lead him to the conclusion that the words are meaningless. Again, in *Intro.* 18–19, appearances to the contrary notwithstanding, he is not denying that meaning depends upon underlying ideas, but rather rejecting the conclusion that for every meaningful general term there must be an abstract general idea. The examination of the particular cases itemized above will show that Berkeley believed *not* that words do not depend for their meanings upon underlying thought processes but that the relation between words and these underlying processes is more complex than Alciphron or the advocates of abstraction had realized. The reason for this complexity, which will in turn be examined in subsequent sections, lies in Berkeley's view of the mind and in his theory of grammar. Let us now take in turn each of the four cases in which Berkeley appears to deny the Lockean principle of analysis.

i. Cases in which the word derives its meaning from its use and can, as a matter of fact, function in use without the users having ideas corresponding to it. The counters in the card game in *A.*VII.5 are of this type, as are the algebraic variables of *Intro.* 19:

> And a little attention will discover, that it is not necessary (even in the strictest reasonings) significant names which stand for ideas should, every time they are used, excite in the understanding the ideas they are made to stand for: in read-

ing and discoursing, names being for the most part used as letters are in *algebra*, in which though a particular quantity be marked by each letter, yet to proceed right it is not requisite that in every step each letter suggest to your thoughts, that particular quantity it was appointed to stand for.

This passage may seem to say that meaning consists in use and not in underlying thought processes; but what it actually says is that although words *do* stand for ideas they can sometimes be used successfully without ideas in mind. The point of the passage is a gloss on the Lockean theory, not a denial of it. The counters in the card game are used for convenience without ideas during the game, but they could not be so used unless a means existed of attaching ideas to them. If there were no way of determining the value of the counters the game could not be played. Similarly, in the algebraic expression "$2x + 4 = 8$" the variable "x" can be used because there exists a procedure in algebra for discovering its value; if there were no such means the expression would be senseless.

The case is not altered if we take the extreme example of a sign for which the value cannot be determined. Berkeley mentions that "the algebraic mark, which denotes the root of a negative square, hath its use in logistic operations, although it be impossible to form an idea of any such quantity" (A.VII.14). Again, it may seem that use is here substituted for the idea as the condition of meaning, but again this is not what Berkeley says. His point is that we have no idea "of any such *quantity*" as $\sqrt{-2}$, not that we have no idea at all corresponding to the term. The idea we might have could be explained by the fact that we do have ideas corresponding to the arithmetical signs "$\sqrt{}$", "$-$", and "2": we would then have an idea of the meaning of $\sqrt{-2}$ without having an idea of any particular quantity. The case is similar to that of words such as "something" or "nothing." I have no idea of any *thing* corresponding to these words, but I may still be said to have ideas of their meanings. For instance, a Lockean theorist might argue that "There is something in my room" and "There is nothing in my room" may be paraphrased respectively as "My room is not empty" and "My room is empty," neither of which would seem to give his theory any trouble.

The general point, in cases of this type, is that words can indeed be *used* without ideas, but only because they *do* signify ideas which, by means of the appropriate analysis, may be discovered. The distinction Berkeley is making is between the meaning of the word and any particular occasion of its use. On particular occasions certain words may be used successfully without ideas, but this is so only because there are occasions on which those words *are* used with the ideas they signify.

ii. Rhetorical uses, where the purpose is not to raise in the audience ideas corresponding to the words used but rather to produce an effect. This case is similar to the first. Berkeley's claim is not that there are meaningful words to which no ideas ever correspond but that there are uses of some words in which the presence of the corresponding idea is not necessary. Besides the *Alciphron* passage, the chief example comes from the Introduction to the *Principles*.

> Besides, the communicating of ideas marked by words is not the chief and only end of language, as is commonly supposed. There are other ends, as the raising of some passion, the exciting to or deterring from an action, the putting the mind in some particular disposition; to which the former is in many cases barely subservient, and sometimes entirely omitted, when these can be obtained without it, as I think doth not unfrequently happen in the familiar use of language. . . . At first, indeed, the words might have occasioned ideas that were fit to produce those emotions; but, if I mistake not, it will be found that when language is once grown familiar, the hearing of the sounds or sight of the characters is oft immediately attended with those passions, which at first were wont to be produced by the intervention of ideas, that are now quite omitted. May we not, for example, be affected with the promise of a *good thing*, though we have not an idea of what it is? . . . Even proper names themselves do not seem always spoken, with a design to bring into our view the ideas of those individuals that are supposed to be marked by them. For example, when a Schoolman tells me *Aristotle hath said it*, all I conceive he means by it, is to dispose me to embrace his opinion with the deference and submission which custom has annexed to that name. (*Intro.* 20)

Berkeley is careful in this passage not to deny that ideas may be, or may have been, associated with the words in question. Indeed, it is obvious that, in his own example, the words "Aristotle hath said it" could not have the effect desired if there were *no* occasions on which the word "Aristotle" was associated with the philosopher of that name.

Cases *i* and *ii* can be made consistent with the ideational theory of meaning by distinguishing between the meaning of the word (which is determined by the idea) and its use on certain occasions (when the idea need not be present)—which amounts to saying that these are secondary uses which are independent of ideas only because there are primary uses in which the words are associated with corresponding ideas.[4] They are in other words non-theoretical uses, to which the Lockean theory is not in any event intended to apply. Another possibility, then, for avoiding the conclusion that Berkeley rejects Lockean semantics in passages such as those just cited, is to distinguish between the use of language for making statements and other uses for purposes such as calculation or persuasion. In denying that the theory applies to the latter Berkeley might still be consistent with Locke, who as shown in Chapter 1 confined his theory of language to the communication of propositions. We cannot, however, adopt this line in dealing with cases *iii* and *iv*, which involve not special *uses* of words but particular *kinds* of words which might well occur in propositions.

iii. General terms. Berkeley, like Hobbes before him, adopted the nominalist view that only names may be universal, all other things being particular (*Intro.* 15). Nominalism raises immediate questions for an ideational theory of meaning. It is admitted that there are general words but denied that there can be any general ideas to which these words refer; the nominalist perspective seems to involve at least a very large exception to the rule that words signify ideas. Berkeley, however, tries to avoid this conclusion. A word is general, he says, when it refers to any member of a class of ideas. When such a word is used there will be in the user's mind some particular member of the class of ideas referred to, which idea might be called "general" in so far as it represents, in the mind of the user of the general word, the class of ideas of which it is a member.

> But it seems that a word becomes general by being made the sign, not of an abstract general idea, but of several particular ideas, any one of which it indifferently suggests to the mind. . . . Now if we will annex a meaning to our words, and speak only of what we can conceive, I believe we shall acknowledge, that an idea, which considered in it self is particular, becomes general, by being made to represent or stand for all other particular ideas of the same sort. (*Intro.* 11–12)

Berkeley is not, therefore, unwilling to admit *general* ideas—that is, particular ideas which are signs for classes of ideas. He objects, however, to *abstract* general ideas of the kind suggested by Locke in *Essay* II.xi.10–11 and III.iii.6 (*Intro.* 11).[5] The Berkeleian general idea is not an abstraction of common features from the class of particular ideas but is one member of that class taken to stand for the class as a whole.

The doctrine of *abstract* ideas, against which Berkeley's nominalism is directed, arises he thinks from another misapplication of the principle that words signify ideas.

> Let us therefore examine the manner wherein words have contributed to the origin of that mistake. First then, 'tis thought that every name hath, or ought to have, one only precise and settled signification, which inclines men to think there are certain *abstract, determinate ideas*, which constitute the true and only immediate signification of each general name. And that it is by the mediation of these abstract ideas, that a general name comes to signify any particular thing. Whereas, in truth, there is no such thing as one precise and definite signification annexed to any general name, they all signifying indifferently a great number of particular ideas. (*Intro.* 18)

There is a great difference, he goes on to say, between having a *definition* which fixes the meaning of a general term and having an abstract general idea corresponding to it (*Intro.* 18). The word "triangle," for instance, may be defined for certain purposes as "a three-sided rectilinear plane figure," but any idea I have corresponding to the word will necessarily be of some particular triangle, which has besides the qualities requisite to satisfy the definition such further individuating qualities as size, color, and particular angles. Misapplication of the Lockean principle leads us to expect an idea which simply corresponds to a general word like "triangle," an idea which is like the definition in being an abstract of particular qualities. The real situation, according to Berkeley, is very different. The word is held to its meaning by a definition, which denotes the class of particulars to which the word applies; use of the word is accompanied by an idea of any of these particulars. Once again, Berkeley does not deny that words signify ideas but argues that the process of signification is more complex than we may suspect.

An obvious objection to Berkeley's explanation of general terms is that it is circular because it explains the meaning of general words in terms of definitions containing other general words. It is no use to say that "triangle" means "a three-sided rectilinear plane figure" when we have no ideas corresponding to general terms such as "plane" and "figure." This problem is the linguistic aspect of the fundamental gap in Berkeley's account of universals; the idea of some particular triangle accompanies the proper use of the word "triangle," but how do we know whether or not any particular idea is an idea of a triangle or of something else? The account we have outlined does not give any solution to the basic problem of classification. To say that the general idea is a particular idea used as a sign of the class of which it is a member begs the very question to which it is offered as a solution: how are these classes formed? It must be admitted that Berkeley has no answer and may not have even seen the difficulty.[6] It is clear, nonetheless, that in his handling of general ideas he intends to preserve the principles of linguistic analysis outlined in *Intro.* 21–24.

iv. Ideas of spirits. Berkeley divides the universe exclusively into ideas and spirits. Ideas are inert; only spirits may be active. Ideas are perceived by spirits and are immaterial. The only substance is spiritual substance (*P.* 2 and 7). We will go into this distinction at greater length when we come to discuss Berkeley's account of ideas, but for the present we are concerned with the semantic problem to which the distinction gives rise. The difference between ideas and spirits is such that there can be no ideas of spirits (*P*.27), yet there are names for spirits in words such as *soul*, *spirit*, *substance*, *I*, *memory*, and *myself*. "But it will be objected that, if there is no *idea* signified by the terms, *soul*, *spirit*, and *substance*, they are wholly insignificant, or have no meaning in them. I answer," Berkeley continues, "those words do mean or signify a real thing, which is neither an idea or like an idea, but that which perceives ideas, and wills, and reasons about them" (*P*.139). Some words, it seems, do not signify ideas but "real things" which are not ideas, and which must consequently be spirits. Some words are therefore exceptions to the principle that all words signify *ideas*—but only if one applies that principle in a strict and literal manner. Locke himself actually observes not the literal version of the principle but rather a version which might be fully stated: "words signify the contents or actions of the mind." The same is true of Berkeley, and names for spirits are no exception to the correct, more liberal formulation of the Lockean principle. Such names stand for whatever are the means whereby the mind has knowledge of spirits. Berkeley's restriction of the term "idea" prevents its use here, and in the first edition of the *Principles* there was in fact no word for these "objects of human knowledge" which "are perceived by attending to the passions and operations of the mind" (*P*.1) and which cover roughly the same territory as Locke's "ideas of reflection." By the time of the second edition (1734) Berkeley had adopted the term "notion" for this purpose, and we may therefore say that names for spirits signify notions (*P*.140 and 142).

There are problems involved with Berkeley's handling of our knowledge of spirits, of which something more will have to be said below. For the present, however, we have shown that each of the four cases which at first seem to show that Berkeley denied the Lockean semantic principle that words signify ideas is in fact deliberately consistent with the proper formulation of that principle. We therefore conclude that Berkeley does indeed subscribe to the doctrine of linguistic analysis outlined in *Intro*. 21–24, according to which verbal propositions must be capable of systematic analysis into underlying thought processes.

THE THEORY OF IDEAS

We come now to the roots of the differences between Lockean and Berkeleian theories of language, which are to be found in the ideas and mental processes which, in both theories, provide the logical base upon which the language of propositional statement is constructed.

Berkeley divides the knowable world into two categories, *ideas* and *spirits*:

> It is evident to any one who takes a survey of the objects of human knowledge, that they are either ideas actually imprinted on the senses, or else such [objects] as are perceived by attending to the passions and operations of the mind, or lastly ideas formed by the help of memory and imagination, either compounding, dividing, or barely representing those originally perceived in the aforesaid ways. (*P*.1)

We therefore have the following classification of objects of knowledge:

```
                           ⎧              ⎧ a) sense
                           ⎪ ideas—from  ⎨ b) memory
OBJECTS OF                 ⎨              ⎩ c) imagination
KNOWLEDGE                  ⎪
                           ⎩ spirits
```

Fig. 7

The relation between the two main categories is of such a kind that spirits may "have," or "perceive" ideas, but there can be no ideas *of* spirits because ideas are essentially inert whereas spirits are essentially active (*P*. 2 and 27). Moreover, ideas are such that they exist only when perceived by a spirit; they have no independent existence, for Berkeley allows no substance but spiritual substance (*P*. 2–3 and 7). As regards ideas, it is correct to say that *esse est percipi*, although in general we should, to accommodate spiritual substance, say *esse est percipi aut percipere*.

For present purposes Berkeley's theory of ideas may be sufficiently clarified by commenting on three aspects of the scheme of Figure 7: (i) the absence of any third category of *things* (which ideas might have been said to represent); (ii) the absence of any further classification of ideas than into those of sense, memory, and imagination; and (iii) the means whereby we acquire knowledge of spirits.

(i) The knowable world consists wholly of ideas and spirits, and yet there are no ideas of spirits—which leaves nothing for ideas to be *of* except other ideas. But we cannot sensibly be said to have ideas of ideas. Suppose I have an idea of a house; why can I not then form an idea of this idea and so have an idea of an idea? To see the answer we must see why it is misleading to speak of an idea *of* a house in the first place. The house "of which" we have an idea does not exist apart from the idea; we must avoid the analogy (loosely appropriate to Lockean theory) of a picture and the possible real existence of the thing depicted. The idea *is* the house and is nothing but the house. We must avoid thinking of the idea as a kind of frame around the picture. Berkeley's ontology leaves room for no alternative: a house *is* a kind of idea. It follows that an idea of a house is just what in ordinary language we call "a house," that an idea of an idea is just what we call "an idea," and therefore that an idea of an idea of a house is nothing different from an idea of a house, which again is simply what we call in ordinary language "a house."

Strictly speaking, ideas are not "of" anything; nothing exists for them to represent. We should say not "an idea of a house" but "an idea which is a house," or simply "a house-idea." The point has bearing upon Berkeley's use of the word "sign," for like Locke he holds not only that words are signs of ideas but also that ideas are signs. In Locke's case, however, ideas are signs in a very different sense from that in which words are signs; whereas words are *arbitrary* signs for ideas, ideas are signs for things in much the same way as a representative picture is a sign for the things of which it is a picture. In Berkeley's philosophy ideas cannot be signs in this latter sense because, as we have just argued, there can be no distinction between the idea and its "contents" (*i.e.*, what it is said to be an idea of). Ideas are signs for Berkeley in precisely the same way as are words, which enables him, as we shall see, to speak of the "language" of ideas and to evolve a recognizably structural basis for his account of linguistic meaning.

(ii) Berkeley does not pursue any classification of ideas beyond their sources in the faculties of the mind (sense perception, memory, and imagination). He does not attempt to classify ideas according to their objects, as does Locke with his categories of modes, substances, and relations. Neither does Berkeley adopt the Lockean atomism and hold that all ideas are either simple or reducible to simples. He does admit the possibility of compounding ideas (*P*.1) and he occasionally talks of "simple ideas" (*e.g.*, *WGB*.II.176), but his use of the terminology is non-technical; he does not hold that all ideas may be analyzed down to simples. (In his early notebooks, the *Philosophical Commentaries* first published in 1871, Berkeley debates with himself the problems of ideational atomism as if initially expecting to adopt this feature of the Lockean theory of ideas, but atomism has no function in any of his public writings. Some of the early writings do make use of a notion of sensible *minima*, which might be regarded as a form of atomism, but apart from one brief mention in the *Principles* the theory of *minima* is not discussed by Berkeley after the *New Theory of Vision*.)

The chief reason for Berkeley's failure to adopt Lockean ideational atomism must surely be that he has no use for it. Locke somewhat gratuitously turns the faculty for combining ideas (needed to make imaginary ideas, such as those of unicorns and golden mountains, consistent with empiricism) into an atomic theory of ideas largely because he is anxious to bring his work into line with that of scientists like Boyle by whom he was greatly influenced. Berkeley takes a more critical attitude towards the sciences (as can be seen by comparing Locke's prefatory "Epistle to the Reader" with Berkeley's *Analyst* or *De Motu*) and sees no need to follow Locke beyond postulation of a combinatory faculty into philosophical atomism. Ideational atomism, moreover, is inconsistent with certain positions which Berkeley wishes to adopt. For example, his denial of abstraction leads him to a relative theory of number, which involves the claim that there is no absolute unit—and therefore no "atom" or "simple idea."

> According as the mind variously combines its ideas the unit varies: and as the unit, so the number, which is only a collection of units, doth also vary. We call a window one, a chimney one, and yet a house in which there are many windows and many chimneys hath an equal right to be called one, and many houses go to the making of one city. In these and the like instances it is evident the unit constantly relates to the particular draughts the mind makes of its ideas, to which it affixes names, and wherein it includes more or less as best suits its own ends and purposes. Whatever, therefore, the mind considers as one, that is an unit. (*NTV*.109)

If a unit idea is a unit only relative to some purpose or consideration the same must be true of a simple idea. A Berkeleian idea may be said to be "simple" relative to a certain perspective, but it is not true that any Berkeleian idea must be either simple or complex in the absolute sense in which this requirement is imposed upon ideas in Locke's *Essay*.

It also follows that Berkeley does not consider ideas to be single or distinct in any absolute sense. What appears as "an idea" at one point may be several ideas or part of an idea at another point. Locke, on the other hand, supposes ideas to be fixed quantities, separate and separable. In Lockean theory this point is bound up with that discussed under (i) above, because Locke demonstrates the absoluteness of unity in his theory of ideas on the supposition that we can have ideas of ideas. Our idea of unity, he argues, comes from the fact that ideas do occur singly and separably in the mind; from the occurrence of any single idea we derive a further idea of unity (*Essay*. III.xvi.1). For Berkeley the way in which the idea of unity is obtained by Locke is void for "abstraction" (*P*.13), and as we have seen he therefore adopts a relative theory of number and inevitably admits the relativity of the notions of unity and simplicity.

Enough has been said to suggest that Berkeley's concept of the idea differs radically from Locke's. In particular, Berkeley does not allow ideas of ideas, he does not distinguish the idea from its contents, and he attaches no meaning to the Lockean notions of the simplicity and singularity of ideas. The consequences for semantic theory are immediately apparent. In Berkeley's account ideas are signs in the same sense as are words, and it follows from the rejection of atomism that we need not search for semantic simples. When it is held that all ideas are either simples or compounded of simples it must follow that words, which signify ideas, have meanings which are either simple or compounded; in abandoning absolute ideational simplicity Berkeley releases himself from this requirement. At the same time, however, he has let go the anchor of Lockean semantics. If the reduction of the idea to simples is *not* possible the way is open to a condition of hermeneutic circularity, in which to explain the meaning of a word we produce a definition which itself consists of words—and so on, with no prospect of an end to the succession of definitions. Lockean atomism ensures an end point to the process by postulating a level of simples to which all meaning must be ultimately reducible. There is no corresponding security in Berkeleian semantics, but as is shown in later sections Berkeley has an alternative foundation for meaning in his theory.

(iii) We have no *ideas* of spirits but we do have *knowledge* of them. To explain how we get this knowledge Berkeley introduces "notions." (The word is used in this special sense in the *Three Dialogues* of 1713, and is introduced into the *Principles* in the revisions made for the second edition of 1734.) Notions are problematic because they do not fit into either of Berkeley's ontological categories, being neither ideas nor spirits, although it would seem they are still "objects of knowledge." Figure 7 should perhaps be revised to include notions along with ideas and spirits. (We would need to add the appropriate rules, *e.g.*, that there can be no ideas of notions or notions of ideas, but that there can be notions of spirits, that spirits "have"—or "perceive"?—notions, and that notions do not exist independent of spirits.) There are at least two different species of notions: those we may call "primary," which derive from intuitive knowledge of the self, and "secondary" notions, which give us our knowledge of other spirits. A revised version of Berkeley's theory of knowledge might then look like Figure 8.

$$\text{OBJECTS OF KNOWLEDGE} \begin{cases} \text{ideas} \longrightarrow \text{of} \begin{cases} \text{a) sense} \\ \text{b) memory} \\ \text{c) imagination} \end{cases} \\ \text{notions} \begin{cases} \text{primary—of the self} \\ \text{secondary—of other spirits} \end{cases} \end{cases}$$

Fig. 8

Berkeley's first and clearest account of notions occurs in the third of the *Three Dialogues*, where Philonous, Berkeley's spokesman, says:

> I own I have properly no idea, either of God or any other spirit; for these being active, cannot be represented by things perfectly inert, as our ideas are. I do nevertheless know, that I who am a spirit or thinking substance, exist as certainly, as I know my ideas exist. Farther I know what I mean by the terms *I* and *myself*; and I know this immediately, or intuitively, though I do not perceive it as I perceive a triangle, a colour, or a sound. . . . My own mind and my own ideas I have an immediate knowledge of; and, by the help of these, do mediately apprehend the possibility of the existence of other spirits and ideas.   (*WGB*.II.231–232)

Knowledge of self is intuitive, and from intuition therefore comes our *primary* notion of spirit. Knowledge of other spirits cannot be intuitive for obvious reasons, and it remains for Berkeley to explain why he is not a convinced solipsist believing that, like ideas, other spirits exist only in so far as I perceive them. (In fact Berkeley does not believe this about ideas, but to escape such a conclusion he has *first* to give his reasons for belief in other spirits. Once established, these other spirits provide his means for proposing the continued existence of ideas independent of *my* perception.) His clearest explanation comes in a passage added to the third (1734) edition of the *Dialogues*:

> [The] being of my self, that is, my own soul, mind or thinking principle, I evidently know by reflexion [i.e. intuition]. . . . It is granted we have neither an immediate evidence nor a demonstrative knowledge of the existence of other finite spirits; but it will not thence follow that such spirits are on a foot with material substances . . . if we see signs and effects indicating distinct finite agents like ourselves, and see no sign or symptom whatever that leads to a rational belief of matter.
> (*WGB*.II.233)

There are "signs and effects" which indicate the existence of other spirits. A full explanation might run as follows. Our ideas occur in sequences. On occasion I can govern the sequence of ideas I have, as when I exclude the senses and follow a line of thought or imagination. At other times I cannot: when I open my eyes and look around I cannot by mere choice alter what I see. Intuition enables us to differentiate between these two cases; therefore I know when my ideas are (as we would ordinarily say) "of things outside myself" and when they are only "in my mind." Experience teaches us the way things normally behave—that is, we come to anticipate certain kinds of ideational sequences as usual in reference to what is customarily called "the material world." Because ideas are inert and cannot of themselves effect any change, departure from the normal sequence of ideas in my experience, if not caused by myself, must be caused by another spirit. The sign of the existence of another spirit is therefore any departure for which I am not responsible from the normal sequence of my ideas. I interpret these "signs" as evidence of spirits because I know from intuition what it is to act upon ideas; seeing the "effects" of such action *not* produced by myself I am left with no alternative but to *project*, as it were, my intuitive notion of spirit onto the ideas in question. In this way a *secondary* notion is formed.

Nowhere does Berkeley himself explain this at length, but the process can be pieced together from several passages in his works. Besides the sections of the third *Dialogue* already quoted in part, there are one or two helpful paragraphs towards the end of the *Principles*:

> In a large sense indeed, we may be said to have an idea, or rather a notion of *spirit*, that is, we understand the meaning of the word, otherwise we could not affirm or deny anything of it. Moreover, as we conceive the ideas that are in the minds of other spirits by means of our own, which we suppose to be resemblances of them: so we know other spirits by means of our own soul, which in that sense is the image or idea of them, it having a like respect to other spirits, that blueness or heat by me perceived hath to those ideas perceived by another.
> (P.140)

> From what hath been said, it is plain that we cannot know the existence of other spirits, otherwise than by their operations, or the ideas by them excited in us. I perceive several motions,

> changes, and combinations of ideas, that inform me there are certain particular agents like my self, which accompany them, and concur in their production. Hence the knowledge I have of other spirits is not immediate, as is the knowledge of my ideas; but depending on the intervention of ideas, by me referred to agents or spirits distinct from myself, as effects or concomitant signs. (P.145)

Whatever its precise mechanism, the secondary notion is a thing of some complexity, and is moreover a very common phenomenon, since it is involved in any apprehension of any "activity" (in which Berkeley includes what we would call mechanical causation) other than that of the apprehending self.

This may be as much as it is necessary to say of Berkeley's theory of ideas in order to arrive at a general view of his theory of language. In section 1 it was shown that like Locke Berkeley believes that language (*i.e.*, the propositional language of philosophical discourse) rests upon a substructure of thought processes. The present section has shown some relevant ways in which the materials or contents of these thought processes, "ideas" and "notions," differ in nature from those in Lockean theory. In our account of Lockean theory the next step was to consider the theory of words, but Berkeley has no theory of words apart from his theory of ideas. Ideas are signs, and in Berkeleian theory words are simply a sub-species of ideas. We therefore pass directly to Berkeley's theory of mind, which will show how, from the materials provided by "ideas" and "notions," are built mental structures which serve as the basis for linguistic utterances. We shall then proceed, as we did with Locke, to a tentative reconstruction of Berkeleian grammar.

THE THEORY OF MIND

As in the previous section we shall not here attempt to deal with all the philosophical issues raised by the subject but will only sketch an outline sufficient for the purposes of the theory of language.

Like Locke, Berkeley distinguishes sharply between the having of *ideas* (and notions) on the one hand and the derivation from them of *knowledge* on the other. In *Siris* he presents the distinction in terms of "sense" and "understanding":

> We know a thing when we understand it; and we understand it when we can interpret or tell what it signifies. Strictly, the sense knows nothing. We perceive indeed sounds by hearing, and characters by sight; but we are not therefore said to understand them. (S.253)

> As understanding perceiveth not, that is, doth not hear, or see, or feel, so sense knoweth not: and although the mind may use both sense and fancy, as means whereby to arrive at knowledge, yet sense, or soul so far forth as sensitive, knoweth nothing. (S.305)

The same distinction between the contents of the mind and the mind's knowledge or understanding of what it contains is evident in Berkeley's earliest work—the argument of the *New Theory of Vision* rests upon the distinction between the idea we perceive and the way in which we understand it (*e.g.*, NTV.3.41 and 45). Both Berkeley and Locke could be said to derive knowledge from ideas by means of establishing connections among ideas, but this would be to conceal a fundamental difference between them. Locke, we have seen, forms logical connections between ideas by means of operations based upon "comparison," but Berkeley, as may be evident from the passages just quoted, believes that knowledge arises from what he often calls the "interpretation" of ideas. Interpretation is the process whereby the mind, on being given certain ideas, moves in some regular, non-random way to conceive another idea which is not given. It is a process which is central to his account of human knowledge and which he almost certainly derived in part from the Lockean theory of "judgment" in *Essay*.II.ix.8–10.

Most of Berkeley's major philosophical writings are centrally concerned with exploration of this faculty of interpretation, which is in effect what in his universe takes the place of the old logic. The rules of interpretation show the means whereby the mind derives certain knowledge from the data of experience. To outline the theory, which is far too complex and problematic to treat in full, we may begin with the questions raised in the *New Theory of Vision*, which has the present advantage of being both shorter and more limited in ambit than the later writings. Here Berkeley confronts the fact that we *do* form connections among ideas so as to move from that which is given to some other which is the result of "interpretation." For example, I perceive by sight a tower, looking no larger than my thumb looks when held at arm's length, but I *know* that the tower is in fact much larger than my thumb. I also know that it is at some considerable distance from me, although, as Berkeley argues at length, I do not *see* distance *per se*. Finally, the science of optics tells us that the retinal image of the tower is inverted, but again I connect the image I perceive with an upright object. The question which the *New Theory* poses, in each of the cases of magnitude, distance, and uprightness, is *how* do I move from the mere visual datum to the further idea which constitutes my *knowledge* of the thing perceived?

In each case Berkeley finds two ways in which the connection *could* be made, only one of which he claims is actually involved under ordinary circumstances. One way is, by deliberate application of rules, to calculate or "infer" the connection. Thus, assuming I know the approximate height of the tower, I may estimate its distance from me by calculation from the angle at which the rays of light from the tower enter my eye (*NTV*.6). If I know the distance of the tower I may, again by using these angles, calculate its magnitude (*NTV*.52). And assuming I know the principles of optics I can, from the very fact that my retinal image is inverted, ascertain geometrically that the tower is upright (*NTV*.89). But, Berkeley argues, we do not in fact use these methods of inference in making such connections—although inference is used in many other cases, of course, as for instance in the solution of problems in geometry, or indeed in any case requiring the deliberate application of rules. The basis for Berkeley's rejection of inference as the means of interpretation commonly employed in the cases cited is simply that we are not *conscious* of employing any inference in arriving at the knowledge in question. With reference to the matter of the position or uprightness of the visual object, for example, he writes:

> I appeal to any one's experience, whether he be conscious to himself that he thinks on the intersection made by the radious pencils [*i.e.*, light rays], or pursues the impulses they give in right lines, whenever he perceives by sight the position of any object? To me it seems evident that crossing and tracing of the rays is never thought on by children, idiots, or in truth by any other, save only those who have applied themselves to the study of optics. And for the mind to judge of the situation of objects by those things without perceiving them, or to perceive them without knowing it, is equally beyond my comprehension. (*NTV*.90; *cf.* 12,19 and 27)

Such connections are successfully made by persons who clearly have not the knowledge necessary to make the inferences advanced in the proposed explanations, which means for Berkeley that another explanation must be found.

The second mode of interpretation, the one which applies, Berkeley claims, in the cases under consideration in the *New Theory of Vision*, is one which he calls "suggestion."[7] *Suggested* connections rest upon past experience of associations rather than upon any ability to apply rules, and differ from inferred connections chiefly in that they operate instantaneously and automatically.

> What seems to have misled the writers of optics in this matter is that they imagine men judge of distance as they do of a conclusion in mathematics, betwixt which and the premises it is indeed absolutely requisite there be an apparent necessary connexion: But it is far otherwise in the sudden judgments men make of distance. We are not to think that brutes and children, or even grown reasonable men, whenever they perceive an object to approach or depart from them, do it by virtue of geometry and demonstration.
>
> That one idea may suggest another to the mind it will suffice that they have been observed to go together, without any demonstration of the necessity of their coexistence, or without so much as knowing what it is that makes them so to coexist. (*NTV*.24–25)

The process here described, usually called "suggestion," is virtually identical with Locke's "judgment";[8] it depends upon an accumulation of like connections in past experience, it operates with imperceptible speed, and it is not dependent upon any conscious effort. Suggestion is the key to Berkeley's logic and to many of his departures from Locke in the theory of language.

Berkeley often explains the difference between the two in terms of the difference between the respective connections made by them: connections made by inference are necessary, those made by suggestion are contingent. But this explanation is potentially misleading, because the only observable difference between the two kinds of connection lies in the operations that produce them. Ideas, in Berkeley's logic, are inherently unrelated. They may become connected either by inference or by suggestion, but the connections make no difference to the ideas themselves. Ideas connected by inference may be said to be related "necessarily" because the rules whereby they are connected form an apparently inescapable bond between them. Connections made by suggestion are *no less* inescapable in fact, however, since both kinds are determined ultimately by past experience. The point is best made through an illustration. Suppose a trained meteorologist, a man who has assimilated the theory of his subject and knows as much as can be known about predicting the weather, steps outside his office and looks at the sky. He sees a certain configuration of clouds, feels the wind, and gives a forecast of rain. This is a clear example of establishing a connection between given ideas (the data he discovers on going outside) and another set of ideas (the forecast) by inference (the rules of meteorological forecasting). Now suppose, at the same time and in the same place, an old farmer newly arrived from the country, a man long schooled by experience in weather watching but, we will assume, a man of no theoretical learning, looks up at the sky and knows— feels in his bones, perhaps—that it is going to rain. This is a clear case of suggestion. The *same* relation is established in both cases; it is called "necessary" in the first case only because it is arrived at by means of a body of rules, and it is called non-necessary in the second only because it rests upon nothing but an accumulation of past associations.

There is nothing specious about this example; any connection established by suggestion may in principle become a subject of inference for some actual or putative science, and we can imagine worlds in which connections which we normally make by inference are made by suggestion. All connections rest ultimately on experience because the rules of inference in the various departments of knowledge are simply codifications of experience. The rules are needed because many connections (*e.g.*, that between a complex geometrical problem and its solution) are not part of *everyday* experience, and if they are to be passed on at all such connections must be codified in the simplest way possible. By using the rules we can then re-establish at will connections which, without the rules, we should have to be constantly rediscovering by accident or great effort. Berkeley's view, therefore, is that the relations established by the two modes of interpretation do not differ in themselves but only in the mode of their creation, relations inferred being deliberately made and those suggested being produced involuntarily and imperceptibly.

Having indicated very briefly the chief division within Berkeley's theory of mind—between the two modes of interpretation—we must concentrate now on the second mode, suggestion, because of its importance to Berkeley's view of language. Berkeley's "suggestion," we have said, is very much the same as Locke's "judgment," and in Chapter 2 it was suggested that the Lockean theory of judgment might form the basis for an alternative theory of signs. Berkeley does in fact take his theory of signs from this source; for him a sign is any idea which causes the mind to pass instantly and involuntarily to another idea—*i.e.*, any idea which *suggests* another. Berkeley's theory of language therefore avoids the problems of privacy and semantic idealism arising from the Lockean contention that words are signs for corresponding ideas *in the mind of the speaker*.

A positive outcome of this concept of the sign is that it allows Berkeley to speak of the corpus of suggestions as a "language." Ideas given in perception are signs whose meanings are the ideas they suggest. It is by virtue of our understanding of these meanings that we are capable of ordering our conduct, for even the simplest anticipation of the future—the unthinking expectation that if we put a hand in the fire we shall be burnt or that if we release a heavy object it will fall—are functions of suggestion. All the knowledge we have, including what we regard as instinctive reactions (but excluding conscious theoretical knowledge, which is a product of inference), presumably derives from connections made by suggestion. The corpus of suggestions is, in Berkeley's view, the language whereby God instructs every man—even the least learned—in the practical skills he needs for survival. Thus, in the case of visual data, Berkeley concludes

> that the proper objects of vision constitute an universal language of the Author of nature, whereby we are instructed how to regulate our actions in order to attain those things that are necessary to the preservation and well-being of our bodies, as also to avoid whatever may be hurtful and destructive of them. It is by their information that we are principally guided in all the transactions and concerns of life. And the manner wherein they signify and mark unto us the objects which are at a distance is the same with that of languages of human appointment, which do not suggest the things signified by any likeness or identity of natures, but only by an habitual connexion that experience has made us to observe between them. (*NTV*.147)

The principle of suggestion is the root not only of the divine language of nature but also, as this passage makes clear, of language in the ordinary sense. Human language, Berkeley believes, is simply a special case of the connection of ideas by suggestion. In order, therefore, to appreciate Berkeley's theory of language we must first understand the workings of the divine language of nature.

Ideas are inert and do not themselves give rise to other ideas (*P*.64). Any change in our ideas, the occurrence of any ideational sequence, must be explained in terms of the action of spirits. There are three possible kinds of spiritual action upon ideas. First there is that by the self upon its own ideas, of which we are each aware by intuition. When we are not aware of having ourselves caused the change in our ideas it must have been produced by some other spirit, in which case there are two possibilities: it may have been caused by some other finite spirit or it may have been caused by God. Since God is assumed to be regular and constant in his actions we can discriminate between these two cases. All sequences of ideas which exhibit constant regularity are the result of divine action, and collectively they constitute what we customarily call the "'laws of nature" (*P*.29–31 and 62). Departures from these norms, for which the self is not responsible, must therefore fall into the remaining category of changes caused by other finite (human) spirits (*P*.145–146). Suggestions are built up in our experience from those sequences of ideas caused by God. If, for instance, the sequence of ideas A + B + C is one for which neither the self nor any finite spirit is responsible it gives rise to a suggestion, such that whenever we are given the sequence A + B we automatically move on to C, even though C is not given in perception. This, which might be written AB→C, is a rule in the divine language and is also a "law of nature" in the ordinary sense.

It may seem, since suggestion rules are admittedly established on a basis in experience, that individuals with different backgrounds might acquire different "languages," but in fact this cannot happen except in the harmless sense that some individuals may have a greater "vocabulary" than others (*i.e.*, have assimilated a larger number of the rules). The first reason is that we can safely assume that the sequences for which God is responsible are universal and invariable; the laws of nature do not change. Second, sequences other than those produced directly by God do not give rise to suggestions under normal circumstances; the sane mind does not mistake its own imaginings for reality, and (if we place ourselves in the more innocent days of the eighteenth century) it is scarcely conceivable that a group of people should so consistently impose deception on another person as to eradicate his sense of the normal. The problem raised here is an aspect of a greater problem for Berkeley's immaterialism: how can his account of knowledge, having abolished the material world, distinguish between what is truly known to be the case and what is illusion? Normally the distinction is made with reference to what is independently real, but Berkeley appears to have left himself nothing of this sort to appeal to. Berkeley can, however, meet the problem by allowing us to distinguish between the three kinds of ideational sequence—the normal (sequences given in the divine language), those for which the self is responsible (the imaginary, known to be such by intuition), and the remainder, which being neither normal nor willed must be caused by other finite spirits. Evidently the mind does not build suggestions on the basis of imaginary sequences—no matter how many times I *imagine* myself putting my hand into the fire and feeling cheerful it will still happen that when I *do* put my hand into the fire I get burnt. Sequences caused by other people could, in theory, outweigh my experience of the normal, but ordinarily, for practical reasons, this does not happen to any great degree. The sane mind is in this way able under normal circumstances to distinguish illusions and deceptions from reality.

The language of suggestion is therefore common to all people. Its constancy is guaranteed by the immutability of the divine nature—but we should note that God is not needed to sustain the system. Berkeley used his philosophy to prove the existence of God—what else, in the absence of material reality, could explain the regularity of our ideas?—but the system will still rest upon the *fact* of our experience of normality even if we decline to speculate about ultimate causes.

Another possible objection to Berkeley's claim for a "language" of suggestion rules by which all men interpret their perceptions is that we are not, in general, aware of learning or applying such rules. Today, after Freud, this objection has little force; there now seems no limit to what may be attributed to what we call the unconscious mind. But in the eighteenth century an "unconscious mind" bordered on paradox. The Cartesians, deducing the very existence of the mind from the "*cogito ergo sum*," were committed to the view of the mind as *essentially* thinking, for an unthinking mind would not exist. Locke dismisses unconscious thought as "a very useless sort of thinking" (*Essay*.II.i.15), and perhaps for this reason did not develop the concept of judgment, which as Condillac later objected appeared to involve an unconscious mental operation. The centrality of the automatic, unconscious operation of suggestion in Berkeley's account of the mind makes him something of an innovator. He was, moreover, aware of the difficulties of this kind that his contemporaries would have with the doctrine. His Alciphron raises the objection, to be told by Euphranor in reply that "we have been all practising this language, ever since our first entrance into the world: . . . it doth not seem to me at all strange that men should not be aware that they had ever learned a language begun so early, and practised so constantly, as this of Vision" (A.IV.12). The linguistic analogy supports Berkeley's claim here, for as a matter of fact the great majority of men learn their native language without any conscious effort and normally use it in the same way.

Suggestion is the *unconscious* means whereby connections are established among ideas, enabling us to move from the mere data of perception to what Berkeley calls "knowledge." Collectively the rules of suggestion constitute the divine language of nature, the source of all human knowledge except the relatively small amount which stems from the *conscious* use of rules—*i.e.*, from inference. In illustrating the process of suggestion we have used a simple paradigm: if the normal sequence of ideas in our experience is A + B + C, then whenever we experience A + B we move on to C. If, for example, I *hear* the sound of wheels (A) and *then look* in the direction from which it comes (B) I *expect* to *see* a coach (C); or if I *see* a flame (A) and *then advance my hand* towards it (B) I *expect* to be *burnt* (C). But this paradigm, involving simply the progression from one group of ideas to another, is inadequate to the complexity of our actual interpretive abilities. I shall not expect to see the coach, for example, if I am inside a room, unless the room has a window overlooking the road, and even then I shall not expect to see the coach if I know it is night, unless I also know that the road is lighted. In reality there are few situations so simple as the three-term cases just cited, in which I perceive A and know that if B follows I may expect C. Thus, if I predict pain *whenever* I see flame I shall be wrong more often than right; most sightings of fire are *not* in fact followed by burning—precisely because we know that they *might* be. But what then becomes of the "rule" *visual image of flame → sensation of burning?*

Berkeley is aware of the problem, and his awareness at this point distinguishes his theory of suggestion from the simpler accounts of psychological "association" advanced by Hobbes and Locke. Berkeleian suggestion is a matter of interpretation, not of association, and cannot be reduced to the paradigm "whenever I perceive the sequence of ideas A + B + . . . I think of x" because the factors governing the occurrence of x in most day-to-day situations are extremely complex. No solution is reached merely by increasing the length of the sequences on the left-hand side of the rule, *e.g.*, by saying tht x occurs after A + B + C + D + E but not after A + B + C + D. Such a solution might, in a cumbersome way, deal with problems such as those just raised concerning the sighting of the coach and the sensation of burning, but this kind of solution will not do for Berkeley because it fails to meet the question of *error*.

If I see a flame and extend my hand towards it expecting to be burnt, only to find it is a deception, perhaps a reflection in a mirror, it is difficult to explain the fact that the suggestion rule has failed to work in this instance. Suggestion rules are signs in the language of God, identified with what we commonly call laws of nature, and a case of error such as this appears to be a case in which a divine law has been broken. *We*, of course, can easily explain the mistake with reference to the presence in the material situation of the mirror (or of whatever caused the deception), but Berkeley cannot do this; for him the situation consists only in the sequence of ideas, and here a normal sequence, a rule in the divine language, has failed unaccountably to proceed as expected. He would appear to have no alternative but to admit that, momentarily, the law of nature, the rule *visual image of flame →sensation of burning* was waived or suspended. Yet this is clearly unacceptable because it conflicts with the premise that God is constant and immutable. The solution is to cast the suggestion rules in an altogether different mold.

Suggestion rules of the form *sequence of ideas perceived→idea predicted* are too simple because they leave no room for error. They are mere association rules which, dignified with the status of laws of nature, cannot admit the least infraction without overturning Berkeley's universe. Life is not like this, for as Berkeley knows people do make mistakes. The solution is to introduce the notion of "circumstances" and in effect to make the rules context-sensitive—each rule applies only if a certain set of circumstances is satisfied. The "circumstances" are further ideas of perception—they can be nothing else. Thus, instead of *sequence of ideas perceived→idea predicted*, we have *ideas perceived→idea predicted (in the context of ideas x ... y)*.

In the *New Theory of Vision*, Berkeley claims that the reason the moon appears larger on the horizon is that in that position more of the earth's atmosphere lies between the moon and an observer, causing it to appear fainter than it does in other positions. Since the faintness of a visual object normally suggests that its actual magnitude is greater than its apparent visual magnitude, the observer automatically *thinks* the moon is larger when its appearance is fainter (*NTV*.67–71). To test this hypothesis we might devise a simple experiment. Berkeley seems to be propounding an association rule of the form *visual appearance of faintness→idea of increased magnitude*, according to which any occurrence of faintness in a visual image will automatically induce an idea of the increased magnitude of the object. Accordingly, if we look at the moon high in the sky through a piece of suitably frosted glass we should arrive at the same result as when we see it on the horizon through the extra miles of atmospheric interference. But this does not happen. Berkeley's explanation shows that he is not propounding a simple association rule but a rule which applies only in certain contexts:

> It may be objected that in consequence of our principles the interposition of a body in some degree opaque, which may intercept a great part of the rays of light, should render the appearance of the moon in the meridian as large as when it is viewed in the horizon. To which I answer, it is not faintness anyhow applied that suggests greater magnitude, there being no necessary but only an experimental connection between those two things. It follows that the faintness which enlarges the appearance must be applied in such sort, and with such circumstances, as have been observed to attend the vision of great magnitudes. When from a distance we behold great objects the particles of the intermediate air and vapours, which are themselves unperceivable, do interrupt the rays of light, and thereby render the appearance less strong and vivid: now, faintness of appearance caused in this sort hath been experienced to coexist with great magnitude. But when it is caused by the interposition of an opaque sensible body, this circumstance alters the case, so that a faint appearance

> this way caused doth not suggest greater magnitude, because it hath not been experienced to coexist with it.
>
> (*NTV*.72; *cf*. 28, 36, 56–57)

The suggestion rule *perception of faintness→idea of magnitude* applies only in certain circumstances. The rule therefore does not simply *associate* the idea suggested with the idea perceived in a mechanically regular way, but rather *interprets* the idea perceived in the light of its context. A way out of the difficulty presented by the fact of human error is now available. When a prediction made on the basis of suggestion fails we need not say that a law of nature has been broken; we can instead say that there has been a failure of *interpretation*—a human error, not a divine whim. The operation of even the simplest suggestion rule involves the active, albeit unconscious, participation of the human mind in evaluating the "circumstances" of the idea perceived. The divine language supplies the rules; human error in their application does not impugn the stability of the divine organization.

By observing the order of ideas in our experience we unconsciously acquire a set of rules of the form

$$A \to B \; (C \ldots D).$$

In other words, "given the idea A in perception we may anticipate B if and only if A occurs in the context of the ideas C and D." Collectively these rules constitute the divine language of nature, through which we acquire all our practical, non-theoretical knowledge of the world. Theoretical knowledge, all knowledge involving *conscious* application of rules, also depends upon the observation of order among our ideas, but is achieved not through suggestion (which is unconscious) but through inference. An inference rule, as we saw in the example of the meteorologist, may in fact make the same connection between ideas—yield the same prediction or interpretation—as does the process of suggestion, and we might therefore wish to say that it is the same rule in both cases. Berkeley's point, however, is that as soon as a suggestion rule is used consciously it becomes an inference rule, which is a very different thing. He insists upon the difference because he wishes to keep suggestion rules free from reliance upon signs and from the difficulties of classification.

A rule which applied on one unique occasion would be no "rule" at all.[9] A rule must have general application and must therefore be formulated in general terms. But only "signs," as we know from the Introduction to the *Principles*, can be possessed of generality. We have seen that our immediate knowledge of the world consists in the ability to interpret *signs* by means of suggestion *rules*. If Berkeley is obliged to admit that the rules of suggestion, which are supposedly the basis for our understanding of signs, are themselves dependent upon signs—that we need to understand signs in order to apply the very rules from which our understanding of signs is derived—then his purpose is obviously defeated. He avoids this obligation by confining the operation of suggestion rules strictly to the realms of the unconscious. Since the rules are never consciously formulated—perhaps never "formulated" in any sense at all—the problem of generality does not arise here. Berkeley allows himself to assume (since God is operating the system) that as each idea is given to the mind we know automatically whether or not it is "the same" as any other idea already experienced. Indeed, we *must* know this in order to assimilate the rules in the first place, although *how* we know it, short of divine inspiration, is never clear from Berkeley's exposition. Inference rules, however, because they are consciously formulated, *do* depend upon the use of signs. Here is the source of Berkeley's desire to keep the two faculties distinct, even though they may, in a sense, utilize the same rules to make the same connections. Suggestion rules must remain unconscious in order to avoid the requirement that they be formulated in general terms, which would render them useless for Berkeley's purpose.

Rules of inference depend upon signs and therefore, in Berkeley's view, they give rise to a different kind of knowledge. Suggestion rules, it might be fair to say, yield all our practical knowledge, but all theoretical knowledge depends upon inference. The difference between the two kinds of knowledge may be expressed as a matter of language: practical knowledge is independent of language and is the foundation of our ability to *use* language of any kind, but theoretical knowledge *depends upon* language and in a sense consists in the study of language. Berkeley expounds this doctrine best in a passage from *Alciphron:*

> To trace things from their original, it seems that the human mind, naturally furnished with the ideas of things particular and concrete, and being designed, not for the bare intuition of ideas, but for action and operation about them, and pursuing her own happiness therein, stands in need of certain general rules or theorems to direct her operations in this pursuit; the supplying which want is the true, original, reasonable end of studying the arts and sciences. Now, these rules being general, it follows that they are not to be obtained by the mere consideration of the original ideas, or particular things, but by the means of marks and signs, which, being so far forth universal, become the immediate instruments and materials of science. It is not, therefore, by mere contemplation of particular things, and much less of their abstract general ideas, that the mind makes her progress, but by an apposite choice and skilful management of signs: for instance, force and number, taken in concrete, with their adjuncts, subjects, and signs, are what every one knows; and considered in abstract, so as making precise ideas of themselves, they are what nobody can comprehend. That their abstract nature, therefore, is not the foundation of science is plain: and that barely considering their ideas in concrete is not the method to advance in the respective sciences is what every one that reflects may see; nothing being more evident than that one who can neither write nor read, in common use understands the meaning of numeral words as well as the best philosopher or mathematician.
>
> But here lies the difference: the one who understands the notation of numbers, by means thereof is able to express briefly and distinctly all the variety and degree of number, and to perform with ease and despatch several arithmetical operations by the help of general rules. Of all which operations as the use in human life is very evident, so it is no less evident that the performing them depends on the aptness of the notation. If we suppose rude mankind without the use of language, it may be presumed they would be ignorant of arithmetic. . . .
>
> If I mistake not, all sciences, so far as they are universal and demonstrable by human reason, will be found conversant about signs as their immediate object, though these in the application are referred to things. (*A*.VII.11–13)

All theoretical knowledge—all "science"—depends upon *signs* because it involves the formulation of *rules* which are necessarily *general*, and generality is a quality of *signs* alone. Berkeley's example of the arithmetician makes the same point as the example of the meteorologist used above: man may acquire considerable practical knowledge by unconsciously observing patterns of ideas in his experience, but to make any deliberate and consciously systematic use of this knowledge he must *formulate* the rules upon which his practical knowledge was based. In some cases the resultant *sciences* will arrive at the same conclusions as were already made on the basis of suggestion, but the process of deriving the conclusions will be altogether different.

Knowledge derived from inference depends on signs, and all signs, in Berkeley's broader use of the term, derive from the divine "language" of nature. We have therefore taken his theory of mind as far as we can without considering the theory of language itself. The latter must be constructed on the basis of what we know of the mind, its materials, and the processes of knowledge. This basis, in summary, consists of ideas and notions, and of the operations performed upon them to derive knowledge. Berkeley's chief difference from Locke in this connection lies in his use of "interpretation" instead of "comparison" as the operational source of knowledge; for Berkeley ideas are not compared to yield propositions concerning their compatibility but are interpreted in the light of the "circumstances" of their perception to yield a prediction of what perceptions will follow. The meaning of an idea, its interpretation, is the idea or ideas which, under the given circumstances, we are likely to experience in the immediate future.

The Berkeleian account of interpretation as the foundation of knowledge depends upon the sequential occurrence of ideas. There are, we have seen, three kinds of sequences: those caused by the self, those caused by God, and those caused by other people. Normally only the second of these contributes to establish suggestion rules in the unconscious mind. The corpus of suggestion rules constitutes the divine language of nature from which we get all our experiential, non-theoretical knowledge. The same sequences of ideas may also give rise to consciously formulated rules, inference rules, upon which all scientific knowledge is based. But inference rules, as we have seen, depend upon the use of signs, which in turn requires an understanding of the principles of language.

In Figure 8 a tentative outline of the *objects* of knowledge is given; Figure 9 represents the *processes and sources* of knowledge just described.

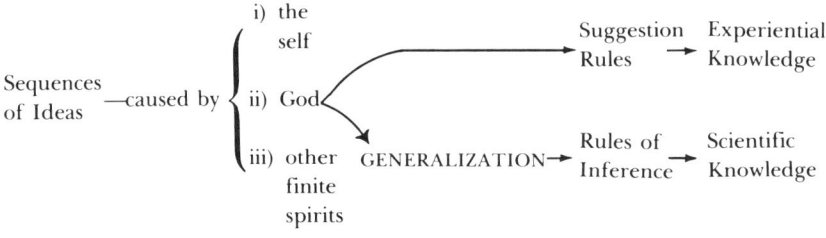

Fig. 9

Language holds an integral place in this account of knowledge. Locke makes particular areas of knowledge dependent upon language in a relatively piecemeal fashion by showing how certain kinds of ideas are, in different ways, conditioned by words. But the Berkeleian scheme of Figure 9 shows all "scientific" knowledge as dependent upon the power of generalization, which (for a nominalist) can be exercised only in some language. And the scheme of Figure 9 still does not show the full extent of the involvement of language and knowledge in Berkeleian theory, which is encompassed in Berkeley's reference to the order of ideas in our experience as a "language" spoken by "the Author of nature."

Because the sequences of ideas generated in the human mind by the action of God are regular, they can be interpreted—that is, recurring patterns can be discovered among them, on the basis of which predictions may be made as to what ideas will follow a given idea in the context of certain other ideas. The regularities discovered are what we call "laws of nature," and when predictions are unconsciously made on the basis of these regularities the process is one of "suggestion."

> Now the set rules or established methods, wherein the mind

> we depend on [*i.e.*, the mind of God] excites in us the ideas of sense, are called the *Laws of Nature*: and these we learn by experience, which teaches us that such and such ideas are attended with such and such other ideas, in the ordinary course of things.
>   This gives us a sort of foresight, which enables us to regulate our actions for the benefit of life. And without this we should be eternally at a loss: we could not know how to act any thing that might procure us the least pleasure, or remove the least pain of sense (*P*.30–31)

This process of learning from regularities in past experience is frequently referred to as understanding or interpreting the divine language of nature (*NTV*.147; *P*.107–108)—a process of which the acquisition and use of ordinary language is a special case. Every sane man understands this divine language to some extent. Less common than the ability to understand the language, however, is the ability to state the rules of its grammar. Berkeley distinguishes sharply between the understanding of the divine language, which rests upon suggestion, and the scientific ability to analyze that language by formulating and using its structural rules, which ability is a matter of inference.

> Those men who frame general rules from the phenomena, and afterwards derive the phenomena from those rules, seem to consider signs rather than causes. A man may well understand natural signs without knowing their analogy, or being able to say by what rule a thing is so or so. (*P*.108)

All science is therefore in a sense a study of the grammar—the structural rules—of the divine language (the "analogy" of its signs). Everyday learning from experience is *understanding* the language of ideas; science is the *formulation of its grammatical rules*. In this way Berkeley's whole view of human knowledge is bound up with linguistic principles.

The theory of knowledge seen in this light suggests that Berkeley would make a sharp distinction between two kinds of statement. First there would be statements about *particular* things and events, statements of knowledge derived from the application, conscious or unconscious, of the rules of the divine language.

Second there would be statements *of* these rules, "scientific" statements, which would necessarily be *general*. There must also be a third kind, to which most of Berkeley's own published statements belong: *philosophical* statements which neither pertain to particulars nor formulate general rules but which discuss the nature and workings of the divine language and its rules. Statements of the first kind reflect the *use* of the divine language, scientific statements give its *rules*, and statements of the third kind are *about* it. For Berkeley all *philosophy* (statements of the third kind) is philosophy of language—which is itself, for him, a department of theology.

THE THEORY OF LANGUAGE

Berkeley accepts the principle that language—at least, the language of informative statement—derives its significance from its relation to underlying mental structures. He agrees, in a general way, with the Lockean view that a word without an idea is without meaning. Meaningful utterances are therefore to be analyzed in terms of their underlying structures: the theory of language, by the principle of analysis, rests upon the theories of the mind, of ideas, and of knowledge. Berkeleian grammar, no less than the Lockean, is fundamentally of the generative type.

Lockean generative grammar is a relatively simple matter. Locke considers the underlying structure to consist in ideas and a few operations, to each of which words stand in a more or less one-to-one relationship. The simplicity of this scheme is permitted largely by Locke's choice of "comparison" as the basic logical operation. Comparison, he asserts, gives rise to mental propositions which correspond very closely in structure to simple sentences. Berkeley's grammar is more complex because his logic is based not upon comparison but upon interpretation, which does not yield mental propositions or any mental structure remotely resembling that of the sentence. More apparatus is therefore needed in Berkeleian theory to mediate between the mental base and the linguistic surface. And because the purpose of this apparatus includes considerable structural reorganization of the base in deriving the surface structures, there is a sense in which

Berkeleian grammar is not only generative but also "transformational."

In Lockean theory the answer to the question "what does the word X mean?" is the corresponding idea or operation *x*. Locke claims that ideas are also signs, which suggests that we should then proceed to ask "what does *x* mean?"—to which he would answer, "the object of which *x* is an idea." It is deceptive, however, to call the idea a "sign" for its object, because in the first place (as shown in Chapter 2), this is not the same sense in which the word is a "sign" for the idea, and second there is no epistemological distinction in Lockean philosophy between the idea and the object— we know the object only through the idea, which means that what Locke speaks of here as signification is in fact identity. In Berkeleian theory, on the other hand, ideas are signs in just the same sense as are words. Having by analysis discovered the meaning of a word in an underlying idea Berkeley must therefore face the further question: "what does the idea mean?"

A starker way of putting the same point is this: for Locke ideas *are* meanings, whereas for Berkeley ideas *have* meanings. For Locke ideas have values fixed by their reference to a supposed non-ideational reality. If we ask him "why is this idea an idea of [for example] a house?," Locke can theoretically point to the thing in reality and say that what makes the idea an idea of a house is its being in some sense a representation of that thing. The relationship between the idea and the object fixes the idea; it is an idea *of* that thing and can change only by becoming the idea of another thing (which would make it a different idea). The idea does not really *mean* or *signify* its object but *represents* the object to mind. Berkeleian ideas, however, have no such fixed values. Berkeley cannot say the idea of a house is an idea *of a house* by virtue of any relationship between the idea and anything not an idea which is a house, because in Berkeley's world there are no houses other than ideas of houses. The idea is a sign which derives its meaning not from any non-ideational reality but from the rules of interpretation. Moreover, since the rules are context-sensitive, the meaning of an idea can vary from one occurrence to the next as its context varies. Because the meaning of an idea can vary, because its value is not fixed but depends upon the context of its occurrence, the

Berkeleian idea stands in need of interpretation while the Lockean idea, with its constant value determined by its object, does not.

We have seen that the rules of interpretation are context-sensitive; in the example from *NTV*.72 the perception of faintness is a sign for magnitude only in the appropriate circumstances. Thus the meaning of the idea which corresponds to a word in a sentence is a function of the contextual ideas—*i.e.*, the ideas corresponding to the other words of the utterance. Consequently (abbreviating somewhat) the meaning of a word in an utterance is determined by the words with which it occurs. Berkeley draws this conclusion from the same example of faintness in the *New Theory of Vision*:

> Faintness, as well as all other ideas or perceptions which suggest magnitude or distance, doth it in the same way that words suggest the notions to which they are annexed. Now, it is known a word pronounced with certain circumstances, or in a certain context with other words, hath not always the same import and signification that it hath when pronounced in some other circumstances or different context of words.
> (*NTV*.73)

The discovery of the meaning of a word is achieved by the same process of interpretation (suggestion or inference) as is used to determine the meaning of an idea. It is, in fact, a special case of that process, for words *are* ideas. Therefore, just as the meaning of an idea depends upon its contextual ideas so the meaning of a word depends upon the contextual utterance.

In abandoning material reality as the foundation for semantic theory, Berkeley appears to have involved himself in hermeneutic circularity. For Locke the meaning of the word is an idea, and if it makes sense to ask what the idea means, the idea plainly means the thing of which it is an idea. But for Berkeley, although words still signify ideas, ideas are of uncertain meaning until they have been interpreted in the light of *other ideas,* and in the same way the meaning of a word depends upon the *other words* of the utterance. It does not appear possible in Berkeley's system to give a non-circular answer to the question of meaning. Besides ideas (which include words), there are only spirits and notions. But there can be no ideas of spirits, and the status of notions is altogether uncertain. The only road left open to Berkeley is the one he takes: the meanings of ideas (including words) are determined by other ideas (including words).

The true basis of Berkeley's theory of meaning lies in the order, regularity, or structure in the sequences of ideas given in experience—*i.e.*, in the divine language of nature. The idea receives the interpretation it does when it occurs in a given context because our experience tells us that the idea in that context normally precedes certain other ideas. If it is then objected that the further ideas suggested by the first idea in its given context are themselves in need of interpretation, and that—the quest for meaning being endless—the semantic theory is inadequate, Berkeley might offer a pragmatic defence. Our ideas, he might say, occur in temporal sequences, and knowledge consists in being able to anticipate impending ideas on the basis of given sequences. The purpose of interpretation is satisfied when this prediction or anticipation is achieved; when, for example, in a visual idea in an appropriate context I predict magnitude on the basis of faintness, I do not *need* to go on to query the idea of magnitude, because in this situation magnitude is what is signified and does not itself yet function as a sign for anything else. The general success of my predictions in securing my survival (and allowing for a percentage of errors) is the practical justification for the semantic theory. The foundation of Berkeleian grammar is therefore the *patterning* of given ideational sequences—the structure of the divine language.

The meanings of ideas in Berkeleian theory are fixed by their places in ideational patterns, but in the special case of words—of language in the strict sense—meaning is still to be discovered by analysis of underlying mental processes. Berkeley's grammar, like Locke's, is of the generative type, distinguishing between surface (verbal) and deep (ideational) structures. Because Berkeley gives the subject virtually no direct attention it is not possible to outline with confidence the machinery which generates linguistic statements from the mental sequences of the base. Certain central features of the generative process may nonetheless be discovered from Berkeley's handling of related issues. We can be reasonably sure of how names for things, spirits, and general ideas respectively relate to sequences of ideas, and we can make a guess at how the structure of simple statements is generated from these basic sequences. It should be observed, however, that from this point we are reconstructing a grammar on Berkeleian principles and not summarizing a grammatical theory to which Berkeley is expressly committed.

In Berkeley's universe there are only a few kinds of entity for which words might stand. They include the objects of human knowledge (from Figure 8), and among them are "signs" (general, but not abstract, ideas). The list is therefore:

1. *Ideas* (including words),[10] which are either:
   a. ideas of particular things as such, or
   b. general ideas ("signs")
2. *Notions* (or "spirits"; we have notions *of* spirits, and words signify the spirits by way of the notions in much the same way, it seems, as Locke's words signify things by way of ideas in Figure 2), which are either:
   a. primary notions (intuitions of the self), or
   b. secondary notions (notions of other spirits— including the divine spirit)

There must therefore be four kinds of expressions in Berkeleian grammar, classified according to what it is they signify. The list must be exhaustive (although further subdivision within it might still be possible) because there is nothing else in Berkeley's world to be signified. (In the Lockean classification of Figure 5 there were also words signifying mental operations, but for Berkeley these must fall under *Notions* in the list because all action is spiritual; words designating action or causality are names for notions.) Each classification is examined below to show how, on the basis of what Berkeley says about ideas and notions, words of each type relate to the underlying sequences of ideas. Specification of the relations between words and underlying ideational sequences, combined with the principle of contextual meaning (the system of the divine language) discussed above, will complete the outline of a Berkeleian theory of language.

1a. Names for particular things present the simplest case. Particular things, in Berkeley's philosophy, are nothing other than collections of ideas:

> And as several of these [ideas] are observed to accompany each other, they come to be marked by one name, and so to be reputed as one thing. Thus, for example, a certain colour, taste, smell, figure and consistence having been observed to go together, are accounted one distinct thing, signified by the name *apple*. Other collections of ideas constitute a stone, a tree, a book, and the like sensible things; which, as they are pleasing or disagreeable, excite the passions of love, hatred, joy, grief, and so forth. (*P*.1)

A name for any particular thing therefore signifies immediately a collection or subsequence of ideas within a sequence. All such words are grammatically proper names; general names fall into the next category.

1b. Berkeley's handling of general names, we have seen, leaves much to be desired. All that need be done here is to offer a summary of his position without any attempt to resolve its difficulties. What Berkeley intended is reasonably clear: use of a general name is properly accompanied by some particular idea which in turn represents the class of ideas of which it is a member and which by means of that idea the word denotes.

> Thus when I demonstrate any proposition concerning triangles, it is to be supposed that I have in view the universal idea of a triangle; which ought not to be understood as if I could frame an idea of a triangle which was neither equilateral nor scalenon nor equicrural. But only that the particular triangle I consider, whether of this or that sort it matters not, doth equally stand for and represent all rectilinear triangles whatsoever, and is in that sense *universal*. All which seems very plain and not to include any difficulty in it. (*Intro*.15)

Berkeley evidently assumes a powerful generalizing faculty in the mind, the operation of which remains mysterious but which must account for our ability to understand a particular idea as representative of a class of ideas. The general name therefore signifies *immediately* some particular idea or collection of ideas, but it *also* signifies, by way of the operation of this generalizing faculty, a whole class of ideas any member of which presumably *might* be called to mind (*P*.11).

2a. Words such as *I*, *myself*, and *me* refer to the spirit of the speaker, of which he has notions by way of intuition. It seems simplest to say that the words signify the notions.

2b. Words referring to other spirits or to actions or causality of any kind (except acts of the self, which fall under the previous category) also signify notions but do so in a more complex way. Notions of other spirits are, as we have seen, projections of a notion of spirit onto a sequence of ideas which, because it is neither imagined nor normal (*i.e.*, generated by God) must be generated by some other finite spirit. Corresponding to words such as *you*, *William the Conqueror*, *God*, *lifting*, *cause*, and *effect* are ideational sequences of a certain kind onto which notions are projected. Names for these secondary notions may be either particular (*William the Conqueror*, *God*) or general (*lifting*, *cause*); where the word is general the ideas of the underlying sequence would also be "signs" in the sense of 1b.

The ways in which words relate to underlying mental structures in Berkeleian theory suggest at once that the grammar will be more complicated than the Lockean grammar, which requires little more than substitution of words for mental acts and ideas in mental propositions. The suggestion is confirmed when we turn to syntactic issues. The syntax of the statement (the linguistic function with which Berkeley, like Locke, is almost exclusively concerned) is traditionally discussed in terms of predication. Locke believes in the existence of an underlying structure corresponding closely to predication because in his view the operation of comparison, when it leads to certain knowledge, is not unlike the linguistic act of predication. In Berkeleian theory, however, there is no mental operation corresponding to predication and therefore no propositional structures in the base. The base consists only of ideational sequences and their accompanying notions and generalizations. To move from such a base to the syntactic structure of the statement therefore requires a relatively complex set of procedures.

Predication is not an exclusively linguistic operation for Locke because he accepts the Aristotelian categorical distinction between substance and qualities: substance is that of which qualities may be predicated, because in reality qualities inhere in substances. The syntax of the proposition, the SUBJECT + PREDICATE structure, corresponds to the structure of the world and is reflected in the Lockean classification of ideas. But for Berkeley there is no substance other than spiritual substance and no qualities other than ideas—and it is not the case that ideas inhere in spirits in anything like the way in which qualities are traditionally said to inhere in material substance. Ideas are all of the same kind and it makes no sense to Berkeley to talk of *predicating* one idea of another. The impossibility of seeing ideas as predicates is discussed at one point in the *Principles*:

> Fifthly, it may perhaps be objected, that if extension and figure exist only in the mind, it follows that the mind is extended and figured; since extension is a mode or attribute, which (to speak with the Schools) is predicated of the subject in which it exists. I answer, those qualities are in the mind only as they are perceived by it, that is, not by way of *mode* or *attribute*, but only by way of *idea*; and it no more follows that the soul or mind is extended because extension exists in it alone, than it does that it is red or blue, because those colours are on all hands acknowledged to exist in it, and no where else. As to what philosophers say of subject and mode, that seems very groundless and unintelligible. For instance, in this proposition, a die is hard, extended and square, they will have it that the word *die* denotes a subject or substance, distinct from the hardness, extension and figure, which are predicated of it, and in which they exist. This I cannot comprehend: to me a die seems to be nothing distinct from those things which are termed its modes or accidents. And to say a die is hard, extended and square, is not to attribute those qualities to a subject distinct from and supporting them, but only an explication of the meaning of the word *die*. (P.49)

The two last sentences of this passage give a clue as to Berkeley's view of what it is in the mind that underlies a linguistic act of predication. In a sentence of the form "The S is P," "S" is a name referring to ideas in the mind and "is P" indicates that there are one or more ideas within the collection referred to by "S" which belong to the class of ideas signified by the idea corresponding to "P." The "is" of predication becomes an indicator of what we might call class inclusion; the subject idea is said to be one of the ideas signified by any general idea corresponding to the predicate term. In Berkeley's view the predicate term simply tells part of the meaning of the subject term; the sentence says that among the ideas signified by "S" is an idea belonging to the class denoted by "P." By extending the predicate to list all the ideas in the collection of ideas signified by "S" we could give a complete description of S—i.e., a complete definition of "S."

This analysis of sentences of the form "The S is P" (where "S" names a particular thing and "P" is a general term) is supported by the analysis of the proposition "Melampus is an animal" given by Berkeley in the rejected draft of the Introduction to the *Principles*:

> Suppose I have the idea of some one particular dog to which I give the name Melampus and then frame this proposition Melampus is an animal, where 'tis evident the name Melampus denotes one particular idea. And as for the other name or [term] of the proposition there are a sort of philosophers will tell you thereby is meant not only a universal conception but also corresponding thereto a universal nature or essence really existing without the mind whereof Melampus doth partake. . . . But if a man may be allow'd to know his own meaning I do declare that in my thoughts the word animal is neither supposed to stand for an universal nature nor yet for an abstract idea which to me is at least as absurd and incomprehensible as the other. Nor does it indeed in that proposition stand for any idea at all. All that I intend to signify thereby being only this, that the particular thing I call Melampus has a right to be called by the name animal. And I do intreat any one to make this easy tryal. Let him but cast out of his thoughts the words of the proposition and then see whether two clear and determinate ideas remain in his understanding whereof he finds one to be conformable to the other. I perceive it evidently in my self that upon laying aside all thought of the words 'Melampus is an animal' I have remaining in my mind one only naked and bare idea viz that particular one to which I gave the name Melampus.
> (*WGB*.II.136)

This passage reaches the same conclusion as the passage from the *Principles*: that only one collection of ideas is involved in the sentence, the collection named in this case by "Melampus." The general predicate term is again said to do no more than tell something further about Melampus, to explain the meaning of the subject term by specifying some of the ideas among those it names. The rejected passage goes beyond the published statements on the working of general terms by claiming misleadingly that *no* idea corresponds to "animal." The published versions, as we have seen, are more complex and more intelligible. According to them "animal" corresponds to some particular idea in the mind which itself signifies a class of ideas (the class normally said to be denoted by the word) some particular member of which class is among the ideas signified by "Melampus."

If our statement involves spirits or actions the analysis is somewhat more complex. If I say "Peter is running," I cannot be saying simply that the ideas signified by "Peter" include a member of the class of ideas denoted by "running," because "running," in so far as it refers to an action, has no properly corresponding *ideas*. "Peter" signifies a collection of ideas which is such as to attract projection of a notion; in short, it signifies what we have called a "secondary" notion. What causes the ideas signified by "Peter" to receive the notion is the fact that their sequential order is not that of inanimate nature (*i.e.*, such as would be attributed to the action of God), nor is it controlled by the spirit of the perceiver. In ordinary language we would describe this situation by saying that Peter is active; he is doing something which, experience and intuition tell us, is the result of his own volition. Exactly what Peter is doing is, in this case, running. The word "running" also signifies a secondary notion. The ideas onto which this notion is projected are the same ideas onto which the notion signified by "Peter" is projected, but the predicate term, as in the two previous examples, makes the subject term more precise—by saying, in this case, just what *kind* of action in the sequence of ideas gives rise to the notion of Peter. Again there is one sequence of ideas underlying the statement and again the predicate in some sense serves to explain the meaning of the subject term. "Running," however, does not *define* "Peter" in the same way as "animal" defines "Melampus." "Running" rather specifies one of the actions which enable us to see the sequence of ideas named by "Peter" as involving a notion of spirit.

The case is slightly altered when an action is predicated of an inanimate subject. When I say "the tree is falling" I cannot, as in the previous example, be saying that "falling" signifies the same notion as "tree," because "tree" does not signify a notion at all but a collection of ideas. What I must be saying is that the sequence of ideas which I name "tree" is also such as to attract a secondary notion (of the activity of falling), but with the proviso that the source of the activity is elsewhere. Trees are not properly capable of activity; in this case I am therefore reporting either an imaginary sequence of ideas or an act of some spirit not specified in the statement. The sentence strictly states that a spirit is acting but does not say which spirit. "Tree" is not the logical subject of "the tree is falling" in the same way as "Peter" is the logical subject of "Peter is running."

We could go on for some time discussing different kinds of statement. If we accept the classifications offered above we have effectually five different kinds of words—those signifying respectively (i) particular things, (ii) general ideas, (iii) primary notions, (iv) particular secondary notions, and (v) general secondary notions. Any of these categories might occur in either subject or predicate positions, which in theory would give us twenty-five kinds of "S is P" structures (although a number of these kinds might be anomalous in English). The analysis of each of these, in the manner of the examples just discussed, would differ from that of the others. But no point would be served by examining each of the twenty-five possible propositional structures. The general means of reducing them to underlying ideational sequences is contained in the above discussion of word types and the several examples.

Enough has now been said about the relation between deep and surface structures in Berkeleian grammar to show that Berkeley's philosophy has led him into a highly original position in linguistic theory. His denial of material substance and his theory of ideas entail the view that nothing in reality corresponds to the subject-predicate structure of the proposition. Since classical times grammatical theory had been derived more or less closely from the categories of Aristotle. Words were classified according to the kind of thing they represented, with nouns standing for substances, adjectives for qualities, verbs for actions, adverbs for modes of action, and so on, with numerous subdivisions and refinements. Berkeley's total revision of the universe abolishes the Aristotelian categories altogether and yields a new classification of words. Traditional syntax, and in particular the operation of predication, no longer has any justification in the structure of reality. The copula itself, the "is" of predication, becomes in Berkeleian analysis something akin to the "is" of identity or of class inclusion. Had Berkeley himself troubled to reconstruct systematically a theory of language on the basis of his revised view of reality he would unquestionably have produced the first significantly non-Aristotelian grammar in the Western world.

The kind of analysis employed in the above examples explores the relation between surface grammatical structures and their underlying mental structures. It reveals most notably that the subject-predicate form exhibited in surface structures such as "the S is P" has no direct correlate in the base, where there are only ideational sequences, notions, and generalizations. A Berkeleian theory of syntax would therefore require complex rules for generating such structures—rules which would very probably now be called "transformational." To complete the theory of language the account of syntax here suggested would be associated with the semantic theory outlined above. We may discuss syntax in the abstract in terms of the various relations between different types of sentence and their underlying mental structures, but in any given case we are dealing with sequences of particular ideas (at both base and surface levels—for words are also ideas), which ideas are subject to semantic *interpretation*. Interpretation, as we have seen, rests upon the fact of ideational patterning in experience (the divine language) and the mind's ability to derive and employ the rules governing these regularities. The generation of syntactic structures and the semantic interpretation of words and ideas would evidently be closely interwoven processes in a Berkeleian grammar.

Berkeley did not himself construct a complete theory of language. Most of his explicit linguistic doctrine is negative in form, demolishing the presuppositions and foundations of established theories, but he does give clear hints as to the kind of theory we would have if we were to try to explain language in the terms of his philosophy. Historically his work on language has suffered general neglect—originally because of its association with the doctrine of immaterialism, which many people regarded as a philosophical joke or eccentricity, and more recently because fundamental difficulties, such as that over generalization, have been exposed in Berkeley's reasoning. Some of his ideas, however, such as his contextual theory of meaning and his concept of "suggestion," reappear in the writings of his professed antagonists, the Scottish philosophers Reid and Stewart.

Berkeley's achievement should not be measured in terms of historical influence. In conclusion we should observe instead that in his work, almost two centuries before Saussure, we encounter a recognizably structural approach to meaning—a theory in which words signify ideas and the meaning of an idea is determined by its place in an ordered structure or "language" of ideas.[11] Nothing else of this kind exists in the philosophy of language of the eighteenth century. Similarly unique is Berkeley's potential revision of syntactic theory on this same structural basis, which justifies the claim that Berkeleian grammar, had it been brought into existence in Berkeley's own day, could have effected as much of a conceptual enlargement in linguistic theory as did the discovery in the early nineteenth century of grammars outside the Western, Aristotelian tradition.

4. Smith and Monboddo: The Search for Origins

INTRODUCTION

Much of the most important thinking of the mid and late eighteenth century in the fields of ethics, law, anthropology, politics, sociology, and linguistics was directed towards the discovery or speculative reconstruction of origins and principles of growth. The many essays of the period concerned in one way or another with the origins of language are only one stream of this powerful intellectual current—which must have its own origins in some radical reappraisal of man's place in the temporal scheme of things, effected perhaps in the latter half of the seventeenth century. Easily the two most brilliant British studies of this type, both by Scots as it happens, are Adam Smith's *Considerations on the First Formation of Languages* (1761) and Lord Monboddo's *Of the Origin and Progress of Language* (1773–92).

The eighteenth-century search for origins may be attributed largely (but not exclusively) to the philosophy of Locke. Besides specific cases, such as that of government,[1] where Locke attempts to explain the principles of an institution by tracing it to its supposed beginnings, his philosophy contains the general precept that to analyze is to discover the genesis of a concept in so far as all ideas can, and for philosophical purposes should, be traced to their sources in ideas of experience (*i.e.*, of sense and reflection). Much use was made of this method in the century following Locke for the analysis of political and social institutions as well as in the philosophy of language. The notion that we can infer the structural principles of an institution from the principles governing its origin and formation, and conversely that given the structural principles we can infer the genetic, passed virtually unchallenged until Stewart questioned it a hundred years later.

The possibility of this inference between analysis and genesis is one premise of the philosophical search for origins in the eighteenth century. Another is the doctrine which Lovejoy calls "uniformitarianism," the belief that the principles of human nature are everywhere and always the same. This second premise makes the search for origins a worthwhile undertaking for philosophers. Because of the uniformity of human nature the essential principles revealed behind any particular human institution will be universal principles.

The purpose of the search for origins was the discovery not of historical facts, nor even of historical probabilities, but of principles of human nature. The adoption of this method has two corollaries worth particular mention. First, the method rejects as irrelevant the orthodox, biblical view that all things earthly, including man, originated mysteriously in the divine act of creation. According to this view there is no need to speculate on origins because we already know of the single source of all phenomena, and because this knowledge can reveal nothing of human nature—although it might reveal the divine. Second, it is a method based not only on known historical facts but also liberal speculation. It was generally admitted that we cannot obtain certain knowledge of the origins of such institutions as language and social organization because these things necessarily precede recorded history. In the absence of certainty, however, we can build speculative reconstructions based on what facts we have. In eighteenth-century Europe the primary sources of these facts were historical records and reports of primitive peoples sent back by travellers. (Under the principle of uniformitarianism a primitive people would be a proper source for knowledge of the pre-history of any civilized people.) By the standards of twentieth-century historians and anthropologists these sources are inadequate, but such standards are irrelevant to the eighteenth-century undertaking. "Speculative history," as Stewart calls the search for origins, sets itself to reconstruct the origin and formation of institutions in a manner consistent with the given facts and with what is known of human nature.

The first significant application of this method to the philosophy of language is Condillac's *Essai sur l'origine des connaissances humaines*[2] of 1746, a work very much in the Lockean tradition. As the title suggests, the *Essai* has the Lockean object of tracing human understanding to its sources in order to outline its structural principles. Like Locke, Condillac finds that the study of language provides an important key to the philosophy of mind, and accordingly a third of the *Essai* is spent in discussion of the origin and formation of language. Condillac's genetic argument intends to show that the faculty of reason in man depends for its manifestation and growth upon the use of signs. Because reason and language develop reciprocally, the study of linguistic origins is integral to Condillac's primary undertaking, the study of man's intellectual origins.

Language is an instrument of rational development because of what was known as the "linearity of speech," the fact that language consists in structured sequences of articulated elements. In Condillac's account, the fact that language is structured enables it to become an instrument of rational advancement as well as a means to the philosophical analysis of the thought processes it expresses.

Condillac's application of the philosophical search for origins to language and his attention to linguistic structures in both genetic and analytic studies of mind are taken over by many important writers on language in the later eighteenth century, including Smith and Monboddo. Smith does not mention Condillac in the *Considerations* but he does refer to Rousseau's *Discours sur l'origine et des fondemens de l'inégalité parmi les hommes* (1755), in which Condillac's theories receive prominent mention. Monboddo read Smith and Rousseau and he knew Condillac's *Essai* at second hand by way of an English review.

ADAM SMITH

Adam Smith's *Considerations concerning the First Formation of Languages* appeared in the *Philological Miscellany* (1761), I, 440–479, and was reprinted in 1767 as an appendix to the third edition of his *Theory of Moral Sentiments*. The subject had evidently occupied him for many years. Stewart dates Smith's interest in languages from his time in Oxford (1740–47),[3] and it is probable that he lectured on the theory of language in Edinburgh during the years 1748–51. Student notes of Smith's lectures in 1762–63 as professor of moral philosophy at Glasgow, including a lecture on the origin of language, have recently been discovered.[4] The published essay, which is the only one of his lectures Smith saw fit to revise and print,[5] is evidently the outcome of some twenty years' work, and it is accordingly, for an eighteenth-century essay on language, unusually well-defined in its areas of investigation and concise in its exposition. It covers only forty-five pages in Dugald Stewart's edition of Smith's works.[6]

Both the originality and the influence of the *Considerations* are hard to determine. Smith mentions no important linguistic studies other than Rousseau's *Discours sur l'origine de l'inégalité parmi les hommes* (1755), but he is clearly indebted at several points to Condillac's *Essai* of 1746, to the philosophical grammarians, and to the general climate of thought fostered above all by Locke. It has recently been suggested, in addition, that Smith's theory of linguistic typology owes something to Gabriel Girard's *Les Vrais principes de la langue françoise* (1747).[7]

The *Considerations* was highly regarded by Monboddo, who avows his indebtedness to Smith at several points, but outside Scotland few writers on language refer to it. Smith's ideas, however, soon became widely accepted both in Britain and in France and Germany. It is impossible to say, in the absence of many cases of explicit acknowledgment, how far these ideas were directly influenced by the *Considerations* and how far they were developed independently as the issues raised by Condillac were increasingly debated. But there is no doubt that Smith's essay had considerable effect and that it ranks among the essential texts in eighteenth-century philosophy of language. The matter of its influence is best summarized by Stewart's observation of 1814: "From the unpretending simplicity with which [the *Considerations*] is written, it is so little calculated to draw the attention of common readers, that I recollect few instances of its being quoted by later writers; but it has had a visible effect on the speculations of many of them, particularly of those foreigners who have treated of the origin of the Romanic tongues spoken in modern Europe. Some, indeed, of the remarks contained in it, which, as far as I know, were Mr. Smith's original property, are now become so common, that I have heard them criticised as not altogether worthy, from their triteness, of the author of the *Wealth of Nations*."[8]

The title of the essay is misleading as to its subject. Smith is not interested in the question which exercised Condillac and Monboddo: how man, supposing him to be originally without language, might have acquired it naturally (*i.e.*, without divine or other external assistance). That language could have been so acquired Smith takes for granted in his first pages, and then turns at once to the problems that interest him: the genetic order in which various syntactic features of language might have appeared, and the explanatory principles underlying that order. Apart from the short final section in which aesthetic issues are discussed the essay is devoted to this problem of order.

Smith's theoretical discussion is limited in two ways which condition his conclusions. First, he accepts without question the categories of traditional grammar, in particular the "parts of speech," and it is the evolution of these traditional categories that he considers. Second, his linguistic data are drawn from the languages known to him, the languages of Western literary tradition: Greek, Latin, French, Italian, and English. He mentions other languages, such as Hebrew and Armenian, but in no specific detail. His theory is therefore supported by at least some Indo-European languages, but had he considered to the same extent languages from other groups his conclusions might well have been different.[9] In neither of these limitations is Smith unusual among his contemporaries, although within ten years of the appearance of the *Considerations* Monboddo was to publish a study drawing data from American Indian languages and Sir William Jones was to begin his lectures on the languages of Asia.

A brief summary of the argument as Smith presents it will be useful.[10] The essay may be divided into four sections.

i. The formation of common nouns, adjectives, and prepositions (3–26). At first man would use words to name particulars, but eventually, observing similarities between objects already named and others, he would apply the name already in use to the similar objects, turning the original proper name into a common noun. The operation responsible for this move from "denotation" of particulars to the naming of classes or species is "generalization." A further operation, which Smith inadequately calls "comparison," is responsible for the devices which enable language to distinguish an individual within a given class. In modern languages these devices take the form of adjectives and prepositions, but because the development of these separate parts of speech would require "abstraction" as well as generalization and comparison, Smith believes there must be an intermediate stage based on generalization and comparison alone. In this stage the adjectival and prepositional function of signifying the individual within the class is performed by inflection. Only as the human faculty for abstraction develops does language turn from inflection to the use of adjectives and prepositions.

ii. The formation of verbs, verbal auxiliaries, and pronouns (26–39). At first men would use single words to refer to events. These words would be, in effect, "impersonal verbs." Eventually language would evolve devices for distinguishing different personal agents, different times, different moods, of the verb. In modern languages these devices take the form of pronouns and verbal auxiliaries, but because the evolution of these parts of speech requires a high degree of abstraction Smith again supposes that there must be an intermediate stage in which the same end is achieved without separate parts of speech—in this case by systematic variation of the verbal stem. The change from the earlier to the later form comes about when a large number of non-native speakers are put in the position of having to learn the language. Because the highly complex systems of conjugations are difficult to learn, the new speakers would simplify them by using separate words to designate the person, and perhaps the tense and mood also, of the verb.

iii. The "maxim" (39–44). On the basis of the foregoing discussion of the development of linguistic structures Smith offers this summation:

> In general it may be laid down for a maxim, that the more simple any language is in its compostion, the more complex it must be in its declensions and conjugations; and on the

contrary, the more simple it is in its declensions and conjugations, the more complex it must be in its composition. (39)

(By the "composition" of a language Smith means the different parts of speech which it necessarily employs; "simplicity" of composition or of declensions and conjugations consists in paucity of categories and variants.) In each of the first two sections Smith has distinguished between those languages which express distinctions by proliferating parts of speech and those which express the same distinctions by systematically inflecting the word stems. Later these types were designated analytic and synthetic respectively. Smith does not use these terms, although he does speak of "analysis" in connection with the analytic type. Having isolated these two structural possibilities in languages past a certain point in their development, Smith now, in the maxim, presents a relation of inverse proportion between them: the more analytic a language is the less synthetic it must be, and *vice versa*. The maxim is a summary expression in structural terms of the historical claim advanced in sections *i* and *ii* that analytic types are later than, and developments from, synthetic types. Smith illustrates the maxim with a brief discussion of languages from classical Greek through Latin to modern French, Italian, and English.

iv. The aesthetic conclusion (44–48). Smith first approached the theory of language from an aesthetic and philological point of view; the Edinburgh and Glasgow lectures in the context of which he first discussed the subject were given under the general title "Rhetoric and Belles-Lettres." The final section of the published essay, which passes an aesthetic judgment on the linguistic types distinguished in the earlier sections, reflects the context in which Smith first addressed the theory of language.[11] Smith gives three reasons for preferring the synthetic mode of expression to the analytic: analytic languages are "more prolix," "less agreeable to the ear," and more restrictive of word order. This amounts to an expression of preference for the classical languages over the modern, which is not surprising in the mid eighteenth century. Monboddo expounds the same position at great length, but in Smith's case as well as in Monboddo's the aesthetic preference is supported by a philosophical conviction that synthetic forms are (for reasons we will discuss) *more natural* than are analytic.

The fourth section is an appendix largely unrelated to the first three, which are closely interconnected. The third section summarizes the structural point to emerge from the first two, which outline parallel formative processes in the nominal and verbal systems of language. The parallelism of sections *i* and *ii* is emphasized in the text. In both cases the same principles apply and the same stages are developed in the same order. In particular, the difficulty of abstraction in both cases inhibits the development of analytic structures and causes an initial proliferation of declensions and conjugations respectively.

> If the declensions of the ancient languages are so very complex, their conjugations are infinitely more so. And the complexness of the one is founded upon the same principle with that of the other, the difficulty of forming, in the beginnings of language, abstract and general terms. (26–27)

> As in the beginnings of language, therefore, mankind seem to have evaded the invention of at least the more abstract prepositions, and to have expressed the same relations which these *now* stand for, by varying the termination of the co-relative term, so they would likewise naturally attempt to evade the necessity of inventing those more abstract pronouns by varying the termination of the verb, according as the event which it expressed was intended to be affirmed of the first, second, or third person. (34–35)

A difficulty in the *Considerations* is that Smith does not pursue this parallelism between sections *i* and *ii* at all points; contrary to expectation, and with no clear purpose, he offers different explanations of the transition from synthetic to analytic structures in the two cases. Separate adjectives and prepositions come to replace the inflections of the noun stem as man develops the necessary capacity for abstraction, but separate pronouns and auxiliary verbs are said to replace inflection of the verb stem when a sufficiently large number of people have to learn a second language. Smith is interestingly aware of the difference between first and second language learning, which provides his explanation of the development of the analytic verb.

> As long as any language was spoke by those only who learned it in their infancy, the intricacy of its declensions could occasion no great embarrassment. The far greater part of those who had occasion to speak it, had acquired it at so very early a period of their lives, so insensibly and by such slow degrees, that they were scarce ever sensible of the difficulty. But when two nations came to be mixed with one another, either by conquest or migration, the case would be very different. (36)

For example, a Lombard learning Latin would have difficulty memorizing declensions, and would ease the burden by using prepositions "and instead of *Romae*, would say, *ad Roma*, and *de Roma*" (37). Similarly, having difficulty with the conjugations he would employ pronouns and auxiliaries, so that for *I am loved* he would say not *amor* but *ego sum amatus*, and for *I had loved* he would say not *amaveram* but *ego habebam* or *ego habui amatum* (38–39). We have therefore two different explanations for the transition from synthetic to analytic structures, and there is no reason why one of these, and not the other, should apply to either the nominal or the verbal systems.[12] Smith's first historical thesis, evident from section *i*, is that languages develop structurally with the development of the human intellectual capacities. The second historical thesis accounts for the transition from synthetic to analytic structures in terms of the mixing of language groups: "upon the intermixture of different nations with one another, the conjugations, by means of different auxiliary verbs, were made to approach towards the simplicity and uniformity of declensions" (39).

Another difficulty often observed in the *Considerations* is an apparent inconsistency in Smith's discussion of the earliest parts of speech. He begins by saying that "the assignation of particular names to denote particular objects, that is, the institution of nouns substantive, would, probably, be one of the first steps towards the formation of language" (3), but in the second section he suggests that "impersonal verbs" would be "perhaps even the first words, made use of in the beginnings of language" (39). The contradiction resolves itself, however, because the question to which we appear to have conflicting answers is really nonsensical. We cannot ask which was the first part of speech because, obviously, there can be a *part* of speech only where there are other parts. We cannot sensibly expect to have verbs in a language in which there are no nouns, or nouns in a language in which there are no verbs, because the categories are defined in relation to one another. Smith's "impersonal verbs" and primal substantives differ only in what they denote: the first nouns denote "particular objects" (3) whereas impersonal verbs denote "events" or "matters of fact" (27). Objects and events, as we shall see, are the elemental constituents of reality in the *Considerations*, and it is only because there are two such constituents that the earliest language can be said to comprise two types of words. Smith is easily made consistent here by allowing substantives and impersonal verbs to be coeval, but this does not mean that we now have two parts of speech in the primal language. There is no syntactic relation, in the earliest language, between proper names (or even, in the next stage, common names) and impersonal verbs: each stands alone, for the first languages have no syntax.

The fact that Smith supposes language to be originally without syntax is of the first importance to the understanding of his purposes in the *Considerations* and indeed of the purposes of most eighteenth-century studies of the genesis or formation of languages. The same conviction that grammar (*i.e.*, syntax) is at first totally absent from language and is a later product of increasing intellectual sophistication is evident, for instance, in Vico's *Scienza Nuova* (1725), in Condillac's discussion of the origin of language in terms of signs—a discussion echoed, in this respect, by Reid—and later in the first volume of Monboddo's *Origin and Progress of Language*. The point is put concisely, at about the same time, in Herder's Prize Essay, when he observes: "je ursprünglicher die Sprache, desto weniger Grammatik in ihr seyn."[13] Two reasons probably lie behind the position, which now seems rather odd, that there might be, and at one time was, a language without syntax. First, the tendency to define language in terms of signs fostered the view that language is not different in kind from use of the simplest signals, in which no syntax is involved. Second, the traditional view of grammar as fundamentally a set of categories derived roughly from the categories of Aristotle suggested an association between the use or invention of language and the capacity for philosophical analysis; consequently when it was asked in the eighteenth century what kind of language an intellectually primitive man would use, it was inevitably concluded that primitive language would be virtually devoid of categorical distinctions and therefore without grammar.

A final difficulty in the *Considerations* again concerns the parallelism between the first two sections. Smith emphasizes in the first section that the first substantives would have been names for *particular* objects and only later would names for classes or species of objects emerge. In the second section, however, he neglects to say whether the first impersonal verbs would name particular events or classes of similar events. Presumably the same stages of evolution would be passed through by the event name as by the object name.

If we iron out the several difficulties mentioned, the *Considerations* yields a highly coherent theory of the coevolution of linguistic and mental structures. Let us therefore put aside for the moment Smith's second historical thesis, let us assume that the earliest languages consist of both proper names and impersonal verbs, and let us suppose that Smith does intend the earliest impersonal verbs to name *particular* events. The *Considerations* now yields the outline of the development of linguistic structure represented in Figure 10.

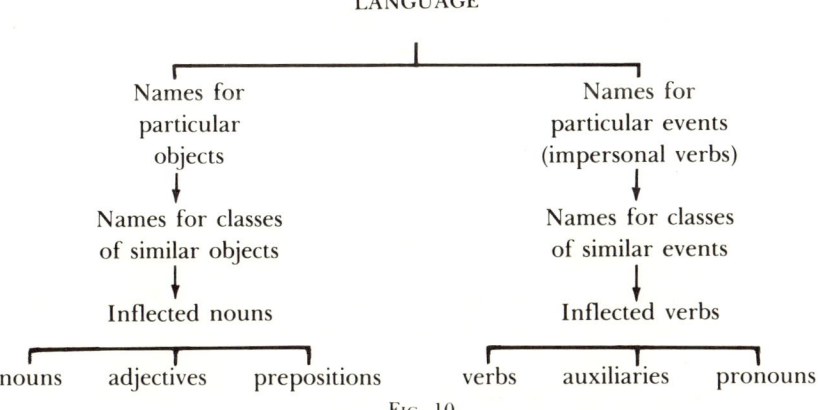

Fig. 10

The history of linguistic structure shown here, however, is only superficially the concern of the *Considerations*. The real concern is with mental principles, which have a genetic order among themselves and which are responsible for this order of language types.

Language begins with denotation, in which Smith sees no difficulty. "Two savages, who had never been taught to speak, but had been bred up remote from the societies of men, would naturally begin to form that language by which they would endeavour to make their mutual wants intelligible to each other, by uttering certain sounds, whenever they meant to denote certain objects" (3). What will be denoted is another matter, determined by the natural environment which, it turns out, consists basically of objects and events. The first words will therefore denote objects and events.

Because objects and events in nature are particulars, it might seem difficult to explain how language ever progresses from the denotation of particulars to the use of general names. Rousseau, who follows Condillac in adopting the nominalist position, raises the problem—to which Smith replies with a very broad assertion of realism, avoiding volumes of philosophical discussion. "What constitutes a species," he says, "is merely a number of objects, bearing a certain degree of resemblance to one another, and on that account denominated by a single appellation, which may be applied to express any one of them" (7). If nature consists of objects, events, and "similarities," then there is no reason why, having denoted the objects and events, man should not go on to denote the similarities. This he would do, Smith holds, by extending a proper name already in use to denote phenomena similar to that which the name originally designated.

> Afterwards, when the more enlarged experience of these savages had led them to observe, and their necessary occasions obliged them to make mention of [for example] other caves, and other trees, and other fountains, they would naturally bestow, upon each of these new objects, the same name, by which they had been accustomed to express the similar object they were first acquainted with. The new objects had none of them any name of its own, but each of them exactly resembled another object, which had such an appellation. It was impos-

sible that those savages could behold the new objects, without recollecting the old ones; and the name of the old ones, to which the new bore so close a resemblance. (4)

The linguistic device of extending a proper name to other objects in some respects resembling the original object of the name is called "antonomasia" (6), but underlying this device is the mental principle of generalization that enables us to apprehend similarities in nature. The act of generalization, however, demands little or no intellectual acuity because the similarities are *given* in nature.

Man's next step, having progressed from naming individuals to naming classes, would be to devise verbal means of distinguishing individuals within classes, so as to avoid the necessity of a proper name for every individual object and event. In analytic languages this function is performed by adjectives and prepositions used to specify the reference of a common noun, and by noun subjects, pronouns, and auxiliaries used to specify the agent and tense of a verb. How might this step be taken?

> Let us suppose, for example, that the word *venit*, *it comes*, was originally an impersonal verb, and that it denoted, not the coming of something in general, as at present, but the coming of a particular object, such as *the Lion*. The first savage inventors of language, we shall suppose, when they observed the approach of this terrible animal, were accustomed to cry out to one another, *venit*, that is, *the lion comes*; and that this word thus expressed a complete event, without the assistance of any other. Afterwards, when, on the further progress of language, they had begun to give names to particular substances, whenever they observed the approach of any other terrible object, they would naturally join the name of that object to the word *venit*, and cry out, *venit ursus*, *venit lupus*. By degrees the word *venit* would thus come to signify the coming of any terrible object, and not merely the coming of the lion. (29)

The impersonal verb *venit* denotes any event involving the approach of a lion, but the device of verbally indicating the subject of the verb gives us a way of distinguishing between similar events (*e.g.*, events involving the approach of any kind of dangerous animal) without giving each event a different name. As a result the word *venit*, now become a personal verb, is free to take on a much more general reference. The evolution of auxiliaries to indicate the time and mood of the event can be explained in the same way. The parallel case of the development of adjectives and prepositions to specify the reference of the common noun is a little simpler. Given a general name, such as *tree*, which denotes a class of objects, man finds a verbal means of distinguishing individuals within the class by isolating and naming the qualities or relations by which in fact individuals are distinguished. A particular tree may be distinguished from others by a particular quality, which would be expressed as an adjective qualifying the common noun, or by its relation to other objects, which would be expressed by prepositional phrases.

To isolate the mental principles underlying these various linguistic devices we look at the procedure common to all of them, which is best represented in abstract terms. Suppose we have two elements of reality, ABC and ABD, which may be either both objects or both events. In the earliest stage of language each of these would have its own particular name, but in the second stage, by the principle of generalization, they would share a common name by virtue of their similarity with respect to AB. The next stage requires man to observe that these two entities, which belong to a single class (of either objects or events) and share a common name (either a common noun or generalized impersonal verb) nonetheless differ from each other with respect to C and D, and to find a verbal means of indicating this distinction without reverting to the first stage by simply giving different names to ABC and ABD. The generalization achieved in the second stage must be preserved in the third and combined with a capacity for verbally isolating the particulars. This can be done only by introducing systematic relations into language, which in the first and second stages is merely a collection of unrelated names. Smith directs our attention to the possibility of different kinds of systematic relations in the third stage, distinguishing two kinds in particular, which we now call synthetic and analytic types.

Smith contends that the two ways of meeting these requirements involve different underlying mental principles, and for this reason one type, the synthetic, necessarily precedes the other in the development of language. In order to emphasize this difference Smith discusses the analytic devices first and indicates what he calls the "abstraction" which they involve. He then introduces the alternative synthetic devices as achieving the same ends without the abstraction. As this is the heart of the typological classification of languages in the *Considerations*, we shall follow Smith closely through the several analytic devices he discusses—adjectives, prepositions, and pronouns.

The invention of adjectives involves generalization, comparison, and abstraction.

> An adjective is by nature a general, and in some measure an abstract word, and necessarily presupposes the idea of a certain species or assortment of things, to all of which it is equally applicable. The word *green* could not, as we were supposing might be the case of the word *cave*, have been originally the name of an individual, and afterwards have become, by what grammarians call an Antonomasia, the name of a species. The word *green* denoting, not the name of a substance, must from the very first have been a general word, and considered as equally applicable to any other substance possessed of the same quality. The man who first distinguished a particular object by the epithet of *green*, must have observed other objects that were not *green*, from which he meant to separate it by this appellation. The institution of this name, therefore, supposes comparison. It likewise supposes some degree of abstraction. The person who invented this appellation must have distinguished the quality from the object to which it belonged, and must have conceived the object as capable of subsisting without the quality. (9–10)

Smith first dismisses the notion that adjectives might be accounted for, like common nouns, by generalization of particular names. There can be no adjectival particulars from which general adjectives could develop. The evolution of the adjective must involve a combination of all three principles, generalization (the realization of similarities), comparison (the realization of differences within similarities), and abstraction (the realization of the distinction between substance and quality). It is important to see how comparison, in Smith's view, differs from generalization and is necessarily a subsequent operation. To generalize is to observe similarities to the extent of grouping phenomena in classes and employing general names. Comparison consists in the observation of differences among the members of a single class.

Prepositions are even more difficult of invention.

> Now, I say, the original invention of [prepositions] would require a yet greater effort of abstraction and generalization, than that of nouns adjective. First of all, the relation is, in itself, a more metaphysical object than a quality. . . . Secondly, although prepositions always express the relation which they stand for, in concrete with the co-relative object, they could not have originally been formed without a considerable effort of abstraction. A preposition denotes a relation. But before men could institute a word, which signified a relation, and nothing but a relation, they must have been able, in some measure, to consider this relation abstractedly from the related objects. . . . Thirdly, a preposition is from its nature a general word, which, from its very first institution, must have been considered as equally applicable to denote any other similar relation. The man who first invented the word *above*, must not only have distinguished, in some measure, the relation of *superiority* from the objects which were so related, but he must also have distinguished this relation from other relations, such as, from the relation of *inferiority* denoted by the word *below*, from the relation of *juxta-position*, expressed by the word *beside*, and the like. He must have conceived this word, therefore, as expressive of a particular sort or species of relation distinct from every other, which could not have been done without a considerable effort of comparison and generalization. (15–17)

(The first point in this passage advances a general claim—that prepositions involve "metaphysics"—which is explained in the second and third points.) Like adjectives, prepositions, which Smith thinks of as denoting relations, are essentially general terms; language apparently would not name individual instances of relation. To name particular kinds of relations involves the comparison of different kinds, just as the denotation of particular qualities requires discrimination among qualities. And the designation of relations by prepositions demands abstraction because, just as in nature the quality never occurs apart from substance, so relations never present themselves but in connection with objects related.

The same three principles are required for the transition from impersonal verbs to the use of personal verbs with noun or pronoun subjects. In the passage quoted above concerning the verb *venit*, it is clear that the transition from the impersonal *venit* meaning *the lion comes* to the use of *venit* as a personal verb in sentences such as *venit ursus* and *venit leo* requires both generalization (the initial use of the impersonal verb to refer to a class of events and not one particular event) and comparison (the distinction of different agents or different actions in events which are in some more general way similar). The transition to SUBJECT + VERB structures also requires abstraction because, in Smith's view, the event is a natural unit in which agent and action are always combined, much as quality and substance are always combined in objects.

> Impersonal verbs, which express in one word a complete event, which preserve in the expression that perfect simplicity and unity, which there always is in the object and in the idea, and which suppose no abstraction, or metaphysical division of the event into its several constituent members of subject and attribute, would, in all probability, be the first species of verbs invented. The verbs *pluit, it rains*; *ningit, it snows*; *tonat, it thunders*; *lucet, it is day*; *turbatur, there is a confusion*; &c. each of them express a complete affirmation, the whole of an event, with that perfect simplicity and unity with which the mind conceives it in nature. On the contrary, the phrases *Alexander ambulat, Alexander walks*; *Petrus sedet, Peter sits*; divide the event, as it were, into two parts, the person or subject, and the attribute, or matter of fact, affirmed of the subject. But in nature, the idea or conception of Alexander walking, is as perfectly and completely one simple conception, as that of Alexander not walking. (27–28)

In each of these three cases Smith argues that the analytic feature is too "metaphysical" to develop immediately from the second stage of language. There must therefore be a less metaphysical stage between the use of general names for objects and events and the evolution of analytic structures. The language of this stage must fulfill substantially the same function as analytic language: the specification of individuals within the classes or species denoted in the second stage. Since Smith believes abstraction to be the principle largely responsible for the "metaphysics" in analytic structures, the difference between analytic structures and the intermediate stage of language we are seeking will be accounted for by the presence or absence of abstraction. The intermediate stage is that of the synthetic type of language, which achieves the same ends as the analytic type without evolving new parts of speech and without the use of abstraction. The linguistic device employed in this stage is *inflection*.

In the case of adjectives Smith argues that there is "another expedient for denoting the different qualities of different substances, which as it requires no abstraction, nor any conceived separation of the quality from the subject, seems more natural than the invention of nouns adjective, and which, upon this account, could hardly fail, to be thought of before them. This expedient is to make some variation upon the noun substantive itself, according to the different qualities it is endowed with" (10–11). He instances the use of different endings to indicate gender in Latin. This device still requires the underlying principles of generalization (to achieve a common noun in the first place) and comparison (to differentiate distinctive qualities among the referents of the common noun), but it does not require abstraction because it makes no separation of quality from substance. The stem is modified by the variable ending, the inflection, much as the substance is modified by the qualities it possesses.

The preposition is similarly metaphysical and its function can be taken care of by inflection in much the same way.

> The different cases in the ancient languages is a contrivance of precisely the same kind. The genitive and dative cases, in Greek and Latin, evidently supply the place of prepositions; and by a variation in the noun substantive, which stands for the co-relative term, express the relation which subsists between what is denoted by that noun substantive, and what is

expressed by some other word in the sentence. In these expressions, for example, *fructus arboris, the fruit of the tree*; *sacer Herculi, sacred to Hercules*; the variations made in the co-relative words, *arbor* and *Hercules*, express the same relations which are expressed in English by the prepositions *of* and *to*. (17–18)

This device does not require abstraction, Smith claims, because the relation "is expressed here, as it appears in nature, not as something separated and detached, but as thoroughly mixed and blended with the co-relative object" (18). Smith confusingly goes on to say that this device does not require "any effort of generalization" or "any effort of comparison." It requires no generalization, he argues, because the words *arboris* and *Herculi* (for example), although they include the meanings of the prepositions in the English phrases *of the tree* and *to Hercules*, "are not, like those prepositions, general words, which can be applied to express the same relation between whatever other objects it might be observed to subsist" (18), which is obviously true in the sense that *arboris* means *of the tree* and cannot mean *of the man, of the house*, or *of Rome*.

But this is not the sense in which Smith has earlier been taken to claim that a system of declensions involves generalization. According to Smith's earlier statement, the motive behind the progression beyond the second stage of language is the need for a verbal means of distinguishing individual objects or events within classes.

> When the greater part of objects had thus been arranged under their proper classes and assortments, distinguished by such general names, it was impossible that the greater part of that almost infinite number of individuals, comprehended under each particular assortment or species, could have any peculiar or proper names of their own, distinct from the general name of the species. When there was occasion, therefore, to mention any particular object, it often became necessary to distinguish it from the other objects comprehended under the same general name, either, first, by its peculiar qualities; or, secondly, by the peculiar relation which it stood in to some other things. (7)

If this is so, then generalization does in fact precede the use of declensions. The word *arboris* must indeed mean *of the tree* (and not *of the man, etc.*), but it is nonetheless general in the sense that it does not necessarily refer always to any one particular tree. Smith's other example, *sacer Herculi*, perhaps misled him here into inconsistency. We might possibly imagine a language in which all nouns were proper nouns and were nonetheless declined, but if generalization is to be avoided we must stipulate that the declensions in this language would be completely unsystematic; the declension of *Hercules* would not be analogous to the declension of *Petrus*. Systematic declension, such as Smith actually finds in Latin, must involve generalization in so far as each noun exhibits the *same* cases in its declension—there is something conceptually common to *Herculi, Petri, Romae*, in so far as they are all genitives. Smith's denial that comparison is required for declension seems similarly inconsistent with earlier passages in the text. Declension does not require comparison, he says, because "the words *arboris* and *Herculi* [for example] are not general words intended to denote a particular species of relations which the inventors of those expressions meant, in consequence of some sort of comparison, to separate and distinguish from every other sort of relation" (18–19). But it is very hard to see how language can signify, whether by means of inflection or in any other way, one instance of a particular relation between particular objects without also signifying other relations and differentiating relations one from another by means of what Smith calls comparison. Just as we do not notice a quality in a particular object unless we can compare it to other qualities, or to the same quality in other objects, so we do not observe a particular relation unless we know of other instances of the same relation or of contrasting relations. Smith himself seems to express this insight in his discussion of the development of adjectives (9–10). Again, to suppose declensions arise independent of comparison is inconsistent with the motivation that Smith attributes to the development of linguistic structures in the passage quoted (7).

Pages 18 and 19 of the *Considerations* undeniably offer the view that declensions—and, by implication, synthetic structures in general—arise directly from the first stage of language and depend no more on generalization and comparison than on abstraction. Although this is not the theory which will be followed here in exposition of the essay, it should nonetheless be emphasized as an alternative interpretation of Smith's position. According to this view inflection begins immediately after the stage of the denotation of particulars. Particular qualities and relations are discovered in particular objects and the names for the objects declined accordingly—with the proviso that there is no system of declension in the language, each set of qualities or relations being peculiar to the objects in connection with which they occur, and each name therefore having its own peculiar set of declensions. Suppose there are two objects A and B, and that A has the qualities (or enters into the relations) M, N, and O, and that B has the qualities (or enters into the relations) P, Q, and R. There are then six possible binary combinations among these elements in nature: AM, AN, AO, BP, BQ, and BR. Using small letters to name the elements designated here by the corresponding capitals, we can say that the language Smith is describing would include words of the form *am*, *an*, *ao*, *bp*, *bq*, and *br*. The stems *a-* and *b-* are inflected, but there is no analogy between their inflections; we cannot say, for instance, that *am* is, or is not, the same case as *bp* because there is no generalization (since -*m* occurs uniquely in the context *a-*, and -*p* occurs uniquely in the context *b-*) and there is no comparison (since the meaning of -*m* is completely independent of the meaning of -*p*). There are two problems in this account of the origin of inflection. First, it is not at all clear that a language of this type could be arrived at without generalization and comparison. In order to see that AM is similar to AN and to name them by *am* and *an* instead of by two unrelated words, a degree of generalization is surely needed; and to see that AM is different from AN and to name them by different terms instead of by a single term (as would probably be done in the earliest stage of language) surely presupposes a degree of comparison. Second, it is hard to see how a language of independently declined proper names could ever give rise to systematic inflection, such as we find in Latin, without generalization and comparison.

Smith has a solution to the latter problem. After outlining this theory of the origin of declensions without generalization or comparison he argues that declensions would become systematic by means of a principle of analogy inherent in the development of languages.

> The example, indeed, of this contrivance would soon probably be followed, and whoever had occasion to express a similar relation between any other objects would be very apt to do it by making a similar variation on the name of the co-relative object. This, I say, would probably, or rather certainly happen; but it would happen without any intention or foresight in those who first set the example, and who never meant to establish any general rule. The general rule would establish itself insensibly, and by slow degrees, in consequence of that love of analogy and similarity of sound, which is the foundation of by far the greater part of the rules of grammar. (19)

"Love of analogy" is in effect another mental principle which, in this case, explains how inflectional systems might evolve without the more intellectual principles of generalization and comparison, and, as Smith indicates, a principle operating in this way would be the foundation of grammatical (syntactical) system in language.

Smith's explanation of why the verb inflected for mood, person, and tense would precede the verb in which mood, person, and tense are indicated by separate words (pronouns and auxiliaries) is not very clear, partly because of the intrusion here of the second historical thesis, which like the principle of analogy cited in discussion of declensions involves appeal to a formal, non-rational principle in the explanation of linguistic structural development. It is evident, however, that the use of the conjugated verb involves generalization in so far as the stem is a general name for a class of events, and comparison in so far as the different forms indicating different persons or tenses are to be defined with respect to one another. As in the case of declension, the fact that the inflection of the stem is systematic indicates the operation of generalization and comparison as we have defined them, unless the alternative account involving the analogy principle is accepted.

Putting aside the analogy principle and assuming the interpretation which supposes the greater bearing of rational principles on linguistic structures, we find in the *Considerations* the account represented in Figure 11 (where the mental principles requisite to each stage are added to the history of language represented above in Figure 10).

The *Considerations* yields a four-stage account of the formation of language, an outline of the structure in each stage, and an explanation, in terms of mental principles or operations, of the transitions from one stage to the next. The essay is essentially an account of the formation of linguistic structures in terms of mental principles. The explanation rests upon the *ordering* of these principles—there must be clear reasons why the principles come into operation in the order in which they do. We have examined the first three principles and their order of operation. Denotation of particulars is accepted by Smith as simple and in need of no explanation. Generalization consists in the naming of similarities observed among particulars, and is therefore necessarily subsequent to denotation. Comparison consists in the discrimination of individuals within the classes established by gener-

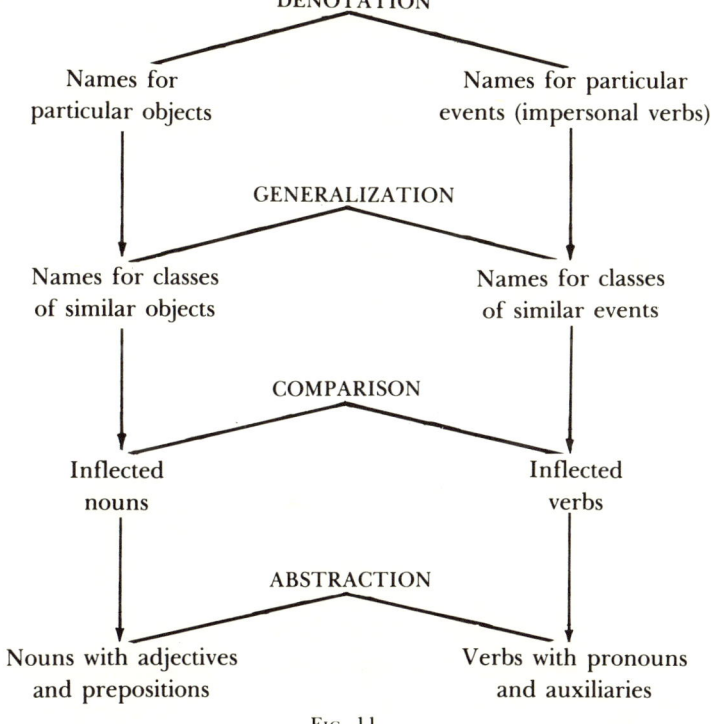

Fig. 11

alization, and is therefore necessarily a still later operation. It remains to see what exactly Smith means by abstraction and why abstraction cannot come into operation until the first three principles are effective. Abstraction is the most important of the principles in Smith's theory because he relies upon it to explain the difference between synthetic and analytic types.

Smith's claim that analytic structures involve abstraction, or "metaphysical" distinctions, where synthetic structures do not is by no means self-evident. He claims, for example, that whereas the distinction between *I love* and *you love* involves the abstraction of agent from action the distinction between *amo* and *amas* does not; he claims that the distinction between *of Rome* and *to Rome* involves abstraction of the relation from the objects related whereas the distinction between *Romae* and *Romam* does not; and he claims that the distinction between *male bear* and *female bear* involves abstraction of the quality of gender from the objects in which the quality inheres whereas the distinction between *ursus* and *ursa* does not. Yet the same conceptual distinction as is made by the analytic structures is in each case made by the inflected forms—the difference in ending between *amo* and *amas* makes precisely the distinction made by the difference in pronoun between *I love* and *you love*, and similarly in the other examples. The manner of Smith's introduction of the various devices of inflection in the *Considerations*, moreover, makes clear that these are alternative devices for expressing the *same* conceptual distinctions as are expressed in analytic structures. The abstraction which differentiates analytic from synthetic types cannot therefore consist in the drawing of conceptual distinctions. The difference between the two types is formal, not conceptual, and abstraction consists in the purely formal operation of embodying the distinctions already expressed by inflection in separate parts of speech.

If abstraction is a purely formal operation and if analytic and synthetic types are merely alternative forms capable of expressing the same contents, the question arises of why Smith considers abstraction to be the most difficult operation and necessarily the last of his formative principles to be applied. Smith's view of abstraction is explicable only in terms of his theory of the structure of reality. Abstraction is the most difficult and therefore the most recent mental operation involved in the formation of language because, unlike the operations of denotation, generalization, and comparison, it introduces a structural change in language which departs from the structure of reality.

Reality consists fundamentally of events and objects. This is evident in the *Considerations* from the fact that when language begins by denoting particulars the particulars it denotes are either objects or events. Objects and events are in effect primitives of the theory; they cannot be defined or further explained. Neither do they explain one another, for although events include objects they are not mere collections of objects. Objects may or may not be similar to one another—this we know from Smith's discussion of generalization in which he emphasizes, against the nominalists, that particulars in nature fall into classes or species. Presumably, although Smith does not say so, the same is true of events, which would be similar or dissimilar on account of the agents, objects, and times they involve. These classes of objects and events are, after generalization, denoted by common nouns and common event names (impersonal verbs) respectively. The qualities of objects and the modifications of events are the basis for comparison, which is in turn the immediate source of synthetic structures.

Reality, then, consists of objects possessed of qualities and relations and of events susceptible of certain modifications. Smith emphasizes that, in nature, qualities and relations occur only in connection with objects, and that agents, actions, and objects of action occur only in connection with events. There are therefore two different kinds of bond in the structure of reality: (1) that between quality or relation and object, or between the event and its several modifications, which is an indissoluble connection; and (ii) that between objects and events, which is not indissoluble. (Objects can occur in events as either the agent or object of action, but considered as part of the event the object is inseparably bound to the event and is not the same thing as the object considered independently.)

From the beginning the structure of language reflects this distinction between the two kinds of bond in nature. Names are bestowed separately upon objects and events, and when generalization and comparison have taken language to the stage of inflection the distinction between objects and events is preserved in that between nominal and verbal roots. The closer bonds between object and quality or relation and between the event and its modifications are expressed in the closer bond between the root and its various terminations. Smith comments at several points on the ways in which synthetic structures reflect the structure of reality.

> Both sex, and the want of all sex, being naturally considered as qualities modifying and inseparable from the particular substances to which they belong, it was natural to express them rather by a modification in the noun substantive, than by any general and abstract word expressive of this particular species of quality. The expression bears, it is evident, in this way, a much more exact analogy to the idea or object which it denotes, than in the other. The quality appears, in nature, as a modification of the substance, and as it is thus expressed in language, by a modification of the noun substantive, which denotes that substance, the quality and the subject are, if I may say so, in the expression, in the same manner as they appear to be in the object and in the idea. (11–12)

> Impersonal verbs, which express in one word a complete event, which preserve in the expression that perfect simplicity and unity, which there always is in the object and in the idea, and which suppose no abstraction, or metaphysical division of the event into its several constituent members of subject and attribute, would, in all probability, be the first species of verbs invented. . . . Every body must observe how much more simplicity there is in the natural expression, *pluit*, than in the more artificial expressions, *imber decidit, the rain falls*; or *tempestas est pluvia, the weather is rainy*. In these two last expressions, the simple event, or matter of fact, is artificially split and divided in the one, into two; in the other, into three parts. In each of them it is expressed by a sort of grammatical circumlocution, of which the significancy is founded upon a certain metaphysical analysis of the component parts of the idea expressed by the word *pluit*. (27–28)

Taking the word as the unit of language corresponding to objects and events, the units of reality, Smith claims that the two kinds of grammatical bond in inflected languages, between (i) the root and its terminations, and (ii) words of different categories, correspond to the two kinds of bond in reality. It is in this sense he claims that prior to the operation of abstraction the structure of language reflects the structure of reality. The operation of abstraction in the formation of language may now be defined as departure from this formal correspondence between language and reality.

The only reason why abstraction comes into effect after denotation, generalization, and comparison, and not before, is that it provides an alternative formal structure for the expression of conceptual distinctions embodied in language by these earlier principles. Smith's implication that abstraction is the source of "metaphysics" and is therefore the most sophisticated and hard-won intellectual capacity is inconsistent with the function actually assigned to abstraction in the formation of language. Abstraction cannot, like the principles of denotation, generalization, and comparison, be defined in terms of its conceptual contribution to the formation of language, as it makes a purely formal deviation from what Smith takes to be the structure of reality.

The representation of Smith's theory in Figure 11 is therefore misleading, in that it lists abstraction as a principle of the same kind as the other three and represents the transition from synthetic to analytic types as being no different in kind from the transitions between the earlier stages. In fact there are two kinds of formative principles in Smith's theory, and two kinds of developmental transition between linguistic stages. There are the principles of denotation, generalization, and comparison, which develop the capacity of language to delineate reality but which do not develop linguistic structures beyond the point of closest correspondence to the structure of reality. And there are the principles of abstraction and analogy, which make no difference to the expressive capacity of language (to what it can say, to its conceptual content) but which do alter its form and which are not bound in any way to the forms supposedly inherent in reality. Let us call these, respectively, *conceptual* and *formal* principles. The order of the conceptual principles is determined by the order of logical complexity among the distinctions they introduce. The formal principles can operate at any time after the conceptual principles have introduced sufficient material for them to work on.

If we are right in describing abstraction as a purely formal principle the two historical theses of the *Considerations* are not alternatives but are complementary. The first historical thesis holds that linguistic structure develops as human intellectual capacities develop; the second explains the transition from synthetic to analytic structures in terms of second language learning. It has been observed that the two theses seem to be alternative explanations of the same phenomenon, but by distinguishing between the two kinds of formative principle involved we can clear Smith's theory of these charges. If the theory involves two different kinds of principles, the conceptual and the formal, the two historical theses are not accounting for the same phenomenon of linguistic development but for different aspects of this development. The first historical thesis obviously covers the operation of the conceptual principles, the second the operation of the formal principle of abstraction. There is no reason why the historical situation Smith describes as the cause of analytic structures should not be accepted as the factor (or one of several possible factors) which triggers the operation of abstraction. Neither historical thesis alone explains the evolution of language, which involves both conceptual and formal principles, but together they seem more or less adequate to the data Smith has isolated.

Smith cannot, however, be wholly exonerated. He does present the operation of abstraction in the first section and elsewhere as if it were an intellectual operation affecting the conceptual content of language, and therefore included under the first historical thesis. If abstraction is a conceptual principle, the use of the second historical thesis to account for it in the second section of the essay is redundant. Abstraction falls under the second thesis only if it is a formal principle. Why does Smith treat abstraction as a conceptual principle in spite of his admissions that it introduces no new conceptual distinctions into language? Presumably he is misled by the importance he attaches to parts of speech into thinking that there are more numerous or sharper conceptual distinctions in analytic than in synthetic structures. In any case Smith does treat abstraction ambivalently as both a formal and a conceptual principle, and it is this ambivalence which seriously flaws his account, not the presence of two historical theses, which become complementary once abstraction is seen to be a purely formal principle.

Smith's account of the formation of languages posits a definite relation between linguistic and mental structures. Language develops through a series of structural stages under the control of an ordered sequence of mental principles, and as a result the structure of language at any stage in its development reflects the structure of thought at that time by revealing which mental principles are in operation. Smith is here on much the same ground as the philosophical grammarians, who also maintained that language is governed by and reflects mental principles. The difference between them lies in the genetic approach which Smith and many philosophers of language adopted after the publication of Condillac's *Essay* in 1746. The philosophical grammarians are concerned with the principles underlying all language, principles which, because they pertain to reason and logic, are necessarily fixed and universal. Changes or diversities in language can be only alternative embodiments of these principles, and for this reason the philosophical grammarians have little interest in the development of languages or in structural varieties among languages. All languages, regardless of structural type or stage of development, are by them supposed to be explicable in terms of one set of philosophical or rational principles, which it is the aim of a philosophical grammar to outline. The grammarians differ from one another in the details of the outlines they produce, but all agree in the premise that one set of universal and invariable principles provides the logical foundation for the grammars of all human languages. Smith, on the other hand, adopts the premise that the mental principles underlying language are themselves evolving. His object is therefore to isolate the differences between languages in different stages of development and to explain these differences in terms of different sets of underlying mental principles.

LORD MONBODDO

James Burnet (who took the title Lord Monboddo when he became a judge of the Court of Session in 1767), although a lawyer by profession, maintained a lifelong interest in philosophy and in language. In his later years he began to publish his thoughts and succeeded in completing twelve volumes[14] before his death in 1799 at the age of eighty-five. For a number of reasons he was largely unread and neglected even in his own time, and has never been revived by linguists or philosophers—although he has received attention from historians of ideas as a possible eighteenth-century evolutionist.[15] The reasons for this neglect are not far to seek: Monboddo's philosophy, being firmly based in Plato, Aristotle, and a host of Aristotelian commentators, inevitably conflicts with the new philosophies of Newton and Locke and appears unforgivably reactionary; his exposition is repetitive and digressive; and he is given to espousing doctrines both quaint (such as the assertion of the humanity of the orangutan) and mystical (such as his later belief that all language originated in the teachings of Egyptian demi-gods). Beneath all this, however, is a linguistic theory which pays closer attention to data and surveys a wider range of languages than was usual in the period, and which considerably advances the kind of speculation recently begun by Condillac and Smith. Monboddo is not an isolated eccentric in the history of linguistic thought (although he may be so in the history of philosophy) but a contributor to the mainstream of eighteenth-century speculation on the nature of language who often anticipates the interests of nineteenth-century comparative philology.[16]

The essence of Monboddo's theory of language is set out in the first two volumes of the *Origin and Progress of Language*.[17] Language is defined as "the expression of the conceptions of the mind by articulate sounds" (I.5), a definition which at once indicates great differences between Monboddo and the earlier genetic theorists Condillac and Smith. The requirement that language be articulate excludes the natural animal cries and other natural signs which, as we see in Reid's *Inquiry*, were often cited as an early stage of language and as a partial explanation of the origin of language as we know it. Monboddo does indeed retain the inarticulate cries and natural signs as part of his explanation of man's development of articulate speech, but he does not suppose that these cries and signs themselves constitute languages differing from language proper only in degree of sophistication. The requirement that language express "conceptions" means for Monboddo that language presupposes considerable rational activity, for in his view the ability to form conceptions is itself an acquired art. It follows that language and mind are not coevolutionary, as the accounts of Condillac and Smith would suggest, but that language depends upon a high degree of prior conceptual development.

The main tenet of Monboddo's theory is that language is not natural but acquired.

> I maintain, that the faculty of speech is not the gift of nature to man, but, like many others, is acquired by him; that not only there must have been society before language was invented, but that it must have subsisted a considerable time, and other arts have been invented, before this most difficult one was found out; which appears to me of so difficult invention, that it is not easy to account how it could at all have been invented. (I.12)

Monboddo emphasizes the intellectual content of even the simplest languages and the complexity of the rational and social structures which must have preceded their development. Herein lies what might be called the rationalism of his theory, as opposed to the empiricisms of Condillac and Smith, who explain the first stages of language in terms of non-rational faculties such as perception, denotation, imitation, and sympathy.

Monboddo's view involves a position on the question of the relation between thought and language: if it is insisted that language proper begins only *after* the formation of the essential faculties of human reason, it must also be accepted that language can have little or no significant influence on the development of the rational structure by which it is itself conditioned. It was generally believed in the period that thought does indeed condition language, but there was also an increasing body of varied doctrines, from sources in Hobbes, Berkeley, Condillac, and Locke, tending to the conclusion that thought also to some extent depends on language and is in some significant respects conditioned by it. In precluding this formative interdependence of language and thought, Monboddo might seem merely to be reviving an older, traditional model according to which the thought invariably comes first, is formulated independently, and is simply expressed or reflected in language. But there is much more than this to Monboddo's account. The *Origin and Progress of Language*, because it treats thought and language as significantly independent of one another genetically, is able—perhaps for the first time in modern linguistic thought—to consider the formal structures of language in isolation from the conceptual structures of which they were usually treated as mere reflections. The *science* of language as we generally think of it begins here with this separation of the study of language from the philosophy of mind.[18]

Monboddo addresses the question of how man acquired language. Because language is not a natural ability like breathing or the power of movement, and because it is evident to Monboddo that the acquisition of language presupposes both the power of forming conceptions and a degree of social organization, he must also discuss man's acquisition of ideas and of a social state. The first volume of the *Origin and Progress of Language* is divided into three books dealing respectively with the origin of ideas or conceptions, the origin of society, and the origin of the first or "barbarous" languages. The second volume deals with the transition from these barbarous quasi-languages to language proper, which Monboddo calls "language of art" and with which his work is thereafter primarily concerned.

In Book I, on the origin of ideas, Monboddo does not use the term "idea" in the usual somewhat extensive sense in which it is employed by Descartes and Locke. Like Reid, but for different reasons, he is dissatisfied with the inclusiveness of the term and with the conclusions which Lockean philosophy builds upon it. Monboddo is most anxious to argue that the data of sense should not be called ideas, although they are indeed necessary to the formation of ideas. Ideas are the result of a number of quite different mental operations upon sense data. According to Locke, says Monboddo,

> the *idea*, as he calls it, of any particular man, or other animal,

is *an idea of sensation*, that is, a perception of the sense: Whereas the fact truly is, however paradoxical it may seem, that no person *sees* (that is, perceives by the sense) either man or horse; for the sense of sight perceives no more than what is pictured in the bottom of the eye, viz. the figure, colour, and size of a certain mass of matter. But, before the mind can pronounce that mass to be a *man*, it must have performed no less than two operations of the intellect; one previous to the perception of sense, the other subsequent. The first is that by which we form the idea of that species of animal we call *man*; and whoever sees a man must have that idea ready formed in his mind: By the second, we compare with that idea the object which the sense presents; and from that comparison conclude, that the object is *man* or *horse*, or belonging to any other species of things. (I.36–37)

A perception is not itself an idea and cannot even be identified until compared with an idea of the species to which it belongs. Ideas are not the same as perceptions but are the universals to which perceptions may be assigned. Ideas are by definition general, and if we accept also Monboddo's definition of language as the expression of ideas it follows that language cannot be supposed to have begun by naming particulars. "No language ever existed, or can be conceived, consisting only of the expression of individuals, or what is commonly called *proper names*" (I.5). Because language must begin by expressing *ideas* the faculties involved in generalization, which Smith supposes to operate only after language has begun, must in Monboddo's view be active before language appears.

How are these general ideas acquired? Monboddo gives a full account of man's progression from mere sensation to the level of generalization attained by metaphysical philosophy. "The materials of the ideas which we form from the perceptions of sense, are all furnished by *sensation*; with which we must begin in our account of those ideas" (I.56), but sensations are "fleeting and transitory" and nothing can be achieved until by means of memory "the perceptions of sense are fixed in such a manner as to become the objects of knowledge" (I.56–57). The next step involves the *comparison* of our perceptions and the discovery of identities and similarities among them. Thus the species is first discovered in the individual. Next, by *abstraction*, we isolate the species from the individual perceptions in which it has occurred.

Abstraction is an important and difficult step, which Monboddo calls "the first act of human intellect," in which man's mental development parts company with that of the higher animals (I.60). His reasons for singling out abstraction involve a theory of the structure of the natural world close to that adopted by Smith.

> For understanding this, it is necessary to observe, that our senses present to us the objects as they exist in nature, that is, mixed and compounded; for, in that way, every thing in the material world appears to the sense: So that, in perceiving even a single object, the sense perceives only so many different qualities united in some *matter* or *substratum*, of which the sense has no perception. Thus, when we perceive a man, or any other animal, the sense takes in at the same time the figure, the colour, the size and other sensible qualities; and the combination of these qualities in one common subject, is the first rude notion, and, as it were, confused sketch, which not only we, but also the brutes, as I have observed, have of the species. But, in order to form the *idea*, a *separation* or *discrimination* is necessary of these qualities from one another.
> (I.59–60)

This view of nature as homogeneous with respect to the traditional categories is of no less importance to Monboddo's account of language than it is to Smith's; they both make use of it as a basis for the explanation of structural types in language and of the relations between these types. Monboddo states the theory as the principle that "every thing in nature is mixed with every thing," a saying he attributes to Anaxagoras (I.97). (This is referred to hereinafter as Anaxagoras's principle.)

Abstraction, however, is not the final step in the formation of ideas; it remains by means of *generalization* to see the one (isolated by abstraction) in the many. "For, perceiving that this *one*, which by our *intellectual* faculty we have separated from the natural mass, exists, not only in the individual object from which we have abstracted it, but in many others; then, and not till then, we have the *idea* of a *quality* or property of any substance; and as soon as we perceive a certain combination of them united together in one common subject, then we have the idea of a *substance*; for the intellect first *separates*, and then *unites*" (I.61). Thus, after perception and memory, ideas are formed by the successive intellectual operations of composition, abstraction, and generalization, and only after ideas have been formed can language begin.

The realm of ideas as Monboddo outlines it is differently structured from the realm of nature. He isolates four particular points of difference (in I.138–139).

1. The world of ideas consists of "shadowy forms," whereas nature consists of "substances, compounded of *matter and form*."

2. The natural world is "a composition of infinite variety" according to Anaxagoras's principle, whereas in the ideal world everything is "separated and discriminated," it being "the great business of human intelligence, to untwist, as it were, the great web of nature, and show every thread by itself."

3. "The natural world we perceive by our *senses*, the ideal by our *intellect*; two faculties altogether different in their nature, and manner of operation."

4. The natural world is readily open to us even in infancy, whereas the ideal world is discovered only later as the intellectual faculties develop. (This last difference is really a corollary of the third.)

The question addressed in Book I is therefore how man achieves the transition from the natural world to the intellectual, a problem which Monboddo solves by outlining the gradual sequence of faculties from sense to generalization. The ideal world is constructed by these operations on the basis provided by our perception of the natural world.

Perception and memory provide knowledge of segments of the natural world in which, by Anaxagoras's principle, no categorical distinctions are apparent. But the world we perceive is not an undifferentiated continuum, because among the segments isolated by our knowledge (perception and memory) there are resemblances which provide the basis for comparison. Nature itself, therefore, includes a complex network of relations of similarity and difference, and it is this network of relations, rather than the things related, of which we are properly said to have knowledge.

If this be a true account of the nature of our ideas, we have no knowledge but of the relations which things have to one another. And it will be objected, that things, particularly that class of them we call substances, have a nature and essence of their own, by which they are what they are, without relation to any thing else. And therefore, according to my account, we can have no knowledge of the nature of such beings. To this I answer, that human knowledge does not reach to the essence of any substance. All we know of them is certain properties or qualities; and these are nothing else but relations to other things. . . .

If it be asked, from whence we get this knowledge of likeness and difference, which, I say, is all we know of the nature [of] things? I answer, from the source of all our knowledge in our present state of existence, I mean the senses. (I.69–70n)

Suppose I have two perceptions ABCPQR and ABCSTU. By comparison I know that they are similar, and by abstraction I can isolate the feature ABC with respect to which they are so, even though ABC may never occur in isolation in nature (it might, for instance, be a complex of qualities). By generalization I then discover that the same feature ABC is found in both these perceptions and may in future be found in others. Suppose I then have the perception ABV; by the same sequence of intellectual operations I can now form the idea AB from the ideas ABC and ABV. On the basis of the perceptual complexes the intellect thus forms a hierarchy of ideas, all that is necessary for the formation of a new idea on a higher level than those so far obtained being the discovery of a similarity among two or more ideas or perceptions of which we already have knowledge. Figure 12 shows part of such an ideational hierarchy. The figure presents Monboddo's genetic account of conceptualization, showing how the formation of some ideas depends upon our ability to compare, abstract from, and generalize over others.

The theory of the formation of ideas by means of a hierarchy of generalizations justifies the Aristotelian method of definition by species and genus.

By comparing things together, we discover their differences as well as their likenesses. And hence we may perceive, that

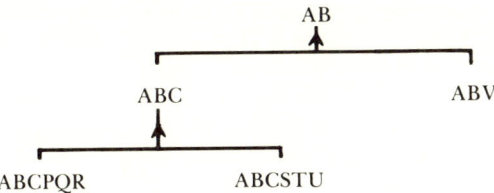

Fig. 12

> Aristotle's notion of *definition* was founded on a perfect knowledge of the human understanding, and the manner in which it acquires knowledge. For, according to him, the definition must contain both the genus and the specific difference; that is to say, what the thing defined has in common with other things, and what distinguishes it from other things. So that, without similitude and difference, there could not, according to Aristotle, be any knowledge of any thing. (I.68n)

Any idea is therefore to be defined with reference to its place in the hierarchy; a proper definition will locate the idea in question under a genus, which genus will be the idea immediately dominating it (as AB dominates ABC and ABV in Figure 12), and will contrast the idea with other ideas of the same genus to indicate its distinguishing features from other ideas dominated by the same generic idea in the hierarchy.

The concepts at the top of the hierarchy, those which are not (yet) dominated by any others, are (for the time being) the ultimate categories of human knowledge. Science, Monboddo believes, depends upon our ability to assign concepts under such categories.

> For there can be no science without definition; and there can be no definition, unless we can tell the genus or class to which the thing defined belongs; and the defintion is not complete, unless we can tell, not only the *immediate* genus, but the *highest*

> genus, that is, the *last class* under which the thing is comprehended. Thus, though I know that *man* is an animal, if I do not know what *animal* is, I cannot be said to know what *man* is. But, further, suppose I know that *animal* belongs to the genus of the εμψυχογ or *animated body*, in order to make the definition complete, I must know likewise to what genus or class of things the εμψυχογ belongs. But is there no stopping in this ascent? or is there an infinite progress upwards? If there be, it is clear there can be no complete definition, and, consequently, no perfect science; because there is no science of what is infinite. Again, suppose there was a limit to this ascent, and that we could determine the *ultimate* genus, beyond which there is no other, that is the *category*, which in the instance I have given, is *substance*; yet, if we could not define the number of those universals, there would, for the same reason, be no science of the principles of things, which, as I have said, the categories are; and all we could say of them would be, that they were infinite. (I.74–75n)

There must be a finite number of discoverable categories if the hierarchy of definitions upon which our knowledge depends is to work. If we could pursue an idea indefinitely upwards through the ranks of the hierarchy our quest for its meaning would never be satisfied, but if we postulate categories, indefinables in terms of which all else may be defined, we have a firm basis for science.

The order of nature is different from the hierarchical order discovered by intellect. In nature perceptions do not necessarily occur in an order based on their elemental composition, and the elements of which perceptions are composed are not necessarily apparent. Intellect isolates and classifies relations among perceptions, bringing similarities together in genera and isolating differences which create new genera, until eventually the elemental composition of nature, the list of the categories, is revealed. Language is a product of the intellectual order and will reflect its structures accordingly. The creation of the intellectual order, however, is a continuing process; it is not accomplished at one stroke, and even though some philosophers may have glimpsed the pattern of the completed structure it still remains for the various sciences to fill in the many details. The intellectual operations of comparison, abstraction, and generalization, therefore, must be continuously applied; it is not the case that each operation applies at only one stage of human intellectual development and is then succeeded by another operation in the next stage. There are, in short, degrees of intellectual achievement. The point is of the greatest importance because it is with reference to this notion of gradually increasing intellectual construction that Monboddo accounts for the transition from one structural type of language to another. Smith's account differs markedly from Monboddo's in this respect. Smith supposes that the operations of comparison, generalization, and abstraction characterize successive stages of intellectual growth and that each stage has its own kind of language. Monboddo believes that all three intellectual operations must be effective before language can begin and that they must continue to be jointly effective as language develops through its successive stages.

In his discourse on inequality Rousseau raised the question, to which he had no answer, of whether language is necessary to the formation of society or society to the development of language. In Book II, on the origin of society, Monboddo has no doubts: "This question I hope I shall be able to solve, by shewing, that society must have been first in the order of things; and that, though it was impossible that language could have been invented without society, yet society, and even political society, may have subsisted, perhaps for ages, before language was invented" (I.216). Monboddo outlines the stages by which man acquires society, just as he outlines in Book I the stages whereby ideas are formed, but since there is no attempt in the theory to suggest any causal correlation between social and linguistic structures we need not examine the genesis of social organization in great detail.

Man is not social in a state of nature, any more than he is intellectual. Book II therefore addresses the question of how man progresses from a state of nature to a relatively complex social state. Monboddo isolates several stages in this "progress of civil society."

1. That of "men living together in herds, like cattle or horses, without even coupling together, or pairing, as we see the males

and females of certain other specieses do; but, nevertheless, carrying on some common business, such as fishing or hunting, or whatever else may be necessary for their sustenance, though without any thing that can be called government or rule." Monboddo finds examples in Herodotus, Diodorus Siculus, and contemporary travel literature.

2. That of men who submit to government on occasions and for purposes of defence. "Under this kind of occasional government, certain inhabitants of the Caribbee islands were, when we first discovered those islands."

3. That of permanent government in public matters, but which leaves domestic and personal matters to settlement by the individuals involved. Such a society, says Monboddo, is found among the Indians of North America.

4. The form of government found in western Europe, which regulates not only public matters but also the protection of its individual citizens in matters of property and personal safety. The private lives of the citizens are still left largely to their own direction.

5. "The last stage of civil society, in which the progression ends, is that most perfect form of polity, which, to all the advantages of the governments last mentioned, joins the care of the education of youth, and likewise regulates the private lives of the citizens." The government of ancient Sparta and the ideal societies described by Plato provide examples (I.362–365).

This sequence does indeed provide a graduated progression but it does not meet Rousseau's problem; it does not explain how men who had no language could form even the simplest social organizations. Monboddo's reply to Rousseau turns upon his definition of language as *articulate* speech, a definition which leaves him free to argue that although early men have not *language* they may still have inarticulate, non-lingual, *means of communication*. The formation of societies in the absence of language can be explained if there are such means—as there are, Monboddo maintains, even among certain gregarious animals.

> For this purpose nothing else is necessary than that there should be among such animals some method of communica-

> tion. If therefore there be other methods of communication, besides that of articulate sounds, there is nothing to hinder a society to be constituted without the use of speech. Now, that there are other methods of communication, is a fact that cannot be doubted: For there are inarticulate cries, by which we see the brutes communicate to one another their sentiments and passions; there are imitative cries; and, lastly, there is the expression of looks, that is, the action of the face; and the gestures of the body. (I.416)

These pre-linguistic methods of making themselves understood provide the means whereby men first formed societies. The motive is supplied by necessity: "And, I say, that the same cause that first produced ideas, and made men rational creatures, did also make them social and political, and, in process of time, produced all the arts of life; and this cause is no other than the necessities of human life" (I.382). The same motive force, and the same means, as we shall see, operate in the early stages of language.

As evidence in support of his claim Monboddo cites several creatures who live in a social state without articulate speech—beavers in particular among the animals, and orangutans (as he supposed) among men. Society must precede the formation of language for the obvious reason that only in a social state will man have the need and opportunity to communicate beyond the range of inarticulate cries. Although Monboddo does not suggest any necessary relation between the various stages of social evolution and the several stages in the progress of man from pre-linguistic to linguistic forms of communication, he does say that as a matter of fact certain kinds of social organization are associated with certain methods of communication. The earliest forms of society rely wholly upon prelinguistic forms of communication. Men in the second social stage "had learned a little articulation, but not so much as to communicate their thoughts to one another, without the help of the natural language of signs." The next stage of society sees the first "barbarous language," of which Monboddo's best example is Huron, a language which is "very rude and imperfect indeed, but such as is sufficient for communication." Only in the fourth stage, that of Western civil society, is the "language of art" attained (I.256–257).

By the beginning of Book III, on barbarous language, Monboddo has explained how, from his initial state of nature, man might have acquired reason (the ability to form ideas) and social organization. It remains to explain how rational, social man might develop a language of articulate speech to express his ideas. The starting point, as Monboddo suggests in Book II, is in the pre-linguistic means of communication available to man in the state of nature. He lists four of these: inarticulate cries, gestures and facial expressions, imitative sounds, and painting ("by which visible objects may be represented") (I.461). These are all "natural signs" in much the same sense as the term is used by Reid, because "even the connexion betwixt inarticulate cries and the things expressed by them, though it appear to be the most remote, is so established in nature, that it is understood by every animal, without any previous compact or agreement" (I.462). Monboddo nonetheless differs from Reid and others who argue that language is a corpus of signs which differ from natural signs only in their institution by compact; he does not allow the possibility of a *language* of natural signs and emphasizes the differences between language proper and these pre-linguistic forms of communication. Even the earliest (barbarous) languages are distinguished by their articulation from natural vocal signs, and the later languages of art involve other formal principles besides.

Of the four pre-linguistic forms of communication Monboddo singles out that of inarticulate cries as the one which would provide a medium suitable to language proper. For vocal cries to become language they must be (i) articulated, and (ii) adapted to the expression of ideas. The two requirements go together because only the articulated voice has the flexibility to express anything approaching the number of different ideas which language must convey. Articulation is the first formal principle of language.

> The alteration made by [the organs of speech] upon the voice is what we call *articulation*; a metaphor taken from the *articuli* or joints of the limb of any animal; for as these divide the limb into parts, so articulation breaks and divides the continuity of the voice, which otherwise would go on in the same tenor,

without any distinguishable parts. And it is in this way that all the variety of sounds is produced, by which men have been enabled to express their conceptions, and to mark every one of them by a different sound. (I.486)

The versatility which gives language its advantage over any corpus of natural signs comes from the adoption of a number of elements (such as articulations of vocal sound) which are in themselves meaningless but which can be combined in a great variety of ways. The significance of signs so formed will lie in the articulation, in the arrangement of the elements, and not in any natural virtues of the elements themselves. Articulation is a very powerful device; from only two elements (or phonemes) we can form two words of one phoneme each, four words of two phonemes, eight words of three phonemes, and so on. From thirty phonemes (many languages have more than thirty) we can form thirty words of one phoneme, nine hundred words of two phonemes, twenty-seven thousand words of three phonemes, and so on. If we assume a rule that no word may contain more than six phonemes our language of thirty phonemes still includes 754,137,930 possible words. (In fact no natural language admits all possible configurations of its phonemes, but there are still more than enough admissible combinations to enable languages to build all the words they need from a relatively small number of phonemes without resorting to words of undue length.)

Articulation is a formal principle because, in itself, it has no conceptual content—Monboddo emphasizes that ideas are formed before articulation is devised for their expression. It is a mathematically powerful, but nonetheless rudimentary device, involving no more than the isolation of a number of distinct sounds within the vocal range and the arrangement of these sounds in short sequences which become the words of the first language. The device, however, leaves open the possibility of further systematization by the introduction of further formal principles, as would occur, Monboddo argues, when man invented a "language of art."

The first articulate speech, like other human institutions Monboddo deals with, does not appear suddenly in its complete and final form but develops from simple beginnings. The device of articulation, Monboddo conjectures, may have been learnt from animal cries (I.492–493) and would in any case have begun by introducing only a very few consonants into the vocalic stream of the inarticulate cry. Consequently, the first stages of language would consist of largely vocal sounds interspersed with few, if any, consonants. Monboddo cites a number of languages in this connection, including Huron, Algonkin, Galibi, and Eskimo, and gives a few examples from the Tahitian language recently made known by Cook's voyages of discovery in the South Seas—from the journal of Sidney Parkinson (a Scot who accompanied Sir Joseph Banks on the *Endeavour*) he quotes the words *eaee* (*neck*), *aiai*, (*armpits*), *eoo* (*nipples*), *eoboo* (*belly*), and *meyoooo* (*nails*) (I.499–507). Because they have only a few sounds, moreover, the first languages will inevitably use longer words in building their vocabulary. "Having very little articulation by consonants, and none at all at first, according to my supposition, it was necessary that they should have a certain length, in order to distinguish them from one another, and give them that variety which was necessary to express various things" (I.507–508). As examples Monboddo gives two Eskimo words, *won-na-we-uck-tuck-luit* (*much*) and *mik-ke-u-awk-rook* (*little*), and prints several lines in the Iroquois tongue (I.509–510).

Regarding the examples given here and elsewhere in illustration of barbarous languages it should be said that Monboddo is very wary of saying simply that such-and-such a language is of the barbarous type. He is well aware of the diversity of factors governing linguistic change, and that some aspects of a language may be developed, under special conditions, more or less rapidly than others. Consequently he is reluctant to place remote and little-known languages in typological categories on the basis of only one or two features. His taking certain words or features of a language to illustrate the characteristics of barbarous languages does not mean that he considers the language used in illustration to be itself of the barbarous type. The only language which he is reasonably sure belongs to this type is the Huron, for which his source was Gabriel Sagard's *Grand voyage du pays des Hurons* (1631). When considering Monboddo in the context of eighteenth-century linguistic study it is worth emphasizing, first, that he employs linguistic evidence, second that a significant proportion of his evidence is from accounts of non-Indo-European languages, and third that his use of evidence is relatively judicious.

As these first languages developed greater degrees of articulation the problem of the length of their words would be alleviated—but the beneficial effects of his development would be to some extent countered by the increase in vocabulary attendant upon ever increasing powers of generalization. We have seen that Monboddo supposes the creation of the intellectual world, the hierarchy of generalization, to be a continuing process once a certain stage in human development is reached. Thereafter the mind is forever introducing further conceptual distinctions and higher generalizations, and as the range of experience is always increasing and providing new materials for the intellect to classify, a considerable pressure is constantly bearing on language. All languages, at any stage of development, are under the perpetual necessity of increasing their vocabulary to accommodate intellectual advancement. The characteristic of barbarous languages which distinguishes them structurally from languages of art is their inability to expand the conceptual range covered by their lexicons without simply adding to their stocks of words. The devices of "derivation, composition, and inflection," which characterize languages of art and enable them to use structurally similar expressions for generically related concepts, are not available to barbarous languages, which simply go on as they begin, proliferating new arrangements of elements for the new concepts to be designated.

Monboddo divides his discussion of the formal structure of barbarous languages into three sections according to the three basic categories which all languages must express: substances and their qualities, actions and their circumstances, and relations (I.516). To understand his arguments in each section it is necessary to bear in mind both Anaxagoras's principle that everything in nature is mixed with everything else and the progressive method of hierarchical generalization which Monboddo outlines in Book I.

i. Substances and their qualities. Early men, the creators of the first barbarous languages, are at a relatively primitive stage of intellectual development. They are, of course, able to formulate ideas as a necessary prerequisite to the use of language, but they will not at first progress beyond a few stages of abstraction and generalization. They are limited in two directions with reference to the kind of hierarchical scheme set out in Figure 12: on the one hand they will fail to reach the lower levels, at which all possible distinctions are observed, and on the other hand they will fail to reach the higher levels of generalization, where the most inclusive categories are discovered. Given the perceptions ABCD, ABEF, and ABCG, the "savage" (as Monboddo calls man at this stage) might see that ABCD and ABEF differ from one another with respect to CD and EF, but he might fail to differentiate between ABCD and ABCG. Again, he might abstract and generalize the idea AB but not the higher level ideas A and B. The reason for these initial failings lies in the principle of Anaxagoras.

> That savages should perform accurately this double operation, of first separating and then uniting, and should in that way form those perfect ideas which only men of science form, must be allowed to be a thing impossible. They will no doubt have some general notion of the species, such as we have seen even brutes have; and consequently some obscure perception of the difference betwixt what is common to the species and what is peculiar to the individual, and making no part of the idea of the species; but they will not make this distinction accurately, so as to take nothing into their idea but what belongs only to the species. To be convinced of this, we need only recollect, that all our ideas arise from perceptions of sense, and that the sense presents every thing to us as it exists in nature; that is, with all its qualities, both those belonging to the species, and those which are peculiar to the individual.
> (I.517–518)

The fact that categorical distinctions are not given in perception but acquired through time and intellectual effort suggests that the earlier stages of language, those prior to discovery of the full range of categorical distinctions, would be simpler than the later because they have less conceptual complexity behind them. But this would not be the case. According to Monboddo the absence of a categorical distinction from the intellectual world leaves a greater number of unrelated elements for language to deal with. In Figure 13, for example, which represents a hierarchy like that of Figure 12, we can completely define the ideas AB, AC, BC, and ABC in terms of A, B, and C.

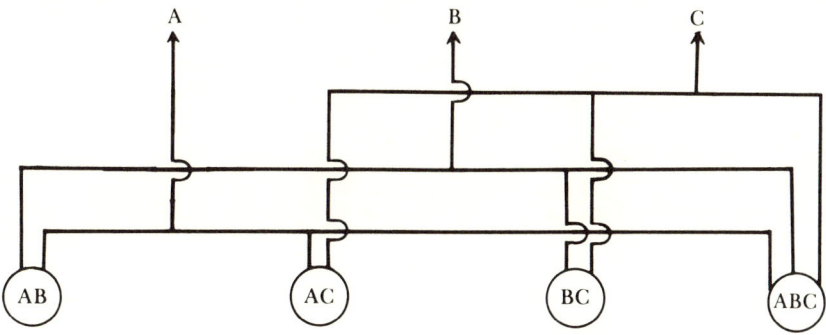

Fig. 13

But if we remove B from this sytem we are left with five indefinables instead of three, as shown in Figure 14.

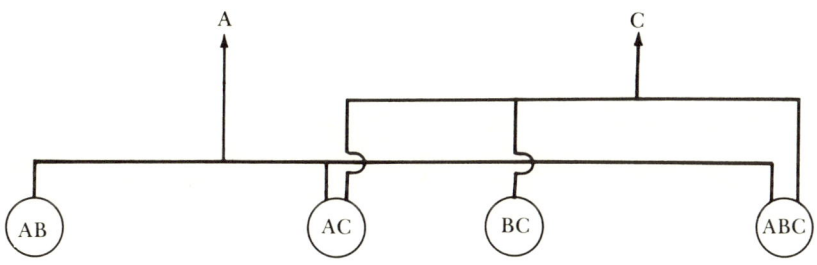

Fig. 14

Here AC can be accounted for in terms of A and C, but AB, BC, and ABC remain, along with A and C, conceptual primitives. The same thing happens in language when parts of the underlying conceptual hierarchy are not available: there is less generalization and consequently a larger number of primitives, which means a larger vocabulary.

The savage, Monboddo argues, will not systematically abstract substance from quality: "the name with which he marks any thing must denote, besides the qualities common to the species, some that belong only to individuals."

> Thus, he will not denote a bear by a name signifying only that species of animal, but he will use a word signifying a *great bear*, or a *small bear*, a *strong bear*, or a *weak bear*, or any other quality of the individual bear that affects his senses or imagination most. They will not have a word for denoting a house, or a hut, in general, but they will have a word signifying a *great* or a *little hut*, or *my hut*, or *your hut*. (I.519)

In this way the want of conceptual distinctions and generalizations places a burden on the vocabulary of early language, but besides these conceptual limitations early languages are further handicapped by want of certain formal principles. Even if we assume that the "savage" has a relatively complete grasp of the intellectual world we must still suppose that his language would be extremely awkward because he would have no way of transferring the system embodied in the intellectual hierarchy into the structure of his speech.

> The last thing I have to observe, with respect to the names of substances and their qualities is, that many substances, as well as their qualities, have a similitude to one another; and therefore they are expressed in the languages of art by words which have likewise a resemblance: Which resemblance is produced either by derivation or composition. . . . The consequence of this will be, that every thing, however like to another, will be expressed by a word quite different; which will occasion a great multiplication of words entirely new, that are saved by the two artifices above mentioned, of composition and derivation; and it will make all the words of the language unconnected with one another: so that there will not be what we call roots in it, nor anything like a system of language. And what will occasion a further multiplication of words in such a language, is the necessity of denoting the same substance joined to a different quality by a different name, and the same

> quality joined to different substances, also by a different name. (I.527)

The intellectual world is hierarchically structured, which means that ideas are systematically grouped and sub-grouped according to their resemblances and differences. In a "language of art" this structuring of concepts is at least to some extent reflected, as when in English the expression *great bear* shares a common element with the related expression *small bear*, and *strong bear* shares a common element with *strong horse*. Monboddo claims that there are no such resemblances between expressions in "barbarous languages"—any resemblances there may be will be random and insignificant—even though the conceptual similarities may be available to its speakers. This is because the barbarous languages do not have the devices of composition and derivation which make possible the linguistic reflection of conceptual systems. In the beginning of language the only formal device is that of articulation, the isolation of distinct sound elements and the creation of different patterns among these elements to express different concepts. Each new concept must be expressed by a new pattern; there are as yet no ways of systematically building patterns among the patterns, of deliberately creating some patterns to resemble others according to some rule so that relations among the concepts expressed may be reflected in the structure of the language expressing them.

Barbarous languages are therefore doubly limited. They have no way of systematically constructing relations among terms, with the result that though they can indeed give a new expression to each idea they cannot convey the hierarchical relations among ideas in the intellectual realm. Moreover, because the intellectual world is continually growing, adding new distinctions and generalizations, the structural inadequacy of barbarous languages is compounded by the passing of time as their vocabularies increase disproportionately. The formal problems here illustrated with respect to the distinction between substance and quality occur also in the case of actions and their circumstances.

ii. Actions and circumstances. The intellectual world discovers a fourfold categorical distinction with respect to action:

> I come now to speak of actions and their circumstances. With respect to which, accurate abstraction considers four things separately: 1*mo*, The action itself; 2*do*, The agent; 3*tio*, The subject of the action, or that which *suffers*; and, *lastly*, The manner in which the action is performed. Let us take, for example, the verb signifying to *beat*. There is first the action of beating; then the agent or person who beats; then the person or thing which suffers, or is beaten; and, lastly, there is the manner of beating, whether quickly or slowly, severely or gently, &c. (I.528)

In a language of art the relations among the concepts here distinguished are reflected in the various aspects or conjugations of the verb. This is possible because abstraction and generalization have produced the higher-level ideas of agent, action, *etc.*, which together with the formal device of inflection allow the evolution of verbal conjugation systems in language.

The savage, however, would not at first attain to conceptual isolation of the categories of action, agent, subject, and manner, because (by Anaxagoras's principle) "all these exist together in nature; and therefore the savage considers them all in the lump, as it were, without discrimination; and so forms his idea of the action; and according to this idea expresses it in words" (I.528). Again, as in the case of failure to abstract quality from substance, the want of categorical distinctions increases the vocabulary.

> For as there is no word expressing the action simply by itself, if there be the least change in any circumstance of the action; nay, if there be but an alteration in person, number, or time, or in the disposition of the mind of the speaker with respect to the action, there must be a new word. For, as they have no idea of those circumstances separate from the action, they can have neither separate words to express them, nor variations of the same word, even if they knew that great secret of artificial languages, I mean inflection. (I.529–530)

By distinguishing agent, subject, and manner from action it is possible to account for many aspects of the verb *to beat* by combining the element *beat* with other elements signifying the various agents, subjects, and manners of beating, but if these distinctions are not made each of the various circumstances of the action becomes itself a primitive not explicable in terms of higher categories, and must therefore be assigned its own word. Moreover, because barbarous languages want the formal device of inflection, each different circumstance will inevitably be expressed by a distinct term even if the conceptual scheme is fully known.

iii. Relations. Under this heading Monboddo considers syntax, which consists, he says, in "expression of the relation or connection of things" one with another. In language of art these connections are accomplished either "by separate words, such as prepositions and conjunctions" (the analytic type), or "by cases, genders, and numbers, in nouns; and, in verbs, by numbers and persons, and also by moods, such as the infinitive and subjunctive, which, in the more perfect languages, are all expressed by inflection or variation of the principal word" (the synthetic type) (I.530). Anaxagoras's principle applies here too, however, and entails the virtual absence of syntax in barbarous languages.

> Now, as every kind of relation is a pure idea of intellect, which never can be apprehended by sense, and as some of those relations, particularly, such of them as are expressed by cases, are very abstract and metaphysical, it is not to be expected, that savages should have any separate and distinct idea of them. They will not, therefore, express them by separate words, or by the variation of the same word, but will throw them into the lump with the things themselves. This will make their syntax wretchedly imperfect, and very much resembling the language which they used before they had words; I mean, the language of *signs*. (I.531)

A language which does not distinguish between substance and quality, or between agent, action, and object, will obviously have no use for the distinction between subject and predicate which in traditional grammar is the very basis of syntax. Barbarous languages begin by simply giving names to segments of experience, and until they can incorporate higher categorical distinctions they are necessarily without syntax. Monboddo's argument, which is on this point very close to Smith's, rests upon the traditional view that the syntactic categories or parts of speech are the linguistic equivalents of the Aristotelian categories—a language which cannot express the distinctions between the categories necessarily has no syntax. But Monboddo is not, like too many eighteenth-century philosophers of language, content with the notion of a language of signs without syntax. "Now, let ever so many words be thrown together of the most clear and determinate meaning; yet if they are not some way connected, they will never make discourse, nor form so much as a single proposition" (I.530). His solution is like Smith's; the words of early languages are each equivalent to a sentence in the language of art: "the first articulate sounds that were formed denoted whole sentences; and those sentences expressed some appetite, desire, or inclination, relating either to the individual, or to the common business which I suppose must have been carrying on by a herd of savages, before language was invented" (I.575).

Monboddo contends that with the increasing burden on the vocabulary of barbarous languages consequent to the continual enlargement of ideas, the point would arrive at which the growing stock of words without syntax or formal interrelations would become impractical, whereupon man would be compelled to impose system on his language and to invent formal principles to generate a language of art. Before this point is reached, however, there is a long and gradual transition from the stage to which Monboddo has brought man by the end of Book II (the beginnings of barbarous language) to the stage reached at the end of Volume I, where the invention of languages of art is imminent. Characteristically, Monboddo does not leave this period in man's development, the age of barbarous languages, unexplored but breaks it down into a sequence of gradations, tracing "the progress of the first operations of the human intellect, I mean abstraction and generalization, as deducible from the progress of language." We have seen that the ability to abstract and generalize, included in the ability to form ideas, is already acquired before language begins, but that these abilities become increasingly powerful with exercise. Monboddo traces, by means of the language it generates, the stages through which the developing powers of intellection pass.

First, language and ideas begin with the generalization of the individual. The individual at this stage is generalized in that an idea is formed of it, but the idea involves as yet but little abstraction, "except of the most general attributes, such as those of time and place." The substance is not distinguished from its qualities, nor the action from its circumstances.

Second, further qualities are abstracted from substance and further circumstances from action, but there would still be no distinct idea of the substance apart from all qualities or of the action apart from all circumstances. "The idea of a *bear*, for example, would be taken off only with the qualities of size, strength, or fierceness; and the idea of the action of *beating*, with circumstances of violent or gentle, with or without effusion of blood." The qualities and circumstances which "attracted the attention of the observer most" would be the first to be abstracted.

Third, substance is completely distinguished from quality, and action from its circumstances. "And thus far," says Monboddo, "the Hurons have gone."

Fourth, genera of a higher level are created, a step involving further removal from the natural world in the direction of the intellectual because a higher genus "would represent something that does not exist in nature, but is intirely a creature of the mind." Monboddo mentions *animal* and *vegetable* as examples of genera reached at this stage.

Fifth, qualities are isolated from substances, a move represented in speech by the creation of the adjective. Because Huron has abstracted substance and action and made some progress towards the higher genera (stages three and four) but has not discovered the use of adjectives, Monboddo is able to establish the order among stages three, four, and five.

Sixth, the isolated quality is abstracted. Abstract nouns are formed in this stage from the adjectives already formed in the fifth stage. This order is established by the fact that "in Greek, and Latin, and, I believe, every language, the nouns of this kind are all derived from the corresponding adjectives."

Seventh, just as the qualities are isolated in the fifth stage, so the circumstances of action are abstracted to form separate ideas. Circumstances include "the time, place, and manner of action—of the persons acting—whether the first, second, or third person—the dispositions of the mind of the speaker with respect to the action—and, *lastly*, whether the action was suffered, or done." In language this stage is reflected in the introduction of adverbs, conjugations of verbs, tenses, moods, and voices.

Eighth, and finally, comes "the formation of ideas of the connections of things upon one another, and their relation to one another in respect of time, place, situation, cause and effect, and the like." Declensions of nouns, and the employment of prepositions and conjunctions, reflect this stage in language. It is here, at last, that syntax is formed (I.569–573).

These eight stages delineate the progress of the mind on the basis of evidence provided by language, but not necessarily the progress of language itself. Monboddo's linguistic examples in the later stages obviously come from languages of art—barbarous languages have no conjugations, no declensions, and no syntax—but this does not mean that the turn from barbarous to artificial language must be accomplished about halfway through the list. Barbarous languages, in an exceedingly cumbersome way, are formally capable of taking us through even the eighth stage—in which case syntax would *not* emerge here. Monboddo does not say precisely when, in terms of this sequence of stages, the linguistic change from barbarous to artificial types would occur. Presumably it would be gradual and variable, a matter of responding slowly to increasing pressures.

In Volume II of the *Origin and Progress of Language*, Monboddo begins discussion of languages of art, which he is convinced are deliberate creations of human reason designed to alleviate the difficulties inherent in the growth of barbarous languages. His approach to the subject is characteristically methodical.

> The art of language appears to consist in *four* things. 1. In expressing accurately and distinctly all the conceptions of the human mind. 2. In doing this by as few words as possible. 3. In marking the connection that those words have with one another. And, *lastly*, The sound of the language must be agreeable to the ear, and of sufficient variety. (II.6)

These are the four conditions which a language of art must meet. The first requires it to do no less than the barbarous languages do in providing a distinct and unambiguous expression for every distinct idea. There must be no loss of conceptual breadth or clarity in the transition from barbarous to artificial language. The second requirement, however, is in effect a demand for a system which will reduce the number of distinct and unrelated expressions, a number which is maximal in barbarous languages. The system will consist in formal devices for the expression in words of the relations (or at least some of the relations) which subsist among concepts in the ideational hierarchy. Monboddo isolates three such devices: composition, derivation, and inflection. The third requirement, that language express relations between words, is a demand for syntax. One way of fulfilling this requirement is by means of inflection (already introduced in order to achieve a systematic reduction of distinct lexical items), but inflection alone is rarely sufficient. The final requirement is largely aesthetic and need not concern us further than the observation that Monboddo desires language to be "very much varied in the sound," "of easy pronunciation," and possessed of words of "a moderate length" (II.17).

The formal principles of languages of art may therefore be reduced to *composition, derivation, inflection,* and whatever more than inflection is needed to establish a *syntax* or means of making connections among words. Composition "is used when the idea to be expressed is composed of two other ideas, to which names have already been given" (II.13). If, for example, we have three concepts, A, B, and AB, related hierarchically as in Figure 15 (i), these need not be given the unrelated names *a*, *b*, and *c*, as they would be in barbarous language and as is represented in Figure 15 (ii). By a process of composition the name for AB can be compounded of the names for A and B, as in Figure 15 (iii). The word *blackbird*, compounded of *black* and *bird*, is an example in English.

Derivation may be applied when "the idea for which a name is sought, is not compounded of two ideas, but is connected with or related to another idea." Suppose x and y are related ideas (*i.e.*, reasonably closely connected ideas in a hierarchy). Instead of

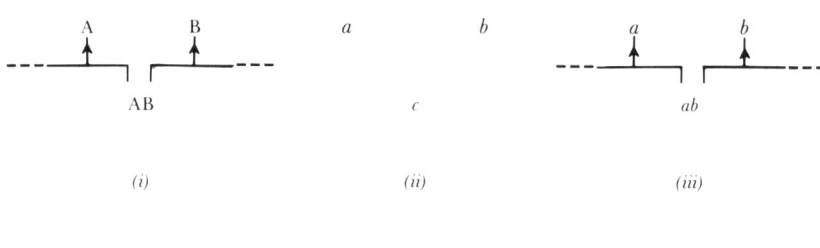

Fig. 15

naming them *x* and *y*, as would be done in barbarous language, we can first name x and then, to express the relation between them, give y a name derived from the name already given to x. The derivation in English of abstract nouns such as *whiteness* or *justice* from their corresponding adjectives would be a case in point.

"But suppose that the idea continues the very same, but some addition [is] made to it, such as that of *time, person, relation* to anything else, or any other necessary adjunct, what is to be done in that case?" (II.14–15). Here a single idea can occur under a number of different higher-level ideas—as, for example, an action may be considered past, present, or future. In such cases the constant idea may be assigned a word-stem which can be systematically inflected to express the idea's various occurrences.

The devices of composition, derivation, and inflection reduce the vocabularies of barbarous languages by making possible the reflection in language of relations established in conceptual hierarchies. The devices are purely formal; the conceptual hierarchy stands before they are applied and is unaffected by their application. Other devices besides these three might achieve the same ends, but these are the three which Monboddo finds actually operative in human language. In effect these devices introduce a system of roots and variations into the structure of language. Barbarous languages, in which words are structurally unrelated one to another, have no roots, but as soon as language incorporates composition, derivation, or inflection some words or elements become roots in relation to others, and the lexicon is reduced accordingly.

How far these principles are applied, the degree to which it is true that the words of a language are either roots or compounds, will vary from language to language and from time to time. In Monboddo's view the language of greatest artifice (and therefore of the highest intellectual and aesthetic value) is that which derives the highest proportion of its lexicon from the smallest number of native roots. Classical Greek, he thinks, approaches perfection: "I have formed a system upon this subject, by which I derive the whole Greek language from combinations in duads of the ω with the five other vowels α, ε, ι, ο, υ, the ω always being last; so that αω, εω, ιω, οω, υω, are the radical sounds from which the whole Greek language, various and copious as it is, may be deduced" (II.192–193). (He expounds this system in a Dissertation appended to the second volume.)

Monboddo defines syntax as "marking the connection and relation that words have to one another" (II.16). To understand this definition we must first look at his discussion of words. In its formal (as opposed to material) aspect language "is ultimately resolvable into *words*" (II.27). Rejecting traditional classifications of words into some eight or nine parts of speech, Monboddo insists on a fundamental division of all words into nouns or verbs. from which two categories all other parts of speech may be derived. A philosophical approach to grammar "requires that every thing of speech should be considered relatively to the nature of the things expressed by it," which things are classified according to the categories of Aristotle. There are indeed ten categories according to Aristotle, but "the nine last are all accidents, that is, things which have no separate existence by themselves, but exist in other things; whereas substance, the first of the Categories, has such a pre-eminence of existence, that it exists by itself, independent of other things" (II.27–30). All words, therefore, express either substance or accident, that is, they are in a philosophical sense either nouns or verbs. Among the categories of accidents are action and passivity ("doing and suffering") which, says Monboddo, "so far as they relate to the mind of the speaker, are to be particularly attended to in the matter of language," because any linguistic utterance must involve not only some account of "the nature of things" but also expression of "some energy, passion, disposition, or, as I would chuse to call it by one word, *affection*, of the mind of the speaker" (II.32).

Monboddo is well aware that a sequence of signs will not constitute a linguistic utterance unless it is also a "speech act"— unless it asks a question, makes a statement, expresses a wish or command, hope or expectation.

> It has been already observed, that any number of words, how great soever, of the clearest and most precise signification, thrown together without being some way connected, would convey to the mind no meaning, except that the speaker had such or such conception; but they would affirm or deny nothing. Now a sentence must necessarily do one or other of these things. (II.338–339)

A sentence therefore expresses not only the relations between the things named by its words but also between these things and the mind of the speaker. Some elements in the sentence must make this "affection" apparent, and the classification of words therefore includes a third basic category.

> As therefore the expression of these accidents or attributes of the mind of the speaker are essential to speech, I would chuse to separate them from other accidents, which may be expressed or not by speech, and to consider them by themselves, calling them *the affections of the speaker's mind*, and leaving to the accidents of substance the common name of *accidents*. We may therefore say, that every word expresses substance, or accident, or the affections of the mind of the speaker. (II.32–33)

The connections among words express both the connection between substance and accident and the connection between substance and accident on the one hand and "affection" on the other. Only when "connections among words" is understood in this sense can Monboddo's definition of syntax be appreciated.

The task of syntax may be accomplished in three ways. "This great business of language appears to me to be performed in one or other of the three following ways: for either the connection betwixt the words is expressed by the words themselves; or, 2*dly*, It is expressed by some other word; or, *lastly*, It is expressed merely by the words standing together in the sentence" (II.339–340). Syntactic connections are expressed by inflection, by separate words (such as prepositions and conjunctions), and by word order. In most languages, although one of these principles may predominate, all three will be found.

Inflection appears among the devices of syntax as well as among the principles for the introduction of roots. Composition, derivation, and inflection all establish paradigmatic relations among words which are semantically related by virtue of the conceptual hierarchy. Inflection differs from composition and derivation in that it can establish the same paradigmatic relations among different sets of words—a number of different roots may be inflected in the same way, whereas composition is limited to three terms and derivation to two, according to Monboddo. His exposition would be clearer if he stated that inflection is the general principle of which composition and derivation are special cases in which only two or three terms are involved, instead of treating inflection as a third principle of paradigmatic construction. Inflection figures in syntagmatic (syntactic) as well as paradigmatic structures because, as different words can be inflected in the same ways, it can be used to show relations of "concord" (agreement) or "regimen" (government) between different words in the same sentence.

The inflectional construction of paradigms, as Monboddo observes at several points, may be achieved either by varying the affixes of a single root word or by associating the root word with a series of other separate words. In Monboddo's observation the former method is characteristic of the "learned" languages, the latter of modern (European) languages.

> In the learned languages, the different distinctions of time are marked by different inflections of the verb. But the modern languages of Europe have not many tenses of that kind, and none at all in the passive voice. Their tenses therefore are mostly formed by the assistance of other verbs, which they call *auxiliary verbs*, but which themselves have but few tenses. Of this kind in English are *have, am, shall, will*; and in French *avoir* and *être*. (II.123–124)

> In the learned languages the numbers in verbs are marked in the same way as in nouns, viz. by inflection; and the three persons are distinguished likewise in that way. This shortens the expression in those languages, by making the use of the pronoun not necessary, besides the advantage it gives them in the variety of composition and arrangement which it allows. In English, as we have but very little variation of our verbs, they must always be accompanied by their nouns or pronouns; and not at a great distance neither, for fear of mistake or ambiguity. (II.163–164)

The structural difference involved here is clearly that isolated by Smith under the notion of "abstraction," the difference now more familiar as that between synthetic and analytic types. Like Smith, Monboddo prefers the synthetic type on aesthetic and philosophical grounds, but unlike Smith he makes it perfectly clear that the difference between the two is purely formal; they convey the same conceptual distinctions.

The analytic equivalent of inflection also has a role in syntax as the second of Monboddo's syntactic types. Obviously whatever syntagmatic relations can be expressed by means of inflection can also be expressed by means of analytic forms. Of the third type of syntactic principle, word order, Monboddo has relatively little to say. It is unquestionably a principle distinct from the other two and is readily observable when English, in which it is important, is compared to Latin, in which it is not. Like many of his contemporaries Monboddo is interested in the question of whether or not there is a "natural" word order, and in what that order might be (II.344–352).

We have now gone as far as is necessary into Monboddo's discussion of languages of art. Much of the remainder of his protracted work is concerned not with structural but with critical and philological considerations. Monboddo's view of the art of language may now be reduced to three principles: (i) the introduction of a system of roots and variations to express paradigmatic relations among words, (ii) the use of these paradigms to express syntactic connections, and (iii) the use of word order to convey syntactic connections. Because synthetic and analytic forms are, in Monboddo's account, simply formal alternatives, they can be subsumed under a single rule for the sake of economy. Monboddo's first two syntactic types are therefore brought together in the second of these principles.

Monboddo's overall account of language involves the following principles—given a basis in sensation and memory and a sufficient degree of social organization:

A. Conceptual Principles
  1. Comparison
  2. Abstraction
  3. Generalization
B. Formal Principles
  4. Articulation (giving rise to barbarous language)
  5. Inflection (including composition and derivation) ⎫
  6. Syntactic Principles ⎬ (giving rise to languages of art)
     (a) Use of the paradigms introduced in principle 5
     (b) Use of word order ⎭

Like Smith's, this theory assumes a theory of the structure of reality (which Monboddo derives from Anaxagoras but which is indistinguishable from the theory tacitly adopted by Smith), and a theory of perception (namely, that what we are given in experience is the structure outlined by the theory of the structure of reality). The conceptual principles in Monboddo's theory are much the same as those to be found in Smith and in the philosophical grammarians. Monboddo's originality among eighteenth-century students of language stems from the sharp distinction he draws between these conceptual principles and the formal principles, an originality which appears most striking when he is compared to Smith or Condillac, who attempt to explain all that they consider to be significant in linguistic form in terms of conceptual principles. Monboddo's insistence that the rational principles which it is the business of language to express must be established *before* the history of language proper begins enables him to discuss the development of the formal structures of language in terms of purely formal principles. As long as linguistic form was considered to be largely conditioned by conceptual structures, as it was by the philosophical grammarians and by most of the genetic theorists who followed Condillac, the study of linguistic structures would remain a subordinate and unempirical procedure within the philosophy of mind.

5. Harris and Reid: Rationalism and Common Sense

JAMES HARRIS

James Harris was born in Salisbury in 1709. His family was well connected, and he was himself nephew to the third Earl of Shaftesbury, whose famous *Characteristics of Men, Manners, Opinions, Times* appeared in 1711. After Oxford Harris read law, but without intending to practice. His father's death in 1733 left him comparatively wealthy and enabled him to pursue careers in both literature and politics. He became a Member of Parliament, was for a short time a Lord of the Admiralty, and in later life was appointed Secretary and Comptroller to Queen Charlotte. He died in 1780 and was buried in Salisbury Cathedral.

Harris was greatly enamored of classical learning, and especially of Aristotle and the early Aristotelian commentators. The four volumes of his own published writings, (i) *Three Treatises: The First concerning Art; The Second concerning Music, Painting, and Poetry; The Third concerning Happiness* (1744); (ii) *Hermes, or a Philosophical Inquiry concerning Universal Grammar* (1751); (iii) *Philosophical Arrangements* (1775); and (iv) *Philological Inquiries* (published posthumously under the direction of his son in 1781), are each concerned to present a broadly Aristotelian position on issues in philosophy, grammar, art, and ethics. The second of these was the work which established Harris's reputation and influence among British philosophers in the latter half of the eighteenth century, and it is with this that we are chiefly concerned—although his other writings, particularly the *Treatises* and the *Arrangements*, are almost indispensable to an appreciation of Harris's philosophical perspectives.[1]

Harris was not an original thinker of any importance and has, quite justly, long been dropped from the roll of significant eighteenth-century philosophers. During his lifetime, however, and for some decades thereafter, the reputation of his *Hermes* was considerable. Its influence is particularly evident in several of the products of the Scottish school which emerged in the front rank of European philosophy after the appearance of Thomas Reid's *Inquiry* in 1764. (Reid's interest in Harris is discussed below.) No less indebted to the stimulus of *Hermes* were James Beattie, whose "Theory of Language" appeared in his *Dissertations Moral and Critical* in 1783, and Lord Monboddo, whose monumental *Of the Origin and Progress of Language* (1773–1792) shares both Harris's rationalist approach to language and his Aristotelian cast of mind. It would be difficult to find evidence that Harris's influence survived the eighteenth century, however, except perhaps indirectly through Reid or through Monboddo (whose work was published in German in 1785, with a preface by Herder, and may therefore have been known to some of the early nineteenth-century philologists). Thus James Harris has long been of interest only to historians, although recent scholarship shows signs of renewed attention to his work: he receives honorable mention in the Chomskyan scheme of linguistic history,[2] and his critical theory has been reappraised.[3]

The reason for including Harris here, in the company of Locke, Berkeley, and Hobbes, is that his *Hermes*, regardless of its philosophical weaknesses and want of originality, was the most influential eighteenth-century English essay in the genre of "universal" or "philosophical" grammar. It may be that when put beside the Port-Royal *Grammar* or the *Grammaire* of Condillac *Hermes* is, in Aarsleff's words, "a poor representative of its kind"[4]—because of its idiosyncratic adoption of a quasi-Aristotelian framework and terminology—but for better or worse it was from the erudite and somewhat archaic words of James Harris that most English readers after 1751 learned the tenets of philosophical grammar. We therefore take Harris as our exemplar of this approach to language in the period.

The label "rationalist" as applied here to this approach must be carefully qualified. The term is justified by the way in which Harris sees language as a product of *reason*, but it should not be taken to imply opposition between Harris's theory of language and the linguistic theories of the "empiricist" philosophers Locke, Berkeley, and Hobbes. On the contrary, the notion of philosophical grammar current in the seventeenth and eighteenth centuries is largely compatible with the linguistic works of these philosophers and is actually incorporated into the linguistic theory of Locke. The point requires emphasis because the widely-known Chomskyan account of linguistic theory in the period postulates an irreconcilable opposition on questions of language between empiricists and philosophers of the "rationalist" (or "Cartesian") tradition, to which the work of the philosophical grammarians is assigned.[5] There is in fact nothing peculiarly rationalist or Cartesian about philosophical grammar in this period—and indeed, *in the theory of language* of the seventeenth and eighteenth centuries there is no clear-cut distinction between empiricist and rationalist (or Cartesian) positions. Nothing shows this more clearly than the fact that the distinguishing features of the "Cartesian" position described by Chomsky—belief in the "creativity" of language use, distinction between "deep and surface" structures, adoption of grammars which are "explanatory" as well as "descriptive," and belief in the innateness of certain universal linguistic principles[6]—can all be found in such major empiricist writers on language as Du Marsais, Condillac, and Locke.[7]

Chomsky has done great service by showing the similarity between many points at issue in contemporary linguistics and those discussed by philosophers of language in the seventeenth and eighteenth centuries. But he is mistaken in seeing the period of Descartes and Locke in terms of a theoretical confrontation broadly comparable to that between himself and the behaviorisms of Bloomfield and Skinner.[8] The importation of the debate of the late 1950s between behaviorists and rationalists in linguistics into discussion of the philosophy of language of the age of Descartes and Locke has caused many writers after Chomsky to lose sight of matters which were clear to an earlier generation of historians.[9]

A related point which has been raised against the Chomskyan

account of the history of linguistics is that philosophical grammar has nothing peculiarly "Cartesian" about it and does not owe its origin to seventeenth-century rationalism but to earlier works, such as the *Minerva, seu de causis linguae latinae* (1587) of Sanctius, which in turn have roots in the speculative grammars of the Middle Ages.[10] Chomsky has responded by differentiating between the methods and purposes of Sanctius and those of post-Cartesian philosophical grammarians,[11] but the point remains that "practically all universal grammarians . . . emphatically and often state their indebtedness to Sanctius."[12] This is certainly true of Harris, who makes passing mention in his *Inquiries* of "those able Writers *Mess. de Port Roial*" but adds a long note on Sanctius which expressly states that his own "*first* rational Ideas of *Grammar* and *Language*" came from reading *Minerva* (I.21–22). Harris also acknowledges medieval antecedents; in later life he was delighted to discover elements of philosophical grammar in the twelfth-century John of Salisbury (I.441–442). He scarcely mentions the seventeenth-century philosophers of language because, like his friend Monboddo, he had conceived a strong dislike of all post-Renaissance philosophy and made the primary purpose of his writings the revivification of classical ideas. If philosophical grammar were in any useful sense a product of Cartesianism or seventeenth-century rationalism Harris would not have been interested in it.

The term "rationalist" as here applied to Harris is not meant to distinguish his philosophy of language as belonging to any definable anti-empiricist tradition in the period. On the contrary, the tradition of universal grammar, whatever its origins, to which Harris's work clearly belongs, comfortably crosses the ill-defined boundaries between rationalism and empiricism, and Harris's position is largely consistent with that of Locke as well as that of the grammarians of Port-Royal. The distinction implied by the label "rationalism" in this chapter pertains to degrees of emphasis and variation in the use of terms rather than to disagreement over fundamentals of linguistic theory. The most important area in which Harris and Reid emphasize matters acknowledged only tacitly by Locke is that of innateness. Locke, of course, accepts innate faculties (such as the ability to perceive the agreement or disagreement of ideas) and admits the existence of certain categories (substances, modes, and relations) in terms of which our knowledge of the world is necessarily framed. These faculties and categories form the basis of his theory of grammar.[13] In a very similar way Harris postulates the universality of certain natural principles and offers a detailed (and broadly Aristotelian) set of categories.[14] Among his natural principles are those governing language, and the categorical schema is the framework of the grammatical structure outlined in *Hermes*. Harris brings the innate universal principles and the logical categories more overtly into connection with grammatical theory than does Locke—who is, after all, not primarily concerned with details of grammar. A further step in the same direction is taken by Reid, whose principles of "common sense" are of the same kind as Harris's intellectual universals.

What we are here calling *rationalism* in eighteenth-century linguistic theory thus consists fundamentally in a dominating interest in the innate universal principles of reason underlying the use of language. No philosopher of significance in the period denied the existence of these principles, but some explored them in greater detail than others and gave them greater prominence in their theories. This tendency to focus on the rational principles underlying language has two particular corollaries in the writings of Harris and Reid. First, consideration of language from the point of view of the mental principles behind it encouraged an approach by way of examining what we *do* with language rather than what we *say*. Different principles are seen as accounting for different kinds of utterance, which are different because they effect different purposes. Both Harris and Reid tend to see language in terms of human action, whereas Locke, Berkeley, and Hobbes concentrate more upon the ways in which language relates to the world. Second, along with the interest in language as action goes a willingness to consider a wide and unrestricted variety of linguistic usages. The philosophers Locke, Berkeley, and Hobbes are primarily concerned with language as a vehicle for propositions which may become the subject-matter of logic, but those who approach language simply as a manifestation of the rational mind have no motive (other than the sheer weight of philosophical and grammatical tradition) to elevate the informative statement to the virtual exclusion of other forms of speech.

The writings of both Harris and Reid exhibit these features. As philosophers the two are very different. The originality of Harris consists chiefly in his efforts to recast the commonplaces of his own day in an antique mold, whereas Reid, with his appeal to "common sense," was genuinely advancing lines of thought which had their roots in the new philosophies of the Enlightenment. They meet, however, in their approach to language by way of innate universal principles, principles which Harris attributed to the logical structure of the world and the common dependence of all minds on the divine mind, and which Reid called the principles of "common sense."

HERMES

At the beginning of *Hermes* Harris defines *Speech* as "the joint Energie of our best and noblest Faculties, (that is to say, of our *Reason* and our *social Affection*) being withal our *peculiar* Ornament and Distinction, as *Men*" (H.1–2). The definition refers to the section in the "Dialogue concerning Happiness" in which he had argued that man is by nature both social and rational ("rational" in the sense of being, unlike other animals, capable of progressing beyond instinct) (T.146–163). In the course of expounding this argument Harris also determines that, given the rational and social nature of man, speech must be *natural* to mankind. The power of speech can be exercised to any purpose only in a social setting, and it would be unreasonable to suppose that nature, having endowed man with "social affections," would leave him to acquire such vital social powers as love, benevolence, and speech (T.155–156). The decision that speech, reason, and society are integral to human nature absolves Harris from the task undertaken by several of his later contemporaries (notably Lord Monboddo) of tracing the origins of language; since man is inherently rational and social, and since language is vital to reason and society, there is no point in speculating as to how man without language could ever have developed it.[15] (Elsewhere Harris writes of the particular conventions of language as being the result of human "compact" [H.328–329, 337; T.57]. His point is that the signs of language are conventional, not natural—in his own terms, words are "symbols," not "imitations" [H.331]—but *the capacity to contrive and employ* these "symbols" is natural.)

Language for Harris is not only natural but also an "energy." He defines "energy" by distinguishing it from both "power" and "work." "THE just Opposite to POWER is ENERGY, which, as it's [sic] etymology shews, implies *the existing in Deed or Act*, as opposed to that existence, which only implies *Possibility*" (A.283). Among *powers* are the human faculties, particularly the essential faculties of reason and social affection. The product of powers, when they are exercised, must be either *energies* or *works*, depending upon whether their parts exist successively or coinstantaneously.

> THIS then, continued he, being the case, and there being this Difference in Productions, call every *Production*, the *Parts of which exist successively*, and *whose Nature hath its Being or Essence in a Transition*, call it, what it really is, a *Motion* or an ENERGY— Thus a Tune and a Dance are Energies; thus Riding and Sailing are Energies; and so is Elocution, and so is Life itself. On the contrary, call every *Production*, whose *Parts exist all at once*, and *whose Nature depends not on a Transition for its Essence*, call it a WORK, or *Thing done*, not an *Energy* or Operation.— Thus a House is a Work, a Statue is a Work, and so is a Ship, and so a Picture. (T.33)

Language is an energy produced uniquely by the rational and social powers or faculties of man. In short, "Speech or Discourse is *a publishing of some Energie or Motion of his Soul*" (H.15). Consequently we can expect a diversity of discourse commensurate with the diversity of "energies" or "motions" of the soul relevant to speech. Harris is thus led into a rudimentary classification of what we would now (after Austin and Searle) call "speech acts," an area of inquiry virtually ignored by earlier philosophers. He begins by discovering two fundamental powers, each of which seems capable of further subdivision.

> NOW the POWERS OF THE SOUL (over and above the meer nutritive) may be included all of them in those of PERCEPTION, and

those of VOLITION. By the Powers of PERCEPTION, I mean the *Senses* and the *Intellect*; by the Powers of VOLITION, I mean, in an extended sense, not only the *Will*, but the several *Passions* and *Appetites*; in short, *all that moves to Action, whether rational or irrational*. (H.15)

Without pursuing the classification further, Harris concludes that "every Speech or Sentence, as far as it exhibits the Soul, must of course respect one or other of these" (*i.e.*, perception or volition) (H.16). He proceeds to assign certain types of "speech or sentence" to each power: an assertion is a product of perception, and interrogatives, imperatives, precatives, and optatives belong to volition (H.16–17).

Speech in general, or "language," is an energy. By way of Harris's rudimentary classification of verbal energies (or speech acts) we arrive at the definition of any *particular* speech (or completed utterance) as the product of one of these powers. The unit of speech, the utterance or speech act, may be defined in Harris's theory not only grammatically (*e.g.*, in terms of subject, verb, and attribute) but also in terms of powers. A speech is the product of a single exercise of one of the powers of perception or volition. Speech in general may be called (consistent with our usage in other chapters) "language," but particular verbal energies, or "speeches," may each be called "sentences" (as in H.16). Harris is careful to show the broad sense in which "sentence" is to be understood in his theory.

> FROM MANNERS we pass to SENTIMENT; a Word, which tho' sometimes confined to mere *Gnomology*, or *moral Precept*, was often used by the *Greeks* in a *more comprehensive* Meaning, *including every thing*, for *which men employ Language*; for proving and solving; for raising and calming the Passions; for exaggerating and depreciating; for Commands, Monitions, Prayers, Narratives, Interrogations, Answers, &c. &c. In short, SENTIMENT *in this Sense* means little less, than the *universal Subjects of our* DISCOURSE. (I.173–174)

A footnote to this passage makes clear that "sentiments" are the same as what Harris calls "sentences." "There are two species of SENTIMENT successively here described, both called in *English* either a SENTIMENT or a SENTENCE; and in *Latin*, SENTENTIA. The *Greeks* were more exact, and to the *different Species* assigned *different Names*, calling the one Διάνοια, the other ἀυώμη" (H.174 note). Harris distinguishes two meanings of "sentence": (i) concise expression of a moral precept, and (ii) a speech act. The latter meaning is the one with which we are concerned and the one Harris intends when he says that "every Speech or Sentence ... must of course exhibit" either perception or volition (H.16). The unit of speech (or language) in Harris's theory is the sentence (or the speech), which is a complete speech act, or in Harris's terminology a verbal exercise of the powers of perception or volition.

Although Harris arrives, by means of his view of the world in terms of powers and energies, at a concept recognizably similar to that of the speech act in recent philosophy of language, he takes the theory no further in this direction. He offers no further classification or analysis of speech acts ("sentences") and builds no more upon the notion of speech as an "energy." Moreover, the unusual terminology which Harris introduces into eighteenth-century philosophy of language can make his arrival at the speech act concept seem more original than it is. Harris does indeed define speech ("language") in terms of action (or "energy"). But Locke is saying something very similar when he points out that "the mind, in communicating its thought to others, does not only need signs of the *ideas* it has then before it, but others also to show or intimate some particular action of its own at that time relating to those *ideas*" (*Essay*,III.vii.1), and Locke is here simply following the Port-Royal grammarians, who base their theories of logic and language upon the three mental *operations* ("*trois operations de nostre esprit*") of conception, judgment, and reasoning.[16] The view of grammatical structures as reflections of mental acts, operations, or energies was in fact commonplace in the period.

On the other hand, Harris's account of speech in terms of energy is no mere repetition of theories already current. Within the general notion that speech (language) is a manifestation of inner energies or operations, two features in particular distinguish *Hermes* from most of its predecessors. First, the order of Harris's presentation, beginning with the concept of energy and clearly defining language at the outset as an energy of a certain kind, emphasizes to a degree unusual in the period the nature of speech as action. At the same time the resultant theory of the "sentence" as the unit of verbal energy reinforces the tendency—which becomes increasingly apparent as the eighteenth century progresses[17]—to take the grammatical sentence, rather than the word, as the unit of consideration in semantic theory. Second, Harris formulates a *general* theory of language in terms of actions, whereas his predecessors, such as Locke and the Port-Royal grammarians, concern themselves primarily with *particular* linguistic usages (usually the statement) and their underlying operations (usually conception and judgment). Locke and the more orthodox philosophical grammarians are more concerned with logic than with language as it is studied by twentieth-century linguistics, and therefore largely confine themselves to the analysis of only those linguistic forms in which propositions are clearly represented. No such confinement is implied in Harris's theory of energies; on the contrary, the second chapter of *Hermes* invites speculation as to the variety of "sentences," and nothing in the ensuing grammatical study limits consideration to any particular sentence type or types. Although Harris himself does little with the broader perspective he achieves he must nonetheless be credited with a theory of language which is more nearly independent of logic than those of the philosophers or the Port-Royal grammarians.

The sentence is the unit in Harris's general theory of language because it is the minimal speech act or unit of verbal energy. The bridge between this general, speech act oriented theory and Harris's grammatical theory rests upon the fact that the sentence is *not* a unit either of sound or of significance. For Harris a sentence is not only an energy but also "a compound Quantity of Sound significant, of which certain Parts are themselves also significant" (H.19–20). The sentence, which as a speech act is simple, is necessarily compound both phonologically and grammatically. (Harris uses the same word, "sentence," to denote both the unit of speech energy and those compounds of significant sound with which grammatical theory is concerned. He nowhere offers any explicit justification for this, but presumably he would have argued that it is only through the notion of a successful speech act that we can distinguish those combinations of significant sound with which grammatical theory is to deal—*i.e.*, distinguish meaningful strings of words from nonsensical strings.) Given this further definition of a sentence it is a simple matter to arrive at the notion of a *word* as "a Sound significant, of which no Part is of itself significant" (H.20), and from this point Harris can proceed to the traditional task of the grammarian—the analysis of utterances into types of words (parts of speech) and the explanation of how words interrelate in utterances.

Just as Harris defines the sentence in terms of both energy and "sounds significant," so speech ("language") may be seen as both "a publishing of some energy" of the soul and as the human use of sound to signify. (The latter definition is in fact more specific in that it excludes other means, such as gestures, which are used to "publish" our thoughts and feelings and which would therefore be included under the former definition.) The two elements of the latter definition, sound and signification, reflect the procedure common in the period of discussing language under these two headings. At first sight these labels may appear to correspond roughly to "phonology" and "semantics" in contemporary linguistics, but this is not so. Here, for example, is the way the distinction is introduced in the Port-Royal *Grammar*:

> La Grammaire est l'Art de parler. Parler, est expliquer ses pensées par des signes, que les hommes ont inventez à ce dessein....
>
> Ainsi l'on peut considerer deux choses dans ces signes: La premiere; ce qu'ils sont par leur nature, c'est à dire, en tant que sons & caracteres.
>
> La seconde; leur signification; c'est à dire, la maniere dont les hommes s'en servent pour signifier leurs pensées.[18]

The Port-Royal grammarians divide their study into two parts, the first dealing with the physical manifestation of signs (which includes not only the sounds of speech but also the characters of writing), and the second with the ways in which signs are used to represent our conceptions and judgments (which include both semantics and syntax). Harris draws the same distinction in terms of *matter* and *form*.

> EVERY thing in a manner, whether natural or artificial, is in its constitution compounded of something COMMON, and something PECULIAR; of something *Common*, and belonging to many other things; and of something *Peculiar*, by which it is distinguished, and made to be its true and proper self.
>
> HENCE LANGUAGE, if compared according to this notion to the murmurs of a fountain, or the dashings of a Cataract, has *in common* this, that like them, *it is a* SOUND. But then on the contrary it has *in peculiar* this, that whereas those Sounds have *no Meaning or Signification*, to Language *a* MEANING *or* SIGNIFICATION *is essential*. Again, *Language*, if compared to the Voice of irrational Animals, has *in common* this, that like them, *it has a Meaning*. But then it has this *in peculiar* to distinguish it from them, that whereas the *Meaning* of those Animal Sounds is derived *from* NATURE, that of Language is derived, not from Nature, but from COMPACT.
>
> FROM hence it becomes evident, that LANGUAGE, taken in the most comprehensive view, *implies certain Sounds, having certain Meanings*; and that of these two Principles, the SOUND is as the MATTER, common (like other Matter) to many different things; the MEANING as that peculiar and characteristic FORM, by which the Nature or Essence of Language becomes complete. (H.309–315)

Meaning or significance, in this formulation, is that which distinguishes the sounds of speech from other sounds. (The second paragraph of the passage quoted shows that, to isolate true—*i.e.*, human—language, the definition should specify that the meaning or significance is artificial—*i.e.*, conventional.) The *matter* of language, in Aristotelian terms, is its substance; its *form* is that which differentiates it uniquely from other substances. Language is distinguished not by its sound but by its meaning, and it is the meaning of language which is the proper study of the philosophical grammarian.

Like the Port-Royal grammarians Harris has relatively little to say about the "matter" of language. Philosophical grammar was primarily concerned with the "form" of language, with what we would call syntax and semantics—two areas of study which were much less sharply distinguished from each other in the eighteenth century than they have been in several prominent schools of linguistic thought in recent decades. The form of language, its meaning or significance, is explained largely by the fact that words stand for things in the world other than themselves. In human language, with only occasional exceptions, this process of representation whereby language can signify things and events in the world is achieved by convention, or what Harris usually calls "compact." In Harris's terminology, words (the meaningful units of language) are "symbols," not "signs." These "signs" (which Hobbes and most writers in the period called "natural signs" to distinguish them from "arbitrary signs," which Harris calls "symbols") are "imitations" which are "derived from *Natural Attributes*" of the thing signified and which are therefore immediately intelligible (H.331). Human languages are clearly not composed of "signs" because they are not immediately intelligible to non-speakers. Human languages, Harris decides, are largely composed of "symbols," which are derived "from *Accidents quite arbitrary*" and are therefore intelligible only to those schooled in the requisite conventions.

Language is conventional, Harris explains, because to try to do the business normally done by linguistic symbols with imitative signs would result in impossible complexity. The business of language is to "publish energies of the soul," which must necessarily be accomplished through a sensible medium.

> NOW THE SENSES, we know, never exceed their natural Limits; the Eye perceives no Sounds; the Ear perceives no Figures or Colours. If therefore we were to converse, not by *Symbols* but by *Imitations*, as far as things are characterized by Figure and Colour, our Imitation would be necessarily thro' Figure and Colour also. Again, as far as they are characterized by Sounds, it would for the same reason be thro' the Medium of Sounds. The like may be said of all the other Senses, the Imitation still shifting along with the Objects imitated. We see then how *complicated* such Imitation would prove. (H.334–335)

Language employs only the medium of sound and is therefore necessarily conventional—except in the relatively rare cases of onomatopoeia.

The argument just outlined turns upon the fact that language is able to represent all sorts of things—not only those things of which sound is an attribute and which would therefore be amenable to "imitation" by "significant sound." Harris does not hold, however, that words signify *things* purely and directly. If such were the case, he argues, all words would be proper names, which would have several absurd consequences, such as that languages would require infinite vocabularies (because the number of particular things is infinite), that language would change as rapidly as things are created and destroyed, and that no general statements would be possible (H.337–340). (Harris is assuming that all sensible things are particular.) If words do not signify things they must signify *ideas*—but not ideas of sense or we are again caught in the aforementioned absurdities. The words of language, therefore, excepting only those which are in fact proper names, must stand for *general* ideas (H.340–343). General ideas are derived from ideas of sense by way of the power of imagination, which allows us to hold particular ideas in mind and to discover by comparison their similarities and differences (H.353–358).

Harris's semantic theory appears much the same as Locke's: words signify ideas, some of which are particular but most of which are general, and general ideas are constructed by the mind from the data of sensible particulars. But Harris is not content with this account of ideas. First, he feels that the doctrine deriving ideas from experiential particulars is only a partial truth. He admits that ideas derive from sense in so far as we can have no ideas without some experience (H.375–379), but he argues that, in so far as all things we experience are a product of either divine or human *design*, and in so far as design presupposes the priority of thought over creation, there is also an important sense in which all things derive from ideas. The overall picture tends to restore the traditional Platonic meaning of the term "idea," which is virtually synonymous with what Harris means by "form."

> HERE then, on this System, we have plenty of FORMS INTELLIGIBLE, WHICH ARE TRULY PREVIOUS TO ALL FORMS SENSIBLE. Here too we see that NATURE is not defective in her TRIPLE ORDER, having (like Art) her FORMS PREVIOUS, HER CONCOMITANT, and HER SUBSEQUENT.
>
> THAT *the Previous* may be *justly* so called is plain, because they

are *essentially prior* to all things else. The WHOLE VISIBLE WORLD exhibits nothing more, than so many *passing* Pictures of these *immutable Archetypes*. Nay thro' these it attains even a Semblance of Immortality, and continues throughout ages to be SPECIFICALLY ONE, amid those infinite particular changes, that befal it every moment. (H.381–388)

Harris sees the things we experience as types or copies of the forms or archetypal ideas in the divine mind.

Harris raises a further problem: how are we to explain the similarity of general ideas in different minds, which must be postulated among speakers of a language if communication among them is to be accounted for? If each man is left to formulate his own general ideas on the basis of experiential data, is it not a remarkable coincidence that most men do arrive at very similar ideas? "NOW is it not marvellous," Harris asks, "there should be *so exact an Identity of our Ideas*, if they were only generated from *sensible* Objects, infinite in number, ever changing, distant in Time, distant in Place, and no one Particular the same with any other?" (H.398–399). Harris does not offer a direct answer but closes the subject with a pointed speculation: given the problem of explaining the similarity of ideas in different minds,

> whence are those Minds, whose Ideas are derived, most likely to derive them?—From MIND, or from BODY?—From MIND, a thing *homogeneous*; or from BODY, a thing *heterogeneous*? From MIND, such as (from the Hypothesis) has *original Ideas*; or from BODY, which we cannot discover to have any Ideas at all?
> (H.400–401)

The empiricist view that we construct general ideas from experience, Harris implies, by itself offers no coherent explanation for the fact that men arrive at ideas sufficiently similar to enable them to communicate one with another. The problem is resolved, he suggests, if we suppose that such ideas are not simply constructed by comparing ideas of sense but are also, in some way he does not attempt to explain, types of the archetypal ideas in the divine mind. In short, Harris plainly inclines to the view, which he expresses in Platonic terms, that general ideas, although in a certain sense dependent upon experience, are actually innate. Only by supposing that the forms or patterns of our general ideas are predetermined in some manner can we explain the similarity of the general ideas of different people.

Even if we take Harris as fully committed to the line of speculation with which he concludes discussion of general ideas, we can still find no fundamental difference between the semantic theory of *Hermes* and that of Locke's *Essay*. Locke would agree that words signify ideas, most of which in common use are general. Presumably Locke and Harris would disagree seriously over the nature and origin of general ideas, but this difference is epistemological and metaphysical, not linguistic. Harris accepts the Lockean "ideational" account of how language relates to the world, but differs on the nature of the world and the means whereby we have knowledge of it.

An objection to Harris's line of argument towards some form of innateness is the admitted fact that although men's ideas may be similar they are in many cases not precisely the same—which they surely would be if they were, as Harris implies, derived uniformly from archetypes in the divine mind. Harris finds a ready reply in those characteristics of human nature which can, in various ways and degrees, interfere with our reception or interpretation of the supersensible forms.

> ORIGINAL TRUTH, having the most intimate connection with the *supreme Intelligence*, may be said (as it were) to shine with unchangeable splendor, enlightening throughout the Universe every possible Subject, by nature susceptible of its benign influence. Passions and other obstacles may prevent indeed its efficacy, as clouds and vapours may obscure the Sun; but it self neither admits *Diminution*, nor *Change*, because the Darkness respects only particular Percipients. Among *these* therefore we must look for ignorance and errour, and for that *Subordination of Intelligence*, which is their natural consequence. (H.403–405)

This explains how it is that "Nations, like single Men, have their *peculiar* Ideas" (H.407), a point which leads Harris to consider differences among languages in terms of the differences among the ideological characteristics of language communities.

Ideological differences—*i.e.*, differences in ideas and habits of thought—which distinguish nations or large groups of people one from another may be expected to be reflected in the respective languages of the groups, "since the *Symbol* [the word] must of course correspond to its Archetype [the idea]" (H.407). Just as we speak of the "genius" or spirit or set of distinctive features of a race or nation, so Harris considers the corresponding "genius" of a language. The genius of a language is determined by the general ideas it signifies, so that an ideologically advanced people, such as Harris considers the Greeks to have been, will not only be better thinkers than other people but will also have a more comprehensive, versatile, and serviceable language (H.408–424).

In his last (posthumous) work, the *Philological Inquiries*, Harris recites a theory of metaphor which he might—although he does not in fact—have adduced to explain further the differences among languages. He defines metaphor as "the transferring of a word from its *usual Meaning* to an *Analogous Meaning*, and then the employing it, *agreeably to such Transfer*" (I.189). The theory in question he states as follows:

> IT has been ingeniously observed,[19] that the METAPHOR took its rise from the *Poverty* of Language. Men, not finding upon every occasion *Words ready made* for their ideas, were compelled to have recourse to *Words Analogous*, and transfer them from their *original* meaning to the meaning *then* required.
> (I.188)

Every new idea thus generates a new metaphor as it finds expression by giving new meanings to old words. We might apply this notion of metaphor to the question of linguistic variety by suggesting that different peoples might well express the same idea in different ways by constructing different metaphors for it. The different metaphors would inevitably have different connotations, and so in the course of time the languages would grow increasingly unlike, even though there remained a sense in which all languages expressed the same ideas.

Although Harris recognizes the real differences between languages which prevent many of them from being mutually intelligible, like any philosophical grammarian (and like the generative grammarians of our own time) he is primarily concerned to examine a "deep" or more fundamental level at which all languages might share common principles. This concern he shares not only with other avowed philosophical grammarians but with all serious philosophers of language in the period. The conceptual distinction between deep and surface levels was not peculiar to any particular school of thought in the age of Descartes and Locke.

We saw how Harris arrives, by way of the notion of a sentence as a compound of significant sounds, at the definition of a word as the least significant part of a sentence. The bridge between the concept of the word so derived and the questions of syntax with which philosophical grammars are centrally concerned is the notion of certain principles of cohesion which at the same time allow words of certain categories to combine in certain ways and exclude illicit combinations as nonsensical. These principles, for Harris, are to be discovered in the logical structure of the world. In his *Philosophical Arrangements* he explains that all things in the world may be exhaustively considered under ten categories (or "arrangements"), which he lists as Substance, Quality, Quantity, Relation, Action, Passion, When, Where, Position, and Habit. States of affairs in the world are to be explained in terms of combinations among these categories. In the same way, those words which denote ideas of *things* (which Harris calls "principal" words) will combine meaningfully among themselves only when the categories of the things they denote can combine in reality.

> SOME things co-alesce and unite *of themselves*; others refuse to do so *without help*, and as it were compulsion. Thus in Works of Art, the Morter and the Stone co-alesce of themselves; but the Wainscot and the Wall not without Nails and Pins. In nature this is more conspicuous. For example; all Quantities, and Qualities co-alesce immediately with their Substances. Thus it is we say, *a fierce Lion, a vast Mountain*; and from *this Natural Concord of Subject and Accident,* arises *the Grammatical Concord of Substantive and Adjective.* In like manner Actions co-alesce with their Agents, and Passions with their Patients.

Thus it is we say, *Alexander conquers; Darius is conquered.* Nay, as every Energy is a kind of Medium between its Agent and Patient, the whole three, *Agent, Energy,* and *Patient,* co-alesce with the same facility; as when we say, *Alexander conquers Darius.* And hence, that is from *these Modes* of *natural Co-alescence,* arises *the Grammatical Regimen of the Verb by its Nominative, and of the Accusative by its Verb.* Farther than this, Attributives themselves may be most of them characterized; as when we say of such Attributives as *ran, beautiful, learned,* he *ran swiftly,* she was *very beautiful,* he was *moderately learned,* &c. And hence the *Co-alescence of the Adverb* with *Verbs, Participles,* and *Adjectives.*

The general Conclusion appears to be this. "THOSE PARTS OF SPEECH UNITE OF THEMSELVES IN GRAMMAR, WHOSE ORIGINAL ARCHETYPES UNITE OF THEMSELVES IN NATURE." (H.262–264)

Harris does not suppose that all intra-sentential syntactic relations are taken care of in this way—indeed, his point at this stage of the text is to show that there are others *not* covered by relations among logical categories which necessitate the introduction into grammar of prepositions and more complex case systems—but he is arguing that the basic relations among parts of speech in a sentence are to be explained as reflections of the logical structure of the world.

It remains only to outline Harris's classification of words into parts of speech—some of the terminology of which occurs in the passage just quoted. Not all kinds of words are explicable in terms of the logical categories; besides prepositions, which have already been mentioned as exceptions, there are also such types as sentential connectives and articles, the function of which is, as it were, purely grammatical. Only relations among words denoting things are to be accounted for in terms of the relations among the things denoted. Accordingly Harris's first step is to distinguish between words which denote things and words which have no denotative value but which nonetheless function syntactically in relation with other words. (This distinction, which was commonplace in the period, was usually presented by English writers in terms of "integral" words and "particles.")

> WITH respect therefore to this Distinction, the first sort of Words may be call'd *significant by themselves;* the latter may be

call'd *significant by relation*; or if we like it better, the first sort may be call'd *Principals*, the latter *Accessories*. The first are like those stones in the basis of an Arch, which are able to support themselves, even when the Arch is destroyed; the latter are like those stones in its Summit or Curve, which can no longer stand, than while the whole subsists. (H.27)

All *things*, Harris continues, must exist as either substances or attributes, and "all Words, *which are significant as Principals*, must needs be significant of either the one or the other." All words which are *principals* are therefore either *substantives* or *attributives* (H.28–30). Words which are *accessories* "acquire a Signification either from being associated *to one Word*, or else *to many*," and are accordingly designated *definitives* or *connectives* respectively (H.30–31). The framework of Harris's grammar consists in these four categories, to one or more of which any word must belong: substantives, attributives, definitives, and connectives. These categories correspond respectively to noun, verb, article, and conjunction in traditional grammar.

Harris's text proceeds through these categories in order, subjecting each to discussion and subclassification. Substantives may be classified in the same way as the substances they denote. Substances are natural, artificial, or abstract (H.37–38), either one or many (H.39–40), and masculine, feminine, or neuter (H.41–61). Substantives may also be classified as primary or secondary, a distinction broadly equivalent to that between noun and pronoun. Primary substantives name substances; secondary substantives (pronouns) are their substitutes, which indicate the thing without naming it. All primary substantives and some pronouns are *prepositive* in so far as they are "capable of introducing a Sentence"; other pronouns are *subjunctive* because they cannot introduce sentences but serve only to "subjoin one to some other, which is previous" (H.77–80). Prepositive pronouns may be of the first, second, or third person.

Attributives, one might suppose, would be represented primarily by the adjectives of traditional grammar, but this is not so. Like other philosophical grammarians Harris begins discussion of this category with the notion of existence, which while it may or may not be properly considered as a predicate by itself is necessarily a component in any other predication.

> For EXISTENCE may be considered as *an universal Genus*, to which all things of all kinds are at all times to be referred. The Verbs, therefore, which denote it, claim precedence of all others, as being essential to the very being of every Proposition, in which they may still be found, either *exprest*, or by *implication*; exprest, as when we say, *The Sun* IS *bright*; by implication, as when we say, *The Sun rises*, which means, when resolved, *The Sun* IS *rising*. (H.88–89)

Verbs which express existence, sometimes called "substantive verbs," may be used either absolutely or with qualification: "Now all EXISTENCE is either absolute or qualified—*absolute*, as when we say, B IS; *qualified*, as when we say, B IS AN ANIMAL; B IS BLACK, IS ROUND, &c." (H.89). Harris outlines in some detail theories of tense and mood which need not be recounted. The final account of attributives is as follows: attributives include verbs, participles, and adjectives; a verb is made up of an atribute, an indication of time (tense), and an assertion; a participle is made up of an attribute and a tense without an assertion; and an adjective denotes an attribute without either tense or assertion (H.184–187). Besides verbs, participles, and adjectives, which are *primary* attributives because they denote attributes of substances, there are also *secondary* attributives, which denote the attributes of attributes; these are adverbs (H.192).

Harris begins a new division of his text (Book II) to discuss those words which he calls accessories. The first type of accessory word is the definitive, the article, the purpose of which is to denote individual members of a known genus or species without bestowing proper names upon them (H.214–216). His treatment of the second type, the connective, is complex, and incidentally shows how closely related to logic was the tradition of philosophical grammar. Connectives are either *conjunctions*, which join sentences, or *prepositions*, which join words (H.237). Conjunctions may be either *conjunctive* (*e.g.*, "because") or *disjunctive* (*e.g.*, "or") (H.240–242). Conjunctives are either *copulatives*, which do "no more than barely *couple* sentences" (*e.g.*, "and"), or *continuatives*, which "consolidate Sentences into *one continuous Whole*" (*e.g.*, "if," "because," "therefore") (H.242–243). Continuatives are either *suppositives* (*e.g.*, "if"), which "denote *Connection*, but assert not actual Existence," or *positives* (*e.g.*, "because"), which imply both connection and existence (H.244). Positives are either *causal* or *collective*: "The Difference between these is this—the *Causals* subjoin *Causes to Effects—The Sun is in Eclipse*, BECAUSE *the Moon intervenes—The Collectives* subjoin *Effects to Causes—The Moon intervenes*, THEREFORE *the Sun is in Eclipse*" (H.245–246). Returning to disjunctives, which "while they *disjoin the Sense, they conjoin the Sentences*," Harris classifies them initially as *simple* or *adversative*, a distinction best explained in his own words.

> Of these DISJUNCTIVES, some are SIMPLE, some ADVERSATIVE—*Simple*, as when we say, EITHER *it is Day*, OR it *is Night*—*Adversative*, as when we say, *It is not Day*, BUT *it is Night*. The Difference between them is, that the simple do no more, than *merely disjoin*; the *Adversative* disjoin, with an *Opposition concomitant*. (H.251–252)

Adversatives are further classified as *absolute* or *comparative* (H.254–255) and as *adequate* or *inadequate* (H.255–256).

There remain the prepositional connectives, which Harris explains as those words employed to create relations among words not accounted for by categorical relations (H.264–274). He observes that in many languages this same end is achieved by proliferation of cases.

Harris's theory of language rests upon two points in particular: first, the account of speech in terms of energy, which gives us the notion of the sentence as a unit speech act; and second, the semantico-syntactic analysis of the sentence in terms of logical categories. The theory is "rationalist" in that both the energies and the logical categories belong to the innate equipment which distinguishes homo sapiens—the energies relevant to speech are products of the unique rational and social characteristics of humanity and the categories are those by means of which the rational intelligence necessarily contemplates the world. The roots of

Harris's approach to language lie in the mainstream of seventeenth-century philosophy of language. Both the essential features of the theory are latent, for example, in Locke's *Essay*, which postulates innate faculties (perception of agreement and disagreement of ideas) at the base of the formation of propositions and which presents an analysis of words against a categorical framework (of modes, substances, and relations). This rationalist approach to language was further developed in the next generation by the Scottish school of philosophy, where Harris's innate universals reappear as Reid's principles of common sense.

THOMAS REID: LANGUAGE AND COMMON SENSE

The Scottish academies produced and fostered a considerable number of eminent philosophers throughout the eighteenth century, but Scottish philosophy did not become a "school" in any real sense until, largely in reaction against Hume (himself a Scot), a number of its leading figures formed a loose association under the leadership of Thomas Reid.[20] Reid (1710–96) was professor of philosophy at King's College, Aberdeen, where he was the founder and leader of the Aberdeen Philosophical Society, the activities of which did much to coordinate the philosophical opposition to Hume on a basis of "common sense." His first important work, *An Inquiry into the Human Mind* (1764), was a product of his years in Aberdeen, although by the time it appeared he had moved to Glasgow where he succeeded Adam Smith as professor of moral philosophy. Chief among Reid's later writings is the *Essays on the Intellectual Powers of Man* (1785), in which his more original thoughts on semantics occur.

The common sense reaction against Hume which Reid initiated began with recognition that the conclusions at which Hume arrived—the skeptical analysis of the self and of causality—were indeed correctly derived from the Cartesian-Lockean philosophy of "ideas," and that the same was true of Berkeley's conclusion that there is no material substance. But these conclusions are counter to common sense and rather than accept them we should reconsider the premises upon which they rest, the so-called philosophy of ideas and the theory of representative perception. We do not need to go into the broader questions of whether the conclusions of Berkeley and Hume do indeed follow from the theory of ideas, or whether Locke actually held a theory of representative perception. What matters for the philosophy of language is the challenge in Reid's writings to the status of ideas in human understanding. Both Locke and Berkeley hold that knowledge consists in the mind's operations upon its contents (normally labeled "ideas," but we must also include Berkeley's "notions"), and language, the chief means of communicating and recording knowledge, is by them analyzed accordingly in terms of ideational structures. Denial of the place of ideas in human knowledge therefore invites—indeed, demands—new approaches in the philosophy of language.

Reid does not provide any complete or systematic discussion of language. Apart from observations on the origin and acquisition of language, he gives only a theory of signs, elaborated from Berkeley and from the Lockean account of judgment, and a number of suggestive but inconclusive pronouncements on semantics. The theory of signs is presented in the early work, the *Inquiry*, and most of the observations on semantics are to be found in the *Essays* written some twenty years later.

Reid defines language in terms of signs: "By language, I understand all those signs which mankind use in order to communicate to others their thoughts and intentions, their purposes and desires" (I.54).[21] The theory of language is therefore part of the wider theory of signs. Reid, like Berkeley, adopts a broadly Hobbesian account of signs as conceptual associations, rather than the Lockean account of signs as public manifestations of mental events or conditions.

Reid gives a much more careful and detailed account of signs than does Hobbes. There are, he says, "two things necessary to our knowing things by means of signs."

> First, That a real connection between the sign and thing signified be established, either by the course of nature, or by the will and appointment of men. When they are connected by the course of nature, it is a natural sign; when by human

appointment it is an artificial sign. Thus smoke is a natural sign of fire; certain features are natural signs of anger; but our words, whether expressed by articulate sounds or by writing, are artificial signs of our thoughts and purposes.

Another requisite to our knowing things by signs is, that the appearance of the sign to the mind, be followed by the conception and belief of the thing signified. Without this, the sign is not understood or interpreted; and therefore is no sign to us, however fit in its own nature for that purpose.

(I.218)

The ambivalence in the Hobbesian definition of a sign over whether the "connection" between signifier and signified resides in the external world or in the mind of the user of the sign is here resolved. The operation of a sign, according to Reid, requires both a "real connection" and a mental movement from "appearance" of the signifier to "conception and belief" in the signified. The requirement that the mental association be backed by a "real connection," however, does not settle all difficulties. The term "connection" is unfortunately vague, for in the absence of any specification we can find "connections" between almost any things in reality. And it is not clear how the absence of such a real connection would affect the operation of the sign, or would even be detectable, provided the movement from "appearance" to "conception and belief" continued to occur.

The *Essays on the Intellectual Powers of Man* published twenty-one years after the *Inquiry*, does not reiterate the theory of signs set out in the earlier work. This may be simply because Reid saw no need to repeat his previously published conclusions, but in the light of the general approach to language in the *Essays* it is more likely to be because he no longer thought these conclusions adequate. The *Inquiry* attempts to define common sense in terms of the theory of signs, as a product of a certain kind of connection drawn by the mind between phenomena and certain conceptions, but the *Essays* presents the principles of common sense as reflected in certain universals of linguistic structure, either syntactic rules or semantic groupings. The earlier work, accordingly, defines language by way of the theory of signs and largely ignores the problems of grammar, whereas the later study inevitably (given its revised approach to common sense) sees language more in structural terms and hardly at all as a body of independently meaningful signs. Reid's later advance beyond the account of language given in the *Inquiry*, which was somewhat archaic even in 1764, is undoubtedly due largely to his reconsideration of the status and exposition of common sense principles, but it may also be attributed in some part to his appreciation of work done on language in the intervening period.[22]

The new approach to common sense in the later book arises broadly from a wish to say in more detail what the most important common sense principles are and to justify the claim that they are indeed *common* to all rational mankind. Reid's chief strategy to this end is citation of features of language which are both reflections of these principles and linguistic universals; the universality of the features then demonstrates the sense in which the principles are common. The procedure is outlined in the opening chapter.

> There are certain common opinions of mankind, upon which the structure and grammar of all languages are founded. While these opinions are common to all men, there will be a great similarity in all languages that are to be found on the face of the earth. Such a similarity there really is; for we find in all languages the same parts of speech, the distinction of noun and verbs, the distinction of nouns into adjective and substantive, of verbs into active and passive. In verbs we find like tenses, moods, persons, and numbers. There are general rules of grammar, the same in all languages. This similarity of structure in all languages shews an uniformity among men in those opinions upon which the structure of language is founded. . . .
>
> The structure of all languages is grounded upon common notions, which Mr. Hume's philosophy opposes, and endeavours to overturn. (E.26–27)

If there are "opinions common to all men" these will be reflected in corresponding "similarities of structure in all languages," and since there are such similarities, Reid claims, the "opinions" or principles of common sense are shown to be common indeed. The argument makes two assumptions in particular: (i) that thought (or "opinion") is regularly reflected in the structure of language, and (ii) that there are linguistic universals. If we grant these assumptions we must conclude that linguistic universals indicate cognitive universals, some of which, Reid wishes to say, are principles of common sense. (Presumably not *all* linguistic universals need reflect such principles, and neither need such principles be invariably reflected in language. It appears that Reid is not attempting to *define* common sense principles in terms of linguistic universals, but simply to demonstrate their universality.)

Both assumptions are problematic. The first will be discussed in the next section. The second really needs no discussion in an exposition of Reid's theory because Reid himself takes it unquestioningly for granted. Like most people in the age of "philosophical" grammar, he believes in the universality of a considerable body of linguistic features. In particular, he believes that all languages exhibit the same parts of speech (E.26, 39, 612), and that verbs in all languages have comparable tense systems, moods, and voices, and agree with their subjects in number and person (E.26, 37, 39, 612). He accepts also the universality of certain "general rules of syntax" (E.39) and of certain linguistic functions (which we might now call "speech acts") such as passing judgment, accepting, refusing, asking questions, threatening, commanding, and promising (E.54, 73). In addition, he outlines in detail a number of specific linguistic features the assumed universality of which he uses to demonstrate particular principles of common sense. It is in his discussion and use of these features that Reid's new attitude to language is most apparent.

Some six linguistic universals are cited in various parts of the *Essays* in support of six corresponding common sense principles. (The order in which they are taken here is arbitrary.)

> [1.] In all languages, we find active verbs, which denote some action or operation; and it is a fundamental rule in the grammar of all languages, that such a verb supposes a person; that is, in other words, that every action must have an agent. We take it therefore, as a first principle ... that every operation we are conscious of supposes an agent that operates, which we call *mind*. (E.37)

The universal syntactic rule is that an active verb requires an agent, which rule, Reid claims, reflects the common sense principle that action, including thought, presupposes the existence of the actor. This principle is Reid's answer to Hume's skeptical analysis of the self; "the thoughts of which I am conscious," Reid asserts, "are the thoughts of a being which I call *myself*, my *mind*, my person" (E.620).

The second rule extends the first:

> [2.] The operations of our minds are denoted, in all languages, by active transitive verbs, which, from their construction in grammar, require not only a person or agent, but likewise an object of the operation. Thus the verb *know* denotes an operation of the mind. From the general structure of language, this verb requires a person; I know, you know, or he knows: but it requires no less a noun in the accusative case, denoting the thing known; for he that knows, must know something; and to know, without having any object of knowledge, is an absurdity too gross to admit of reasoning.
> (E.37–38)

When the active verb is transitive it requires not only an agent but also an object. Reid's example, the verb *to know*, is judiciously chosen, for he wishes to use this rule as evidence of the common sense distinction between thought (or knowledge) and the objects of thought. Thought, Reid argues, "cannot be without an object, for every man who thinks must think of something; but the object he thinks of is one thing, his thought of that object is another thing" (E.160). Locke's use of the term "idea" confuses the object of thought with the act of conception and leads inescapably to the immaterialism of Berkeley. Common sense tells us that the object we think of exists independent of our thinking of it, and language reflects this universal sentiment in its rules governing transitive verbs. Reid frequently uses rules 1 and 2 in combination to enforce the threefold distinction which Hume had questioned between the thought, the thinker, and the thing thought about—between action, agent, and object (E.13–14).

Just as an active verb requries a subject, so an adjective requires a substantive.

[3.] In all languages, we find certain words, which by grammarians, are called adjectives. Such words denote attributes, and every adjective must have a substantive to which it belongs; that is, every attribute must have a subject. (E.37)

Since there are adjectives and substantives in all languages the requirement is universal and indicates a common sense principle that qualities require substances. The offenders are again Berkeley and Hume, who held "that a body is nothing but a collection of what we call sensible qualities." Against them Reid asserts that "every adjective in language must belong to some substantive expressed or understood; that is, every quality must belong to some subject" (E.276–277).

[4.] Divisions and subdivisions of things into *genera* and *species* with general names, are not confined to the learned and polished languages; they are found in those of the rudest tribes of mankind: from which we learn, that the invention and the use of general words, both to signify the attributes of things, and to signify the *genera* and *species* of things, is not a subtle invention of philosophers, but an operation which all men perform by the light of common sense. (E.468)

Reid's object here is to combat the tendency towards nominalism fostered within the philosophy of ideas by Berkeley, Hume, and Condillac. He argues "that there can be no language, not so much as a single proposition, without general words," from which "it is natural to conclude that there must be general conceptions, of which [general words] are the signs" (E.470–471). The formation of general terms in all languages demonstrates to Reid the existence of general concepts which such words denote.

[5.] The simple attributes of things, which fall under our observation, are not so numerous but that they may all have names in a copious language. But to give names to all the combinations that can be made of two, three, or more of them, would be impossible. The most copious languages have names for but a very small part.
It may likewise be observed, that the combinations that have names are nearly, though not perfectly, the same in the

different languages of civilized nations, that have intercourse with another. . . .

From these observations we may conclude, that there are either certain common principles of human nature, or certain common occurrences of human life, which dispose men, out of an infinite number that might be formed, to form certain combinations rather than others. (E.494–495)

Reid accepts the point made by Locke[23] that some words in some languages have no equivalents in others (E.497), but finds more remarkable the fact that most words in most languages *can* be readily translated by single words in most other languages. He is surprised to find himself for once in agreement with Hume, who observed that "among different languages, even where we cannot suspect the least connexion or communication, it is found, that the words, expressive of ideas, the most compounded, do yet nearly correspond to each other: a certain proof that the simple ideas, comprehended in the compound ones, were bound together by some universal principle, which had an equal influence on all mankind."[24] But whereas Hume is content to attribute this phenomenon to association Reid prefers to see it as evidence of "the fitness of the combinations we make, to aid our own conceptions, and to convey them to others by language easily and agreeably" (E.495).

The fourth rule holds that all languages employ general terms, the fifth that in most cases the general terms employed correspond in different languages. The sixth and last rule we shall discuss, which is in many ways the most important to Reid, holds that in all languages general terms are frequently ambiguous between the sensation (*e.g.*, the sensation of smell occasioned by a rose) and the sensible quality (*e.g.*, whatever in the rose causes the sensation).

> All the names we have for smells, tastes, sounds, and for the various degrees of heat and cold, have a like ambiguity; and what has been said of the smell of a rose may be applied to them. They signify both a sensation, and a quality perceived by means of that sensation. The first is the sign, the last the thing signified. As both are conjoined by nature, and as the purposes of common life do not require them to be disjoined

in our thoughts, they are both expressed by the same name; and this ambiguity is to be found in all languages, because the reason of it extends to all.   (E.244; *cf.* I.43–44, 61–62)

The sixth rule interacts importantly with the second. The second rule indicates a common sense principle distinguishing the object of thought from the thought itself. The sixth rule explains how departures from this principle can occur through misguided interpretation of the ambiguities latent in language. The phrase "the smell of a rose," for instance, is ambiguous between the sensation and the quality, which allows the philosophers of ideas to claim that it actually denotes the sensation or "idea." Such ambiguities occur in all languages in connection with all areas of perception, which enables Reid to explain how the philosophers of ideas could command such wide conviction in defiance of common sense.

Other universals besides these six are asserted in the *Essays*, but in comparison they are of little philosophical interest. The six listed are those upon which Reid places particular reliance for the demonstration of common sense principles. The first three are syntactic whereas the last three are primarily semantic universals. In no case is the universality of the feature demonstrated, or even argued; Reid is in fact simply adopting accepted universals from the tradition of philosophical grammar.

The aim of philosophical grammar, very roughly, is to establish the structures of language upon a foundation in mental principles, and its technique, accordingly, consists largely in the explanation of structural linguistic features in terms of underlying mental structures and operations. The features discussed are assumed to be universal because the mental processes upon which they are said to be based are thought to be universal. Although they differ in detail, the many philosophical grammars published in the century or more after that of Port-Royal exhibit a remarkable agreement in the universal structures they seek to explain, an agreement due largely to their overall acceptance of the categories of traditional grammar. The first five of Reid's six universals can be found in almost any philosophical grammar of the period.

The point is easily demonstrated with reference to the *Hermes* of

James Harris, which is the most important English essay in the genre and which was well known to Reid and to other Scottish philosophers in the latter half of the century. Many of Reid's statements on universal grammar may possibly derive directly from Harris.

Harris defines universal (or philosophical) grammar as *"that Grammar,* which without regarding the several Idioms of particular Languages, *only respects those Principles, that are essential to them all"* (H.11). He divides all words into four categories: "substantives," "attributives," "definitives," and "conectives," which are roughly equivalent to nouns, verbs, articles, and conjunctions respectively (H.31–32). These categories are formal universals, each of which Harris examines in turn. In discussion of the verb he clearly enunciates Reid's threefold distinction between agent, action, and object.

> All Verbs, that are strictly so called, denote Energies. Now as all *Energies* are *Attributes,* they have reference of course to certain *energizing Substances.* Thus 'tis impossible there should be such Energies, as *To love, to fly, to wound,* &c. if there were not such Beings as *Men, Birds, Swords,* &c. Further, every Energy doth not only require an Energizer, but is necessarily conversant about some *Subject.* For example, If we say, *Brutus loves*—we must needs supply—loves *Cato, Cassius, Portia,* or some one. *The sword wounds—i.e.,* wounds *Hector, Sarpedon, Priam,* or some one. And thus is it, that every Energy is necessarily situate between two Substantives, an Energizer which is *active,* and a Subject which is *passive.*
> (H.173–174)

Reid's third universal is encompassed in Harris's distinction between substances and attributes. All things that exist fall into one of these categories, depending upon whether they exist "as the Energies, or Affections of some other thing" (attributes) or "without being the Energies or Affections of some other thing" (substances). Words signifying substances are "substantives," those signifying attributes are "attributives" (H.29–30). All attributives are either verbs, particles, or adjectives (H.94). Harris thus arrives at a differentiation between substance and quality reflected in universal grammar.

Harris also believes that generalization is a universal principle reflected in all languages (H.350–374), and from the fundamental uniformity of human reason he further deduces the universality of certain basic generalizations. "In short ALL MINDS, that are, are SIMILAR and CONGENIAL; and so too are *their Ideas*, or *intelligible Forms*. Were it otherwise, there could be no intercourse between Man and Man, or (what is more important) between Man and God" (H.395–397). Here are Reid's fourth and fifth universals.

Hermes therefore reflects each of Reid's first five universals, and the same could be shown of the Port-Royal grammar or almost any essay on philosophical grammar in the period. This explains the confidence with which Reid advances his linguistic universals despite his want of evidence supporting their alleged universality, but it also raises a problem. The philosophical grammarians based their linguistic universals upon the universality of underlying mental principles, upon the nature of which they were able to assume broad agreement. But Reid's procedure is, in effect, the reverse, using the universality of certain linguistic features to support his claim for the reality of corresponding mental principles of common sense. He cannot, therefore, cite the works of the philosophical grammarians in support of the universality of the linguistic features he uses without circularity, and he does not do so explicitly. But cut off from their basis in contemporary grammatical theory Reid's supposed universals of language are left with no support whatsoever.

Reid's sixth universal is essentially his own and is bound up with the procedures and purposes of his philosophy. (The sixth universal is the only one from the above list to figure significantly in the *Inquiry* as well as in the *Essays*.) The universal ambiguity between the quality of the object and the perception of the quality is Reid's chief means of exposing the nature of the errors of the philosophy of ideas. How this is so can best be examined by considering an objection which has been raised against his use of language—particularly his use of supposedly universal linguistic structures as evidence of common sense principles—in philosophical argument.[25]

There is an apparent inconsistency in Reid's maintaining on the one hand that language is an embodiment of common sense principles and on the other hand that the inherent ambiguities of language have led highly reputable philosophers into utter absurdities. Language appears to be cast in a dual role, as both hero of common sense and villain of the philosophy of ideas. The same contradiction is reflected in another problem. The misleading ambiguities Reid finds at the root of the philosophy of ideas are all cases in which ordinary language fails to embody, in either its grammatical structures or its vocabulary, some distinction which can be made conceptually. For instance, color words (including the word "color") generally fail to distinguish between the percept, the visual image, on the one hand, and the quality of the object, whatever it may be, that is the physical cause of the image on the other. Since, as Reid assumes, language reflects thought, the absence of these distinctions from language indicates that they are not customarily made in thinking. They are, in other words, not part of "common sense." The problem is to explain how Reid can consistently rest an avowedly common sense philosophy upon the requirement that we recognize distinctions manifestly foreign to common sense. In short, if the first five universals are evidence of common sense distinctions, the universal ambiguity of the sixth should surely indicate that to draw distinctions in areas of such ambiguity is to transgress beyond the bounds of common sense.

The problem, and an indication of the direction of its solution, are best set out in Reid's own words.

> Almost all our perceptions have corresponding sensations which constantly accompany them, and, on that account, are very apt to be confounded with them. Neither ought we to expect, that the sensation, and its corresponding perception, should be distinguished in common language, *because the purposes of common life do not require it. Language is made to serve the purposes of ordinary conversation; and we have no reason to expect that it should make distinctions that are not of common use.* Hence it happens, that a quality perceived, and the sensation corresponding to that perception, often go under the same name.
>
> This makes the names of most of our sensations ambiguous, and this ambiguity has very much perplexed philosophers. It wil be necessary to give some instances, to illustrate

the distinction between our sensations and the objects of perception.

When I smell a rose, there is in this operation both sensation and perception. . . . But it is here to be observed, that the sensation I feel, and the quality in the rose which I perceive, are both called by the same name. The smell of a rose is the name given to both: so that this name has two meanings; and the distinguishing its different meanings removes all perplexity, and enables us to give clear and distinct answers to questions, about which philosophers have held much dispute. . . .

All the various names we have for smells, tastes, sounds, and for the various degrees of heat and cold, have a like ambiguity; and what has been said of the smell of a rose may be applied to them. They signify both a sensation, and a quality perceived by means of that sensation. The first is the sign, the last the thing signified. As both are conjoined by nature, and *as the purposes of common life do not require them to be disjoined in our thoughts, they are both expressed by the same name*: and this ambiguity is to be found in all languages, because the reason of it extends to all. (E.242–245; my italics)

Here Reid gives a clear instance of what we have called his sixth universal. The problems arise because of his insistence that only by "distinguishing . . . different meanings" covered by a universal ambiguity can we "give clear and distinct answers" to the relevant philosophical questions. Why does the common sense philosopher need to probe beyond the level of common sense? Why is language at once a stronghold of common sense principles and a source of absurdity? The answer lies in the passages italicized in the quotation: those ambiguities which are universal are so because "the purposes of common life" do not require their disambiguation. In other words, there is no effective ambiguity when these words appear in ordinary usage; the ambiguity remains latent because the ordinary man invariably understands such words in *one or other* of their two or more possible senses. For example, in ordinary usage "the smell of a rose" signifies a quality of the object, not the sensation; to make it signify the sensation and not the quality we must utter it in special circumstances or add express qualifications to that effect. Again, the word "toothache" normally signifies not the quality of the object (the physical or chemical condition of the tooth) but the sensation, the pain. Part of the objection raised against Reid may be met on this basis. Because he is not in fact saying that language is *misleadingly* ambiguous in common use, his sixth universal is not used inconsistently with the first five. He does not say at one point that language embodies common sense and at another point that it is a source of confusion. *In normal usage* the ambiguous terms covered by the sixth universal do not cause confusion.

Part of the problem seems yet to remain. Why is the common sense philosopher obliged to disambiguate such words, to find two meanings where common sense discovers only one? The answer seems to be that he is required to do so only in order to meet his opponents' arguments which are based on the latent ambiguities. Only by exposing the ambiguity can the common sense philosopher *show why* the philosophers of ideas are in error. Reid himself adopts this procedure in many places. Here, for instance, he discusses color words, which are commonly understood as referring to a quality of an object but which, being technically ambiguous between quality and image, have been systematically misconstrued by the philosophers of ideas:

> From what hath been said about colour, we may infer two things. The first is, that one of the most remarkable paradoxes of modern philosophy, which hath been universally esteemed as a great discovery, is, in reality, when examined to the bottom, nothing else but an abuse of words. The paradox I mean is, that colour is not a quality of bodies, but only an idea in the mind. We have shown, that the word *colour*, as used by the vulgar, cannot signify an idea in the mind, but a permanent quality of body. We have shown, that there is really a permanent quality of body, to which the common use of this word exactly agrees. . . . Philosophers have thought fit to leave that quality of bodies, which the vulgar call *colour*, without a name, and to give the name *colour* to the idea or appearance, to which, as we have shown, the vulgar give no name, because they never make it an object of thought or reflection. Hence it appears, that when philosophers affirm that colour is not in bodies, but in the mind; and the vulgar affirm, that colour is not in the mind, but is a quality of bodies; there is no difference between them about things, but only about the meaning of a word. (I.102–103)

In this passage from the *Inquiry* Reid is in effect invoking the sixth universal to show, not that color words are deceptive in common use, but that latent ambiguities have been used by the philosophers of ideas to derive their conclusions. To expose what philosophers such as Locke, Berkeley, and Hume have been doing Reid must disambiguate the term in question and show that they have taken the less common of its two potential meanings. The answer to the problem is therefore that the common sense philosopher needs to go beyond common sense only in order to refute his opponents who have already done so. If there were no philosophy of ideas Reid would have no use for the sixth universal. In this respect at least, the purpose of common sense philosophy is "to make itself unnecessary";[26] when all departures from common sense have been convincingly exposed there will be no further need for the philosophy which exposes such departures.

LANGUAGE AND THOUGHT

The overall tendency of Reid's philosophy is to deny the intermediation of ideas between the objectively knowable world and human understanding. He therefore seems obliged to reject also the ideational theory of meaning, according to which linguistic utterances in some way signify or correspond to underlying mental structures or processes, with reference to which their meanings are determined. Reid can hardly discount ideas as intermediaries in our interpretation of the world but retain them as intermediaries in the special case of our interpretation of language. On the other hand, Reid's use of language to demonstrate common sense principles rests upon the supposition that language does reflect thought. Each of the first five linguistic universals listed in the previous section is offered by Reid as evidence of a corresponding intellectual structural universal, which is credible only if we suppose the structure of language to reflect the structure of thought. Reid is thus committed to the existence of a mental structure in some sense underlying meaningful utterances and having structural correspondence with language in at least the areas covered by the list of universals. At the same time, however, he is unable to subscribe to anything very like the Lockean model, in which utterances are generated by operations upon ideas in the mental substratum.

Reid offers little explicit enlightenment. In places he reaffirms the necessity for meaningful utterances to be based upon "conceptions," but elsewhere he clearly criticizes the Lockean theory of meaning. Among the passages in the *Essays* which challenge the ideational theory one of the strongest is a brief and simple discussion of the difference between conception and sensation.

> I can easily distinguish between a notion and a sensation. It is one thing to say, I have a sensation of pain. It is another thing to say, I have a notion of pain. The last expression signifies no more than that I understand what is meant by the word *pain*. The first signifies that I really feel pain.   (E. 193)

Lockean theory holds that to understand a word I must at least have a proper corresponding idea, whereas Reid here says that the idea or "notion" *consists in* the understanding of the word. Locke founds language upon an ideational base but Reid appears to make no distinction between language and understanding. Reid supports his view with a criticism of Lockean terminology. I can, he says, either have a sensation of pain (*i.e.*, be *in pain* in the ordinary sense), or I can have a "notion" of pain (in which case I am not in pain but I might, for example, be understanding the words of another who tells me that *he* is in pain). The Lockean "idea of pain" is evidently not, in most circumstances, to be identified with a *sensation* of pain, but if it is no more than a *notion* of pain, Reid argues, to have an idea of pain can be nothing more than to understand the word "pain." (He implicitly raises the question of what the "idea" of pain could be, other than an understanding of the word, if it is not a sensation of pain.) Reid defines the idea in terms of understanding the word, whereas Locke defines understanding of the word in terms of the idea.

A similar position emerges from another passage in the *Essays*.

> What the precise limits are which divide common judgment from what is beyond it on the one hand, and from what falls short of it on the other, may be difficult to determine; and men may agree in the meaning of the word who have differ-

ent opinions about those limits, or who even never thought of fixing them. This is as intelligible as, that all Englishmen should mean the same thing by the county of York, though perhaps not a hundredth part of them can point out its precise limits. (E.560)

Here again Reid distinguishes between understanding words and having corresponding ideas. Just as I can understand "pain" without being in pain, so I can comprehend "Yorkshire is the largest English county" without knowing anything very definite about the boundaries of the county of York. (This second point would not tell seriously against the ideational theory had it not been generally required that ideas be definite. Locke, for instance, admits that ideas may be "obscure" but denies that they can be "indistinct" or vague [*Essay*, II.XXIX.4–5]. The ideational theorists denied themselves the option of replying that my idea of the county of York might not be precise but is nonetheless an idea. Their theory thus has no satisfactory explanation of my ability to use words without clear and distinct ideas of the referents.)

The direction of such passages in Reid is towards an explanation of language in terms of its use rather than in terms of the mental substratum. The use of the word is taken as evidence of the idea, and the idea is no longer set up as a precondition for the understanding of the word. But Reid does not follow this path with any purpose or persistence. Apart from such short and rare passages as those just quoted he remains committed to the view that "Words are empty sounds when they do not signify the thoughts of the speaker" (E.471), and we are still faced with his use of linguistic universals which rests upon the supposition of some correspondence between distinct linguistic and mental structural levels.

Reid himself does not resolve the difficulty, but an answer may be suggested for him on the basis of the ambiguity that the common sense philosopher discovers in such terms as "idea," "thought," and "conception." In the case of "idea," for instance, Reid concludes "that if the word *idea* in a work where it occurs in every paragraph, be used without any intimation of the ambiguity of the word, sometimes to signify thought, or the operation of the mind in thinking, sometimes to signify those internal objects of thought which philosophers suppose, this must occasion confusion in the thoughts both of the author and of the readers" (E.160). Therefore, when a philosopher says that words signify thoughts or ideas he means one or both of two distinct things: (a) that the meaningful use of language entails a mental *act*, and (b) that the meaning of the utterance is the *object* of that act. Lockean theory confuses these two and tends to identify the meaning of the utterance with the mental act behind it. The common sense distinction between the agent and the object (Reid's second universal) offers a way to avoid this confusion while retaining the notion of a mental level underlying the use of language. The underlying mental act has broad structural correspondence with the language used, but it does not in itself provide the meaning of the language. On this basis it may be possible to reconcile Reid's use of linguistic universals as evidence of underlying mental principles with his occasional claims that the understanding of words does not consist in formulating corresponding ideas.

For example, if I say "the rose is red," two things in particular must be happening. First, assuming I am aware of what I am saying, there must be an act of mind underlying the statement—an act, in this case, of predication, involving the assertion that an object is possessed of a certain quality. But this act of mind is not the meaning of the statement, which meaning must in some sense consist in the object of the act—*i.e.*, in the rose and in the fact that it possesses certain qualities, one of which may be red. Again, taking one of Reid's own examples, if I say "John is in pain," my use of the word "pain" in a meaningful assertion suggests that I understand what I mean—but not that the meaning *is* anything in my mind corresponding to the word. In order to say, in a meaningful way, "John is in pain," I must perform certain mental actions, but the meaning of the words is not bound to these actions.

In short, it is possible to see Reid as intending a distinction between the objects of thought, which constitute (or at least are essential to) the meaning of language, and the acts of mind underlying meaningful utterances, which acts exhibit a measure of structural correspondence with the universals of grammar.

Reid uses this distinction, or something very like it, in his answer to the nominalists who (like Berkeley) argue that all things are particulars and that universals exist only in the general terms of language.

> Every word that is spoken, considered merely as a sound, is an individual sound. And it can only be called a general word, because that which it signifies, is general. Now, that which it signifies, is conceived by the mind both of the speaker and hearer, if the word have a distinct meaning, and be distinctly understood. It is therefore impossible that words can have a general signification, unless there be conceptions in the mind of the speaker, and of the hearer, of things that are general. It is to such that I give the name of general conceptions: and it ought to be observed, that they take this denomination, not from the act of the mind in conceiving, which is an individual act, but from the object, or thing conceived, which is general.
> (E.471)

The act of conception is always particular, but the object of conception, in the case of general terms, is necessarily general. No doubt this answer to the question of universals raises as many problems as it resolves, but we are here no further concerned with it than to see in it Reid's use of the distinction between the mental act underlying a term and the object which the term denotes.

It may seem that the interpretation just given of Reid's philosophy of language is improbably close to recent speech-act theory in its division of the referential meaning of the utterance from the action behind it, and in the claim that there are different basic kinds of underlying act.[27] The several linguistic universals taken in the *Essays* to constitute evidence of mental principles must, if our interpretation is correct, find correspondence in different kinds of acts accompanying the use of these universals in meaningful utterances. Thus, behind "the rose is red" is a predication of a quality, behind "John is running" is an attribution of an action to an agent, and behind "roses are red" is (besides a predication) a generalization. There is clear evidence that Reid did, to a greater extent than most philosophers of the period, consider language in terms of the diversity of its functions, of the various things that can be *done* with it. Here, for instance, he is combatting the view that the only form of utterance the philosopher need contemplate is the declarative statement:

> All languages are fitted to express the social as well as the solitary operations of the mind. It may indeed be affirmed, that, to express the former, is the primary and direct intention of language. . . . In every language, a question, a command, a promise, which are social acts, can be expressed as easily and as properly as judgment, which is a solitary act. The expression of the last has been honoured with a particular name; it is called a proposition; it has been an object of great attention to philosophers; it has been analyzed into its very elements, of subject, predicate, and copula. All the various modifications of these, and of propositions which are compounded of them, have been anxiously examined in many voluminous tracts. The expression of a question, of a command, or of a promise, is as capable of being analyzed as a proposition is; but we do not find that this has been attempted; we have not so much as given them a name different from the operations which they express. (E.73)

Elsewhere Reid asserts that "language is not made either by grammarians or philosophers" (E.269) but "rude and ignorant men" in order to "express their wants, their desires, and their transactions with one another" (E.706). Reid does not elaborate any kind of speech act theory as such, but the approach to language suggested in these passages by way of the "social acts" performed between speaker and hearer is consistent with much of what he says about language elsewhere.

Reid's overall approach to language, in conclusion, is "rationalist" in much the same way as is that of Harris. Both are interested in language as the reflection of mental structures and operations which are in some sense innate, and both are led by this interest into a greater awareness than is discoverable in the other theories here examined of the nature of language as action. Pursuing this notion, both their theories, in different ways, distinguish more sharply than others between the referential meaning of words and the meaningful function of the speech act which contains them.

Of these two philosophers Reid is undoubtedly the more important. His significance in the history of the philosophy of language consists not so much in what he has to say about language—which is sometimes uncertain and often derived from earlier writers— as in the use to which he puts language in his philosophy. His work seems surprisingly modern to a twentieth-century reader because of Reid's frequent employment, especially in the *Essays*, of evidence from common verbal usage to illustrate wider arguments. There is a similarity in this respect between Reid's procedures and those adopted by "ordinary language" philosophers (notably Wittgenstein) after the Second World War. The similarity should not be pushed too far, however, for Reid still works in the eighteenth-century mode, seeing language as the reflection of underlying *thought*, which is for him the true object of study.

Conclusion

Anyone familiar with the main channels of twentieth-century work in linguistics and philosophy will see at once that none of the texts considered here will fit comfortably into either of those categories as we now understand them. The theoretical study of language in the seventeenth and eighteenth centuries seems, from the standpoint of our own time, to make no clear distinction between linguistic and philosophical approaches and to achieve no definition of language as a subject for study independent of broader epistemological, psychological, and anthropological considerations. Even the philosophical grammarians, to whom Chomsky has allied himself, study not grammar in Chomsky's own sense of the term but grammar as an adjunct to logic and the philosophy of mind. For us to see these characteristics of the work of the age as failure is simply unhistorical; as a matter of fact the theoretical study of language in the period was almost invariably encompassed by broader philosophical questions to which answers were sought by means of some kind of linguistic investigation. Of the authors here considered only Monboddo comes close to the borderline we would now be inclined to draw between philosophy and what the nineteenth century was to designate as comparative philology.

The philosophical issue to which the study of language was generally bound in the period was that of the nature of the rational mind—its principles, its operations, and (especially in the later eighteenth century) its origins—a question which, in turn, arose from the philosophers' need to discover a logic, a foundation of certitude upon which to rest their arguments and investigations. All of the theories examined here are centrally concerned with the problem of the relation of language to mind, and it is with respect to this common theoretical center that we may, by way of conclusion, attempt a rudimentary classification of the theoretical positions we have covered.

From this point of view the first and most fundamental question in linguistic theory is whether or not language does reflect thought. More precisely, for the theories we have considered, it is a question of whether linguistic structures and categories rest upon corresponding mental ideas and operations, or whether language functions as an independent formal system which may guide thought but which does not in any direct way reflect it. Of the writers we have discussed only Hobbes takes the latter alternative, the others holding unanimously that language reflects the mind in such a way that the structures of rational thought form the underlying principles of rational discourse. Having taken this stand, all the philosophers here considered (except Hobbes) are therefore committed at the outset to some form of what Chomsky has called the generative theory of grammar.

The Hobbesian exception is by no means unique in the period. Lines of thought on language comparable to that of the author of *Leviathan* were developed on the continent, particularly by Leibniz and Condillac. The roots of this position lay in the Aristotelian tradition of formal logic, which had fostered the view that certain verbal formulae—notably certain figures of the syllogism—could guarantee the validity of an argument whose premises were accepted. The validity of the argument rested not upon the thought but upon the formula; and when, as in Hobbes and Condillac, this notion was combined with some form of nominalism which inhibited the postulation of "general ideas" corresponding to general names, it became easy to conceive of the operation of language as independent of underlying mental structures.

The majority of philosophers in the period, however, clearly preferred the generative model, which postulates a systematic connection of some kind between the patterns of language and the universal (logical) operations of rational thought. Such a model of language is accepted by Locke, Berkeley, Smith, Monboddo, Harris, and Reid. The *kind* of generative model selected depended on the particular theory of mind adopted, but in general the period espoused the form of the theory embodied in what became known as "philosophical grammar." The most influential text of this type was undoubtedly the *Grammaire* of Port-Royal, but there were many others, both earlier and later, among them the *Hermes* of James Harris.

The many philosophical grammars of the period differ among themselves on points of detail, but they agree in the kind of grammatical theory they offer—a theory which traces the forms of language to the universal forms of thought and which tends to view these last in terms of the fundamental categories and operations of traditional logic. This quasi-psychological approach to language appealed widely to philosophers in a period which saw the main issues facing philosophy as epistemological. Once language was seen as a systematic reflection of human thought, then it could be studied—as language was in fact studied by both Locke and Reid—in order to throw light upon the acquisition, employment, and limitations of human knowledge.

Locke's philosophy of language, which incorporates the basic tenets of philosophical grammar, was unquestionably the most influential in Britain throughout the eighteenth century. By the mid century, moreover, it had become dominant in France as well, and was reflected in the writings of Condillac. Locke developed the generative model in directions broadly influenced by seventeenth-century atomism: he adopted a theory of mind based upon the compounding and comparing of ideational units and fostered a view of philosophical analysis as consisting in the tracing of concepts to their origins in simple ideas. The many treatises of speculative etymology written in France and England in the last decades of the century owe more to Locke than to any other single philosophical source.

Reid's opposition to Locke had nothing to do with the doctrines of philosophical grammar—which both philosophers used, each to his own end—but concerned the theory of ideas which Locke had elaborated from Descartes. From a base in philosophical grammar Reid tried to show that the theory of ideas rests upon misconstruction of language and is furthermore a perversion of "common sense" as revealed in the universal presuppositions of reason underlying human speech.

The only significant philosopher of the eighteenth century who accepted the generative model of language without adopting the form of that model expressed by the philosophical grammarians was Berkeley. The reason for this singularity lies in the fact we have observed, namely that philosophical grammar took the basic categories and operations of the mind to be reflections of corresponding categories and operations of traditional logic—specifically such categories as substance and quality and such operations as predication. Berkeley's immaterialism caused him to reject the world in which these categories and operations applied and to construct another in which such traditional notions as predication, substance, and quality had no meaning. His grammar is still generative in that it posits a systematic relation between verbal and underlying mental structures, but beyond this point Berkeleian grammar bears no similarity to any other formulated in the period. It is sad, but perhaps inevitable, that Berkeley's influence on subsequent philosophy of language should have been negligible.

The genetic approach to language, developed in the decades after Condillac in a wide variety of theses and exemplified here in the works of Smith and Monboddo, was again broadly consistent with philosophical grammar. It remained within the generative model and employed the traditional grammatical categories and structures. Conceptually, moreover, the genetic theorists held for the most part to the framework constructed for the philosophy of language by Locke and Condillac (even though some, like Monboddo, opposed Locke on other grounds); they introduced no new theoretical positions with respect to language. Historically, however, they are most important because they widened the horizons of linguistic theory and pioneered a route which was to be a major bridge between the philosophy of language of the age of Locke and the florescence of comparative philology in the next century. In particular, as soon as they began to consider that the structures of thought and language might *change*, the genetic theorists automatically found themselves speculating on the possibility of *varying* relations between language and its mental base—

speculating, that is, upon the possibility of a plurality of different types of language for different stages of mental and linguistic development. The immediate result was a close attention, particularly evident in Monboddo, to structural varieties among languages, varieties which the tradition of philosophical grammar had largely ignored in its wish to emphasize linguistic universals. In this respect the great works of nineteenth-century comparative linguistics must acknowledge the unscientific speculations of Smith and Monboddo as among their immediate progenitors, and it is in this development of a framework for the consideration of structural linguistic types that the abiding importance of the genetic theories lies.

To venture further into historical generalizations would be to go too far beyond the evidence presented in these chapters. Enough has perhaps been said to show that the theory of language in the period from Hobbes to Reid was centrally concerned with the nature of the relation between language and thought, and that its approaches to this problem were varied and original. The questions asked by most of the writers considered are still being seriously debated, and some of the more notable positions adopted in the present century by way of solution have recognizable counterparts in the theories we have examined.

Notes

1. HOBBES: FORMALISM

1. William Kneale and Martha Kneale, *The Development of Logic* (Oxford, 1962; revised edition 1968), p. 302. The historical outline given in this section is abstracted chiefly from Kneale and from Wilbur Samuel Howell, *Eighteenth-Century British Logic and Rhetoric* (Princeton, 1971). Robert Blakey's *Historical Sketch of Logic* (London, 1851) is still informative on the subject. My own account is, of course, greatly simplified.
2. Francis Bacon, *The New Organon*, ed. Fulton H. Anderson (New York, 1960), pp. 18–19.
3. *Ibid.*, p. 20.
4. Kneale, p. 310.
5. The situation is outlined in J. A. Passmore, "Descartes, The British Empiricists, and Formal Logic," *Philosophical Review*, 62 (1953), 545–553.
6. Much has been written upon the linguistic work of the Royal Society and its associates. A good starting point is the Introduction to *The Works of Francis Lodwick*, ed. Vivian Salmon (London, 1973).
7. For discussion of Locke see Chapter 2.
8. References are to *The English Works of Thomas Hobbes*, ed. Sir William Molesworth, 11 vols. (London, 1839–1845).
9. *Cf.* Descartes' presentation of the problem of reliance upon memory in Rule VII of the *Regulae ad directionem ingenii*. *Cf.* also Ludwig Wittgenstein, *Philosophical Investigations* (London, 1953), I, 258.
10. See "The Theory of Ideas" in Chapter 2.
11. For Locke's discussion of judgment and association see "The Theory of Mind" in Chapter 2.
12. This definition is couched in terms of the distinction between marks and signs, which we have seen does not work because the mark fails to obviate the problems of privacy it is intended to avoid. It is clear, however, that most names in language are in fact used as "signs."
13. For further discussion see the relevant chapters of J. W. N. Watkins, *Hobbes' System of Ideas* (London, 1965).

14. Both objection and reply are quoted from *The Philosophical Works of Descartes*, trans. Elizabeth Haldane and G. R. T. Ross (London, 1911), II, 65–66.
15. Hobbes' view of language made more impression on the continent. Both Leibniz and Condillac discuss several of his notions sympathetically.

2. LOCKEAN THEORY: IDEALISM

1. The *Essay* is quoted from the edition by Peter H. Nidditch (Oxford, 1975). References are given in the text.
2. Etienne Bonnot de Condillac, *Essai sur l'origine des connaissances humaines* (Paris, 1746), Introduction.
3. John Horne Tooke, Επεα Πτεροεντα; *or the Diversions of Purley*, 2nd ed. (London, 1798), I, 31.
4. Hans Aarsleff, "Leibniz on Locke on Language," *American Philosophical Quarterly*, 1 (1964), 183. This paper explores Locke's adoption of the principle that words are arbitrary signs, and Leibniz's disagreement with the same.
5. Noam Chomsky, in *Cartesian Linguistics* (New York, 1966), implies by omission that the universal grammarians belonged to a tradition of thought concerning language to which Lockean empiricism is inherently opposed.
6. *Cf.* Ludwig Wittgenstein, *Philosophical Investigations*, I, 377 and *passim*.
7. The distinction between meaning (or sense) and reference was not unavailable to Locke, for it lies implicit in the nominalist tradition, which sees all general terms as signs to which, though they have meaning in the appropriate contexts, nothing in reality corresponds. *Cf.* Berkeley, *Principles*, Intro., 20. It is significant that Berkeley is closer than Locke to the nominalist tradition.
8. Norman Kretzmann, "The Main Thesis of Locke's Semantic Theory," *Philosophical Review*, 77 (1968), 175–196.
9. Kretzmann, 187.
10. Locke evidently believes also that words contribute in several ways to the processes of thinking (Kretzmann, 181–183).
11. These theories are discussed in Chapter 5.
12. The point is argued in Stephen K. Land, *From Signs to Propositions; The Concept of Form in Eighteenth-Century Semantic Theory* (London, 1974), pp. 13–15.
13. R. I. Aaron, *John Locke*, 2nd ed. (Oxford, 1965), p. 113.
14. Aaron, pp. 12–14 and 31–35.
15. Locke's dissatisfaction with this part of the *Essay* is evident from the note added posthumously in the fifth (1706) edition to II.xv.9.
16. Antoine Arnauld and Claude Lancelot, *Grammaire générale et raisonnée, ou, l'art de parler* (Paris, 1660), pp. 26–30.
17. Because *truth* is properly predicated only of *propositions*—IV.v.2.
18. Arnauld and Lancelot, pp. 27–28.

19. Kretzmann, p. 180.
20. Although Locke does not cite the *Grammaire* in his text he certainly knew and respected it. The omission of any open reference may simply reflect the fact that the work was widely known and that its doctrines regarding the classification of words and the analysis of the verb were commonplace by 1690.
21. Arnauld and Lancelot, p. 90.
22. *Ibid.*, p. 91.
23. *Ibid.*
24. *Ibid.*, p. 90.
25. Condillac, *Essai*, I.vi.4.
26. The claim is advanced in Chomsky (1966), pp. 33–35. The attribution of a transformational model to the Port-Royal grammarians has been questioned: Karl E. Zimmer, Review of Chomsky (1966) in *International Journal of American Linguistics*, 34 (1968), 290–303.
27. For recent debate and further references pertaining to Chomsky's view of the history of linguistics see the essays by Arthur C. Danto, Norman Kretzmann, and Jacques Rieux and Bernard E. Rollin in *The Port-Royal Grammar*, ed. and trans. Jacques Rieux and Bernard E. Rollin (The Hague, 1975). See also my review of this volume in *Linguistics* (1979).

3. BERKELEIAN THEORY: STRUCTURALISM

1. Berkeley is quoted from *The Works of George Berkeley, Bishop of Cloyne*, eds. A. A. Luce and T. E. Jessop (London, 1948–57). References given in the text are either to the pages of this edition (abbreviated *WGB*) or to the numbered paragraphs of Berkeley's writings (using the following abbreviations: A = *Alciphron*, Intro = Introduction to the *Principles*, *NTV* = *New Theory of Vision*, P = *Principles of Human Knowledge*, S = *Siris*, and *TVV* = *Theory of Vision Vindicated*).
2. G. J. Warnock, *Berkeley* (London, 1953, rpt. 1969), p. 83.
3. Norman Kretzmann, "History of Semantics" in *Encyclopedia of Philosophy*, ed. Paul Edwards (New York, 1967), VII, 282–283.
4. Jonathan Bennett, *Locke, Berkeley, Hume: Central Themes* (Oxford, 1971), pp. 52–58.
5. Berkeley's account of generality is unsatisfactory. His terminology is confusing and he may not disagree with Locke as much as he thinks he does. See Bennett, *op. cit.*, pp. 47–49.
6. Bennett, *op. cit.*, pp. 49–52.
7. Berkeley's use of this terminology is not consistent in his earliest writings. "Inference" is used in its ordinary, more general sense in several places in the *New Theory of Vision*, although "suggestion" there has already been confirmed in its technical meaning. The special senses are usually followed in the *Principles*, and are given clear authority in the *Theory of Vision Vindicated* by the summary of the theory of which the terms are part.

8. Berkeley himself does not use the term "judgment" in this Lockean sense.
9. Wittgenstein, *Philosophical Investigations*, I. 198–199.
10. The general rule is that words signify ideas. But words can also signify words, as does the word "word." To accommodate this possibility within the general rule we must admit that words *are* ideas.
11. The Saussurean comparison is developed in Stephen K. Land, "Berkeleian Linguistics," *Linguistics*, 213 (1979), 5–28.

4. SMITH AND MONBODDO: THE SEARCH FOR ORIGINS

1. John Locke, *Two Treatises of Government* (1690).
2. For discussion of Condillac's work on linguistic origins see Hans Aarsleff, "The Tradition of Condillac: The Problem of the Origin of Language in the Eighteenth Century and the Debate in the Berlin Academy before Herder," in *Studies in the History of Linguistics: Traditions and Paradigms*, ed. Dell Hymes (Bloomington, 1974), pp. 93–156.
3. *The Collected Works of Dugald Stewart*, ed. Sir William Hamilton (Edinburgh, 1854–60), X, 9.
4. *Adam Smith's Lectures on Rhetoric and Belles Lettres*, ed. John M. Lothian (London, 1963).
5. The point is made in Christopher J. Berry, "Adam Smith's *Considerations* on Language," *Journal of the History of Ideas*, 35 (1974), 130–138, which offers useful background information.
6. *The Works of Adam Smith*, ed. Dugald Stewart (London, 1811), V, 3–48. References given in the text are to this edition.
7. Jan Noordegraaf, "A Few Remarks on Adam Smith's *Dissertation* (1761)," *Historiographia Linguistica*, 4 (1977), 59–67.
8. Stewart, *Works*, IV, 23–24. See also Eugenio Coseriu, "Adam Smith und die Anfänge der Sprachtypologie," in *Wortbildung, Syntax und Morphologie: Festschrift zum 60. Geburtstag von Hans Marchand* (The Hague, 1968), pp. 46–54.
9. Otto Funke, *Englische Sprachphilosophie im späteren 18. Jahrhundert* (Berne, 1934), p. 25.
10. For a fuller summary see Stephen K. Land, "Adam Smith's 'Considerations concerning the First Formation of Languages,'" *Journal of the History of Ideas*, 38 (1977), 677–690.
11. Funke, p. 31; Berry, pp. 130–131.
12. Funke, pp. 29–30.
13. *Herders sämmtliche Werke*, ed. Bernhard Suphan (Berlin, 1891), V, 82–83.
14. *Of the Origin and Progress of Language*, 6 vols. (Edinburgh, 1773–92). *Ancient Metaphysics*, 6 vols. (Edinburgh, 1779–99).
15. Arthur O. Lovejoy, "Some Eighteenth-Century Evolutionists," *Popular Science Monthly*, 65 (1904), 336–340, and "Monboddo and Rousseau," *Modern Philology*, 30 (1933), 275–296.

16. E. L. Cloyd, *James Burnett, Lord Monboddo* (Oxford, 1972), the only full-length study of Monboddo's life and work, discusses the importance of his writings on language (especially pp. 82–84) but perhaps does not do full justice to the intricacy and originality of his theory.
17. I use the second editions of these two volumes, which appeared, with some revisions, in 1774 and 1809 respectively.
18. Hans Aarsleff, *The Study of Language in England, 1780–1860* (Princeton, 1967), locates the origin of "philology proper" in the divorce of linguistic speculation from philosophy, an achievement with which Aarsleff credits Dugald Stewart (p. 102).

5. HARRIS AND REID: RATIONALISM AND COMMON SENSE

1. I have used first editions of Harris's works, except in the case of the *Treatises*, where I have used the fourth edition (1783). References are given in the text using the abbreviations: T = *Treatises*, H = *Hermes*, A = *Philosophical Arrangements*, I = *Philological Inquiries*.
2. *Cartesian Linguistics*, pp. 22, 31–32. This aspect of Harris's work is stressed in Joseph L. Subbiondo, "The Semantic Theory of James Harris: A Study of *Hermes* (1751)," *Historiographia Linguistica*, 3 (1976), 275–291.
3. R. Marsh, *Four Dialectical Theories of Poetry: An Aspect of English Neoclassical Criticism* (Chicago, 1965).
4. Aarsleff (1967), p. 11.
5. Chomsky, *Cartesian Linguistics*.
6. These four features are discussed respectively in the four main sections of *Cartesian Linguistics*.
7. This and related points concerning Chomsky's theory are made in Hans Aarsleff, "The History of Linguistics and Professor Chomsky," *Language*, 46 (1970), 570–585. See also the reviews of *Cartesian Linguistics* by Vivian Salmon in *Journal of Linguistics*, 5–6 (1969–70), 165–187, and Karl Zimmer in *International Journal of American Linguistics*, 33–34 (1967–68), 290–303. See also Chapter 2, note 27.
8. See B. F. Skinner, *Verbal Behavior* (New York, 1957) and Chomsky's review of this in *Language*, 35 (1959), 26–58.
9. The late Otto Funke, for example, summarizing *Hermes*, acknowledges a strong anti-Lockean element in Harris but also affirms that Harris's belief in universal grammar places him, in this respect, squarely within the tradition of Locke and Wilkins. "*Das Problem einer allgemeinen Grammatik im Sinne einer deskriptiven Semasiologie, d.h. die Betrachtung der allen Sprachen gemeinsamen geistigen Grunstrukturen und ihrer Spiegelung in ihnen entspricht zweifellos dem Universalismus des Aufklärungszeitalters; auf dieser Basis hatte bereits* Wilkins *in seinem* 'Essay towards a Real Character and a Philosophical Language' (1668) *die Skizze einer Universalgrammatik entworfen, und* Locke's *sprachphilosophische Untersuchungen fussen auf denselben Voraussetzungen.*" Funke (1934), pp.

11–12. See also Funke's *Studien zur Geschichte der Sprachphilosophie* (Bern, 1928), pp. 1–48.
10. Robin Lakoff, "Review of Grammaire générale et raisonnée," *Language*, 45 (1969), 343–364, and Aarsleff (1970).
11. Chomsky, *Language and Mind* (New York, 1968), pp. 15–16. He receives some support from Zimmer (1968), p. 291.
12. Aarsleff (1970), p. 573.
13. See Chapter 2, especially "The Theory of Grammar."
14. See his *Philosophical Arrangements*.
15. A similar point was made twenty years after *Hermes* in Herder's celebrated *Abhandlung über den Ursprung der Sprache*.
16. Arnauld and Lancelot, pp. 26–30. Harris's presentation of the distinction between energies, powers, and works seems unusual for the eighteenth century because he looks back in his terminology beyond the psychological theorizing of Locke to the Aristotelianism of the late Middle Ages.
17. See Land (1974).
18. Arnauld and Lancelot, p. 5.
19. Harris does not give the source of this observation, which can be found in several writers earlier in the century, including Vico, Blackwell, and Warburton. See Land (1974), pp. 50–74.
20. The history of Scottish Philosophy is chronicled in James McCosh, *The Scottish Philosophy, Biographical, Expository, Critical, from Hutcheson to Hamilton* (New York, 1875). The doctrines of the Scottish school are subjected to close scrutiny in S. A. Grave, *The Scottish Philosophy of Common Sense* (Oxford, 1960).
21. References are to Reid's *Inquiry into the Human Mind*, ed. Timothy Duggan (Chicago, 1970), and his *Essays on the Intellectual Powers of Man*, with an Introduction by Baruch A. Brody (Cambridge, Mass., 1969), distinguished by the letters I and E respectively.
22. Particularly the works of his fellow-countrymen Smith and Monboddo, discussed in Chapter 4.
23. *Essay*, II.xii.6.
24. Hume, *Enquiries*, ed. L. A. Selby-Bigge, 2nd ed. (Oxford, 1902), p. 23.
25. Aarsleff (1967), pp. 100–101.
26. Grave, p. 130. In this respect Reid's view of common sense philosophy is close to Wittgenstein's concept of philosophy in the *Philosophical Investigations*.
27. *Cf.* John R. Searle, *Speech Acts: An Essay in the Philosophy of Language* (Cambridge, 1969).

Bibliography

1. PRIMARY SOURCES

Arnauld, Antoine, and Claude Lancelot. *Grammaire générale et raisonnée, ou, l'art de parler*. Paris, 1660.

Bacon, Sir Francis. *The New Organon*. Ed. Fulton H. Anderson. New York, 1960.

Berkeley, George. *The Works of George Berkeley, Bishop of Cloyne*. Ed. A. A. Luce and T. E. Jessop. 9 vols. London, 1948–57.

Burnett, James—see Monboddo.

Condillac, Etienne Bonnot de. *Essai sur l'origine des connaissances humaines*. Paris, 1746.

Descartes, René. *The Philosophical Works of Descartes*. Trans. Elizabeth Haldane and G. R. T. Ross. 2 vols. London, 1911.

Harris, James. *Hermes, or a Philosophical Inquiry concerning Universal Grammar*. London, 1751.

——. *Philological Inquiries*. London, 1781.

——. *Philosophical Arrangements*. London, 1775.

——. *Three Treatises: The First concerning Art; The Second concerning Music, Painting, and Poetry; the Third concerning Happiness*. London, 1744.

Herder, Johann Gottfried von. *Herders sämmtliche Werke*. Ed. Bernhard Suphan. 33 vols. Berlin, 1891.

Hobbes, Thomas. *The English Works of Thomas Hobbes*. Ed. Sir William Molesworth. 11 vols. London, 1839–45.

Hume, David. *Enquiries*. Ed. L. A. Selby-Bigge. Oxford, 1902.

Locke, John. *Two Treatises of Government*. London, 1690.

——. *Essay concerning Human Understanding*. Ed. Peter H. Nidditch. Oxford, 1975.

Monboddo, Lord (James Burnett). *Of the Origin and Progress of Language*. 6 vols. Edinburgh, 1773–92.

——. *Ancient Metaphysics*. 6 vols. Edinburgh, 1779–99.

Reid, Thomas. *Essays on the Intellectual Powers of Man*. Rpt. with an intro. by Baruch A. Brody. Cambridge, Mass., 1969.

——. *Inquiry into the Human Mind*. Ed. Timothy Duggan. Chicago, Ill., 1970.

Smith, Adam. *Lectures on Rhetoric and Belles Lettres*. Ed. John M. Lothian. London, 1963.

———. *The Works of Adam Smith*. Ed. Dugald Stewart. 5 vols. London, 1811.

Stewart, Dugald. *The Collected Works of Dugald Stewart*. Ed. Sir William Hamilton. 11 vols. Edinburgh, 1854–60.

Tooke, John Horne. Επεα Πτεροεντα; *or the Diversions of Purley*. 2nd ed. London, 1798.

2. SECONDARY SOURCES

Aaron, R. I. *John Locke*. 2nd ed. Oxford, 1965.

Aarsleff, Hans. "Leibniz on Locke on Language." *American Philosophical Quarterly*, I (1964).

———. *The Study of Language in England, 1780–1860*. Princeton, N.J., 1967.

———. "The History of Linguistics and Professor Chomsky." *Language*, XLVI (1970).

———. "The Tradition of Condillac: The Problem of the Origin of Language in the Eighteenth Century and the Debate in the Berlin Academy before Herder." *Studies in the History of Linguistics: Traditions and Paradigms*. Ed. Dell Hymes. Bloomington, Ind., 1974.

Bennett, Jonathan. *Locke, Berkeley, Hume: Central Themes*. Oxford, 1971.

Berry, Christopher J. "Adam Smith's *Considerations* on Language." *Journal of the History of Ideas*, XXXV (1974).

Blakey, Robert. *Historical Sketch of Logic*. London, 1851.

Chomsky, Noam. Review of B. F. Skinner's *Verbal Behavior*. *Language*, XXXV (1959).

———. *Cartesian Linguistics: A Chapter in the History of Rationalist Thought*. New York, 1966.

———. *Language and Mind*. New York, 1968.

Cloyd, E. L. *James Burnett, Lord Monboddo*. Oxford, 1972.

Coseriu, Eugenio. "Adam Smith und die Anfänge der Sprachtypologie." *Wortbildung, Syntax und Morphologie: Festschrift zum 60. Geburtstag von Hans Marchand*. The Hague, 1968.

Funke, Otto. *Studien zur Geschichte der Sprachtypologie*. Berne, 1928.

———. *Englische Sprachphilosophie im späteren 18. Jahrhundert*. Berne, 1934.

Grave, S. A. *The Scottish Philosophy of Common Sense*. Oxford, 1960.

Howell, Wilbur Samuel. *Eighteenth-Century British Logic and Rhetoric*. Princeton, N. J., 1971.

Kneale, William, and Martha Kneale. *The Development of Logic*. Oxford, 1962.

Kretzmann, Norman. "Semantics, History of." *Encyclopedia of Philosophy*. Ed. Paul Edwards. New York, 1967.

_____. "The Main Thesis of Locke's Semantic Theory." *Philosophical Review*, LXXVII (1968).

Lakoff, Robin. Review of the *Grammaire générale et raisonnée*. *Language*, XLV (1969).

Land, Stephen K. *From Signs to Propositions: The Concept of Form in Eighteenth-Century Semantic Theory*. London, 1974.

_____. "Adam Smith's 'Considerations concerning the First Formation of Languages'." *Journal of the History of Ideas*, XXXVIII (1977).

_____. "Berkeleian Linguistics." *Linguistics*, CCXIII (1979).

Lovejoy, Arthur O. "Some Eighteenth-Century Evolutionists." *Popular Science Monthly*, LXV (1904).

_____. "Monboddo and Rousseau." *Modern Philology*, XXX (1933).

Marsh, Robert. *Four Dialectical Theories of Poetry: An Aspect of English Neoclassical Criticism*. Chicago, Ill., 1965.

McCosh, James. *The Scottish Philosophy, Biographical, Expository, Critical, from Hutcheson to Hamilton*. New York, 1875.

Noordegraaf, Jan. "A Few Remarks on Adam Smith's *Dissertation* (1761)." *Historiographia Linguistica*, IV (1977).

Passmore, John A. "Descartes, The British Empiricists, and Formal Logic." *Philosophical Review*. LXII (1953).

Rieux, Jacques, and Bernard E. Rollin (eds.). *The Port-Royal Grammar*. The Hague, 1975.

Salmon, Vivian. Review of Noam Chomsky's *Cartesian Linguistics*. *Journal of Linguistics*, V–VI (1969–70).

_____(ed.). *The Works of Francis Lodwick*. London, 1973.

Searle, John R. *Speech Acts: An Essay in the Philosophy of Langage*. Cambridge, 1969.

Subbiondo, Joseph L. "The Semantic Theory of James Harris; A Study of *Hermes* (1751)." *Historiographia Linguistica*, III (1976).

Warnock, G. J. *Berkeley*. London, 1953.

Watkins, J. W. N. *Hobbes' System of Ideas*. London, 1965.

Wittgenstein, Ludwig. *Philosophical Investigations*. Oxford, 1953.

Zimmer, Karl E. Review of Noam Chomsky's *Cartesian Linguistics*. *International Journal of American Linguistics*, XXXIV (1968).

Index

This index includes a number of crucial terms used in a special or technical sense by the writers discussed. Such terms are indicated by quotation marks and are followed by the name of the writer in whose works they occur—*e.g.*, "Abstract ideas" (Berkeley).

Aarsleff, Hans, 3, 194
"Abstract ideas" (Berkeley), 90–91
"Abstraction" (Locke), 46, 66, 69; (Smith), 136, 138, 144–149, 151, 153–155, 156–159, 190; (Monboddo), 164, 166, 168, 169, 176, 180, 182–183, 191
"Analogy" (Smith), 151–152, 157
Analytic type of language, 137–139, 143–145, 147–148, 154, 157–158, 181, 190
Anaxagoras, 164–165, 175, 176, 180–181, 191
Aristotle, 5–6, 124, 128–129, 141, 160, 166–167, 187, 193, 194, 197, 204, 238
Arnauld, Antoine, *see* Port-Royal grammarians
"Art, Languages of" (Monboddo), 162, 171, 173, 175, 178–180, 184, 185–191
"Articulation" (Monboddo), 170–175, 179, 191
Association of ideas, 12, 16, 66–67, 69, 73, 109–112
Atomism, 44, 47–48, 95–97, 237
Austin, John L., 199

Bacon, *Sir* Francis, 3–8, 25, 27, 29, 81
Banks, *Sir* Joseph, 174
"Barbarous languages" (Monboddo), 162, 171–186
Beattie, James, 194
Berkeley, George, *Bishop of Cloyne*, 1, 2, 4, 8, 16, 19, 27, 42, 71, 74, 79–130, 161, 194–195, 197, 215–216, 220–221, 229, 233, 238, 240
Bernier, François, 48
Boyle, Robert, 48, 95
Burnett, James, *see* Monboddo, *Lord*

Charlotte of Mecklenburg-Strelitz, *Queen Consort*, 193
Chomsky, Noam, 2–4, 76, 194–196, 237–238
"Combination" (Locke), 46, 51, 54–55, 65–66, 69
"Comparison" (Locke), 46, 65–70, 75, 101, 115, 118, 124; (Smith), 136, 145–153, 155, 157; (Monboddo), 163, 165–166, 168–169, 191
"Composition" (Monboddo), 175, 178, 185–186, 189, 191

Condillac, Etienne Bonnot de, 3, 32–33, 59, 73, 108, 133–135, 140, 142, 159, 160–161, 191–192, 194–195, 221, 238–240
Cook, James, 174

"Derivation" (Monboddo), 175, 178–179, 185–186, 189, 191
Descartes, René, 3, 7–8, 10, 14, 22, 24–27, 29, 43, 81, 108, 162, 195–196, 210, 239
Diodorus Siculus, 170
Du Marsais, César, 195

"Energy" (Harris), 199–203, 214

Freud, Sigmund, 108
Funke, Otto, 2

Galileo, 10
Gassendi, Pierre, 48
"General ideas" (Locke), 46–47, 51, 66, 75; (Berkeley), 89–91, 121–123, 128; (Monboddo), 163; (Harris), 206–208
"Generalization" (Smith), 136, 142–157; (Monboddo), 164–166, 168–169, 175–180, 182–183, 191; (Harris), 225
Generative grammar, 3, 70, 74, 76, 79–80, 118–119, 121, 210, 238–240
Girard, Gabriel, 134
Grammar: Lockean, 74–76; Berkeleian, 118–130; *see also* Generative grammar, Philosophical grammar, Transformational grammar

Harris, James, 1, 193–215, 224–225, 234, 238–239
Herder, Johann Gottfried, 140, 194
Herodotus, 170
Hobbes, Thomas, 1, 3–4, 8–29, 89, 109, 161, 194–195, 197, 205, 216–217, 238, 241
Hume, David, 12, 215–216, 220–221, 229

"Ideas" (Locke), 43–51, 119–120; (Berkeley), 91–100, 119–120; (Reid), 229–231
Ideas, theory of, 7–8
"Inference" (Berkeley), 102–105, 109, 112–117, 120
Inflection, 136, 138, 148–152, 154, 175, 179–180, 184–186, 188, 190
"Interpretation" (Berkeley), 101–105, 109, 112, 115, 117–121, 129

John of Salisbury, 196
Jones, *Sir* William, 135
"Judgement" (Locke), 16, 42, 69, 71–74, 80, 101, 103, 105, 108, 215

Kretzmann, Norman, 37–40, 63, 82

Lancelot, Claude, *see* Port-Royal grammarians
Leibniz, Gottfried Wilhelm, 1, 34, 238
Locke, John, 1–4, 7–8, 15–16, 18, 22, 24, 26, 27, 29, 31–77, 79–97, 100–101, 103–105, 108–109, 115–116, 118–122, 124–125, 131, 133–134, 160–162, 194–197, 201–202, 206–208, 210, 215–216, 220, 222, 229–232, 238–240
Logic, 5–8, 14, 24–29, 31, 77, 101, 104, 197, 202, 237–239
Lovejoy, A. O., 132
Lucretius, 5

"Marks" (Hobbes), 13–15, 21
"Modes" (Locke), 15, 44–45, 47–48, 50–51, 53–59, 63, 75, 77, 197
Monboddo, *Lord* (James Burnett), 1–3, 131, 133–135, 137, 140, 159–192, 194, 196, 198, 237–238, 240–241

"Names" (Hobbes), 18–23
Newton, *Sir* Isaac, 51, 160
Nominalism, 19–21, 23–29, 89–90, 142, 155, 221, 233, 238

"Notions" (Berkeley), 82–83, 92, 97–100, 115, 120–124, 127–128

Parkinson, Sidney, 174
Philosophical grammar, 3, 34, 159, 192, 194–196, 202, 204, 210, 212, 219, 223–225, 237–241
Plato, 5, 160, 170, 206–207
Port-Royal grammarians, 22, 34, 61–65, 74, 76, 194, 196, 201–204, 223, 225, 239
"Propositions" (Hobbes), 22–26; (Locke), 69–70, 124–125; (Berkeley), 124, 128

Ramus, Petrus, 5
Rationalism, 194–197, 214–215, 234
Reid, Thomas, 1, 41, 140, 160, 162, 172, 194, 196–198, 215–235, 238–239, 241
"Relations" (Locke), 44–47, 51–53, 55, 57, 59, 67, 75, 77, 197
Relativism, 26, 34, 53–55
Rousseau, Jean-Jacques, 133–134, 142, 169–170
Royal Society, 3, 7, 40, 61, 66

Sagard, Gabriel, 174
Sanctius, 196
Saussure, Ferdinand de, 130
Searle, John R., 199
Shaftesbury, *Third Earl of* (Anthony Ashley Cooper), 193
"Signs" (Hobbes), 14–21; (Locke), 34–35, 37–42, 70–71, 73–74, 94, 119–120; (Berkeley), 80, 94, 105, 113–116, 119, 122, 124; (Harris), 205; (Reid), 216–218
Skinner, B.F., 195
Smith, Adam, 1, 131, 133–159, 160–161, 163–164, 169, 181–182, 190–191, 215, 238, 240–241
Stewart, Dugald, 19, 41, 130, 132–134
Structuralism, 129–130
"Substances" (Locke), 44–45, 47, 51, 53, 55, 57–59, 75, 197
"Suggestion" (Berkeley), 103–113, 115–117, 120, 130
Syllogism, 6–7, 25, 28–29, 62, 238
Synthetic type of language, 137–139, 144–145, 148, 150, 154–156, 157–158, 181, 190

Tooke, John Horne, 32–33
Transformational grammar, 74, 119, 129
Truth, 15, 23–25, 27–29, 69–70

Universals: philosophical, 19–21, 23, 28–29, 91, 163, 232–233; linguistic, 217–221, 223–233, 241

Vico, Giovanni Battista, 140

Warnock, G. J., 82
Wilkins, John, 61, 66–67
Wittgenstein, Ludwig, 47–48, 235